Information Work
with Unpublished Reports

Institute of Information Scientists
657 High Road, Tottenham, London N17 8AA
MONOGRAPH SERIES
Hon. General Editor:
Dr D. J. Campbell

Information Work with Unpublished Reports

PART I

WORK IN LARGE NATIONAL INFORMATION CENTRES

by

A. H. Holloway
*formerly Head,
Naval Scientific and Technical Information Centre (UK)*

and

Elizabeth H. Ridler
Defence Research Information Centre (UK)

with supplementary (North American) material by

Domenic A. Fuccillo

and

a section on 'Mechanization' by

Marvin E. Wilson
*Assistant Director, Operations,
National Technical Information Service (USA)*

PART II

WORK IN COMPANY-BASED INFORMATION UNITS

by

B. Yates
*Director, Australian National Science and Technology Library
formerly Group Technical Communication Manager
Pilkington Brothers Limited*

A Grafton Book

Westview Press
Boulder, Colorado

IN ASSOCIATION WITH
THE INSTITUTE OF INFORMATION SCIENTISTS

Published 1977 in the United States of America
by Westview Press, Inc.
1898 Flatiron Court
Boulder, Colorado 80301
Frederick A. Praeger, Publisher and Editorial Director

First published 1976 in London, England, by
André Deutsch Ltd.

Copyright © 1976 by the authors

All rights reserved. No part of this publication
may be reproduced or transmitted in any form or by
any means, electronic or mechanical, including photocopy,
recording or any information storage and retrieval
system, without permission in writing from the publishers.

> **Library of Congress Cataloging in Publication Data**
>
> Main entry under title:
>   Information work with unpublished reports.
>
>   (Monograph series — Institute of Information Scientists)
> (A Grafton book)
>   Includes bibliographies and index.
>   CONTENTS: Holloway, A. H. and Ridler, E. H. Work in
> large national information centres. — Yates, B. Work in
> company-based information units.
>   1. Libraries — Special collections — Reports.
> I. Holloway, Arthur Herbert. Work in large national
> information centres. 1976. II. Yates, Bryan,
> 1928-   Work in company-based information units.
> 1976. III. Series: Institute of Information Scientists.
> Monograph series — Institute of Information Scientists.
> Z692.R45153   025.17'3   76-43306
> ISBN 0-89158-717-9

Printed in Great Britain by
Ebenezer Baylis and Son Ltd.
The Trinity Press, Worcester, and London

Introduction to the Series

The Monograph Series has been planned and organized by the Institute of Information Scientists, in consultation with the publishers. The aim is to provide a series of texts to fill (so far as may be practicable) the considerable gaps in the monograph literature of this fairly new subject, which have greatly complicated the teaching of it; the monographs should be suitable also for people learning on the job, and for information scientists who want to brush up their knowledge of particular fields.

The importance of clear, readable English has been stressed to all authors and, as far as human frailty (my own as well as others') allows, I have tried to insist on it in editing.

The authors are all well known experts in their fields. Every monograph has been read and criticized by two referees, one of whom is normally a North American and one a Briton, and changes have been made where necessary to meet their comments. The series is intended for English-reading people interested in the subject all over the world.

D. J. CAMPBELL

Contents

LIST OF FIGURES	11
LIST OF PLATES	12

PART I

PREFACE	15
INTRODUCTION	17

17 – Definition of 'unpublished report'; 17 – Changing attitudes to unpublished reports; 22 – Unpublished reports in various kinds of centre; 22 – Kinds of reports; 22 – Structure of the monograph; 23 References.

1. MATERIAL   25

   25 – Definitions; 26 – Reports as primary documents; 27 – Kinds of reports; 34 – State-of-the-art reports; 35 – Theses; 38 – Physical form of reports; 39 – References and selected bibliography.

2. PRODUCTION OF REPORTS   40

   40 – Report writing; 42 – Form of reports; 43 – Parts of a report; 51 – References and selected bibliography.

3. SOURCES AND ACQUISITION   53

   54 – Governments as sources; 54 – Report centres in the United Kingdom; 59 – Report centres in the USA; 67 – Sources in other countries; 68 – Some international sources; 72 – Sources of theses and translations; 73 – Specialized information centres; 74 – Various kinds of organization as sources; 75 – Information on current research; 76 – Acquisition; 79 – References and selected bibliography.

4. REPORT PROCESSING AND ABSTRACTING   82

   82 – Physical form of catalogues and indexes; 83 – Cataloguing: 90 – Abstracting; 92 – References.

5. SUBJECT ANALYSIS AND INFORMATION RETRIEVAL 93
93 – Indexing systems; 93 – Pre-co-ordinate systems; 94 – Post-co-ordinate systems; 95 – The thesaurus; 98 – Subject analysis; 100 – Indexing by computer; 102 – Computer-aided indexing; 103 – Evaluation of indexing systems; 104 – Information retrieval; 108 – On-line retrieval systems; 111 – References and selected bibliography.

6. ANNOUNCEMENT 117
118 – Bulletins; 120 – Some important bulletins: 129 – Indexes to bulletins; 129 – The future of bulletins; 130 – References.

7. SELECTIVE DISSEMINATION OF INFORMATION (SDI), OTHER SERVICES AND USER NEEDS 131
131 – SDI; 132 – Computerized SDI; 137 – Requests; 142 – Special bibliographies; 142 – State-of-the-art-reports; 143 – Translations; 144 – Users; 148 – References.

8. PHOTO- AND MICROCOPYING 150
150 – Advantages; 150 – Copyright; 153 – Photocopying; 155 – Microcopying and Microforms; 163 – References and selected bibliography.

9. MECHANIZATION 167
167 – Simple mechanization; 167 – Tape-typewriters; 169 – Data preparation; 172 – Library 'housekeeping'; 173 – Minicomputers; 174 – Preparing for an in-house computer; 175 – Practical problems of installing a computer.
176 – Section by Mr Marvin E. Wilson on Mechanization; 176 – Definitions; 178 – Equipment; 179 – Microcopying and microforms; 182 – Data in machine-readable form; 183 – On-line information retrieval; 185 – Decision-making; 186 – References and selected bibliography.

10. SECURITY, STORAGE AND WEEDING 189
189 – Security of material; 193 – Access to protected information; 194 – Storage; 199 – Weeding; 202 – Reference and selected bibliography.

11. ORGANIZATION AND MANAGEMENT 203
203 – The information centre: sub-units and centraliza-

tion; 208 – Staff; 214 – Training; 215 – Assessment of staff; 216 – Assessment of methods; 219 – References and selected bibliography.

Conclusion 222

Other Relevant Literature 223

Appendix 1: Acronyms and Abbreviations 225

Appendix 2: Names and Addresses of National Information Systems outside the UK and USA 231

PART II

INTRODUCTION 237
237 – What reports are for; 237 – Definition of reports; 238 – Staffing; 239 – Aims of the monograph.

1. THE ORIGINS OF REPORTS AND HOW TO FIND THEM 241
241 – Internal reports; 243 – Laboratory notebooks; 244 – External reports; 247 – Theses; 248 – Form of reports; 249 – How to locate reports; 252 – References and selected bibliography.

2. EDITING, PRODUCING AND NUMBERING REPORTS 253
253 – Types of report; 254 – The editorial function; 259 – Reproducing reports; 261 – Numbering reports; 265 – Creating an internal series code and numbering system; 265 – References.

3. CATALOGUING, CLASSIFICATION, INDEXING AND DISSEMINATION 266
266 – Cataloguing; 267 – Classification and indexing; 269 – Centralized versus decentralized indexing; 270 – Access to reports index; 270 – Dissemination of information; 273 – References and selected bibliography.

4. STORAGE AND SECURITY CONTROL 276
276 – Arrangement; 278 – Storage methods; 280 – Weeding; 280 – Security grading; 283 – Records; 286 – Selected Bibliography

Other Relevant Literature 287

Index to Parts I and II 289

List of Figures

PART I

1. Time in the dissemination of information in psychology (adapted from Garvey & Griffith) — 28
2. Information output of US-Government-sponsored health projects (adapted from Orr & others) — 30
3. Layout of catalogue-card sheet for inclusion in a report — 47
4. Reverse side of catalogue-card sheet (Fig. 3) — 48
5. Report documentation sheet or standard title-page — 56
6. A *Notice of research project* sheet issued by Smithsonian Science Information Exchange Inc. — 62
7. A flowchart for report processing — 89
8. Typical entries from *Government Reports Announcements (GRA)* — 122
9. A typical entry from *Scientific and Technical Aerospace Reports (STAR)* — 123
10. Part of a page from *R & D Abstracts*, with explanations — 127
11. Request for photocopies (to illustrate copyright declaration) — 152
12. Reverse of request for photocopies (Fig. 11) — 153

PART II

1. Internal progress sheet for an editorial department — 255
2. Approval form for reports — 257

List of Plates

Plates 1 and 3 are used by courtesy of the Technology Reports Centre, Plate 7 by courtesy of the Defence Research Information Centre (both United Kingdom). All other plates are used by courtesy of the National Technical Information Service (USA) and were kindly made available by Mr Marvin E. Wilson, Assistant Director, Operations.

Facing page

1. Station Square House, St Mary Cray, Kent, which houses DRIC and TRC — 96
2. The front of the National Technical Information Service building, Springfield, Va. — 96
3. The RECON terminal at the Technology Reports Centre — 97
4. A Xerox Micro-Enlarger Processor — 97
5. Computer Output Microfilm reading stations — 128
6. The computer facility at the National Technical Information Service — 128
7. Storage of reports at the Defence Research Information Centre — 129

PART I

Preface

In the field of national report centres, it is for security reasons almost impossible for nationals of one country to have detailed knowledge of the experience and problems of report centres in another country. For this reason efforts were made over several months to find a North American author of suitable experience to collaborate in writing this monograph, but all the people approached were too busy to accept another task.

When the search had been virtually abandoned, Mr William T. Knox, Director of the National Technical Information Service (USA) kindly suggested Mr Domenic A. Fuccillo, a gentleman 'of extensive US Government experience in the technical report area', who kindly undertook to supply some North American information, and secured the help of others in doing so. We are most grateful to Mr Fuccillo, and also to Mr Marvin E. Wilson (also suggested by Mr Knox), for providing the material they have. We hope that if a second edition is called for, it may be possible to find contributors from Canada, Australia and other countries.

We wish gratefully to acknowledge the help and advice given in connection with this monograph by Mr William T. Knox, and Mr A. C. Nicholas of the UK Department of Industry.

D. J. Campbell
A. H. Holloway
Elizabeth H. Ridler

Introduction

DEFINITION OF 'UNPUBLISHED REPORT'

An unpublished report may be defined as one which, at the time of its first issue, cannot be obtained by the public as of right. While this is not entirely satisfactory as a definition it implies that an unpublished report may at a later stage be generally available or even openly published. It also implies that the reports may be made available to certain requesters if they can prove that they have a need for the information. Some unpublished reports are sent to large numbers of selected recipients, which would constitute publication for the purpose of copyright, but the reports remain 'unpublished' since they are not available to the general public. Unpublished reports, in fact, normally have a distribution controlled by their originators, or by an authorized distribution centre. The book trade does not touch them. Reports may be unpublished to deny the use of their contents to rival organizations, or because this is a condition of a contract, or because a patent is being sought on some development which is described, or for a number of other reasons, and these reasons may or may not lose their force with the passage of time.

CHANGING ATTITUDES TO UNPUBLISHED REPORTS

The report is an important source of information. Its elusive character in the past has caused some librarians, publishers, and documentalists to despise it as a source, but its vitality and flexibility as a medium of communication have assured its survival.

Unpublished reports, perhaps because they have been casually prepared, printed, and bound, have been casually treated in the library and elsewhere. The result has been a bewildering profusion of cataloguing and shelving practices. Of late, however, the generation and treatment of report literature, especially technical reports, has become formalized. In some respects, particularly in subject cataloguing and indexing, the handling of reports is more sophisticated than that of other types of literature.

Johanna E. Tallman has sketched the history of the report from early times until 1942. It is a fascinating story that at present can only be read through the unpublished literature itself. (Tallman, 1972.) The same author has also produced a wide-ranging bibliography on reports (Tallman, 1973).

In rapidly developing fields of technology reports have been an important source of information for over sixty years. In the United Kingdom the Aeronautical Research Council's *Reports and Memoranda* series began in 1909, and in the USA the National Advisory Committee for Aeronautics (now the National Aeronautics and Space Administration – NASA) issued its first report in 1915. The (UK) Association of Special Libraries and Information Bureaux (Aslib) was founded in 1924. The important function of special libraries was early recognized by industrial research associations, which were themselves considerable producers of reports, and from its foundation Aslib has been a source of information on report literature and its treatment.

The Second World War

The greatest stimulus to interest in the report came with the Second World War. Innumerable reports were circulated during wartime in an informal communication network. Much of the literature was security-classified or limited in scope and distribution. Eventually this material was assimilated into other reports, became available only through informal channels, or was lost. Most of the formal activities to capture significant amounts of this information came at the war's end.

During the Second World War, a great deal of research and development was carried out which could not be published at the time. Publication was impracticable partly because of the shortage of paper and facilities, but mainly because the work was in support of the military operations and wartime security frowned upon, even when it did not specifically forbid, the publication of anything which could conceivably be of use to the enemy, even though an actual paper might contain no reference to any piece of military equipment. Report production was especially high in the USA, where the Office of Scientific Research and Development (OSRD) sponsored many hundreds of technical reports.

After the Second World War

Immediately after the war, more than 1,500 teams of Allied specialists were sent to Germany and Japan to collect information. Their objectives were two: to *capture* as many enemy documents of a scientific and technical nature as possible and to *interrogate* scientists, manufacturers, factory personnel, and others and to record unpublished information. The specialists amassed thousands of reports, and in one massive effort the United States Army Air Corps acquired many tons of the documents, flew them to Dayton, Ohio, housed them in aircraft hangars behind wire fences, and catalogued them. By November 1947, about 56,000 German and 3,000 Japanese documents of aeronautical interest were catalogued and indexed. A Central Air Documents Office (CADO) placed its mark on many of these documents. Dr Vannevar Bush, then head of the US Office of Scientific Research and Development, recommended the formation of an Office of the Publication Board. This Board was to release systematically to the public and to American industry as much of the technical report literature as could be declassified in a 'crash' programme. By use of data processing machines of the day, information about these reports was disseminated to the American aerospace industry. Top policy-making decisions accompanied these activities. Another eminent figure in this early work was Dr Ralph Shaw, who advised Bush's office on report policy. The working idea of the Board, according to Shaw, was that of 'announcing and making known' rather than 'printing and distributing' reports. Documents were to be treated in an orderly way and sent to co-operating libraries. The government libraries were the Library of Congress, Army Medical Library (now National Library of Medicine), and National Agricultural Library. The reports were filed by Publication Board (PB) number. In 1951, CADO was merged with the Office of Naval Research into the Armed Services Technical Information Agency (ASTIA). In 1953 ASTIA acquired an additional 150,000 documents from the Library of Congress. At the end of the war the US Armed Services, the newly established

Atomic Energy Commission, and other Federal agencies were busily writing, editing, and publishing reports. The private sector, too, recovering from wartime restrictions, also produced abundant reports. In 1950 the US Congress established within the Department of Commerce a clearinghouse function. By that time the Office of the Publication Board became known as the Office of Technical Services (OTS) within the Department of Commerce. Later, in two departmental reorganizations, OTS was renamed (1964) the Clearinghouse for Federal Scientific and Technical Information and (1970) the National Technical Information Service.

Also in 1945 appeared an article by Vannevar Bush, 'As we may think'. Dr Bush was then Director of OSRD and he wrote that men of science should turn to the massive task of making more accessible the store of knowledge, that instruments were at hand which if properly developed would give access to and command over the inherited knowledge of the years and that perfection of these instruments should be the first objective of scientists as they emerged from war work. This article can be said to be the origin of information science as a discipline in its own right.

In 1948 the Royal Society held a conference on scientific information at which subjects discussed included production and distribution of scientific literature, abstracting, subject classification, mechanical selection and mechanized distribution of information.

Throughout the 1950s and 1960s technical reports and other scientific publications were issued in such numbers that an 'information explosion' was said to be occurring, with an exponential growth of documentation in many scientific disciplines, and new techniques had to be developed to deal with the problem. Several hundred specialists in information handling were brought together for the 1958 International Conference on Scientific Information. Possibly the strongest stimulus, however, was the report of the President's Science Advisory Committee Panel on Science Information (Chairman, Dr A. Weinberg). The resulting publication, *Science, government, and information: the responsibilities of the technical community and the government in the transfer of information*, was widely read and acted upon in and outside government. It spurred the formation of numerous information centres, which amassed and organized report collections. The US Government still sponsors information centre work. A recent directory (National

Referral Center) lists 108 of them. It is still too early to judge the impact of these and private sector information centres on the progress of science, technology, education, and other fields. But there is little doubt that the scientific community has heeded the dictum of Weinberg and fellow panel members that they must share many of the burdens that have been traditionally carried by the professional documentalist. They have shared especially in the preparation of extended abstracts, index terms, and in the construction of thesauri for indexing in their subject fields. The report literature has also been influenced by these scientist-aided adjuncts, and many reports today are accompanied by them.

Although great improvements have been made, very little has been written about procedures which are either peculiar to unpublished reports or adapted to them with special modifications.

As the number of reports increased, so did methods of handling them improve. The student should be aware that the bibliographic landscape is littered with both successful and unsuccessful attempts to handle reports. Among the co-operating libraries in the early 1950s, the Library of Congress probably had the best record with Publication Board reports. The late Dr Mortimer Taube is considered a pioneer in establishing rules and procedures for the cataloguing of reports. He developed these rules through working with operating government agencies. His early paper on the subject (Taube) led him into an intellectual controversy with the proponents of conventional cataloguing systems. Echoes of these arguments can still be heard today.

Yet another historical key to report handling can be traced to the ASTIA attempts to develop a thesaurus of subject terms. These starts culminated in the elaborate systems of subject headings, thesauri, and microthesauri used in today's information centres.

We have also inherited a sense of urgency about the report. This may be attributed to its consistently 'perishable' nature, real or imagined. It may also be traced to the somewhat frantic, mechanical work in the Dayton, Ohio, aeroplane hangars. That work led to the early use of the Hollerith card, sorting by category by a succession of devices, and finally to today's automated methods of computer handling of reports.

UNPUBLISHED REPORTS IN VARIOUS KINDS OF CENTRE

The title 'information centre' covers a number of different kinds of organization which will be dealt with in more detail in Chapter 3. An information centre in a specialized branch of science or technology will hold all sources of information relevant to its speciality, whether published or not, but will give special attention to the unpublished sources since these commonly deal with current scientific and technical research and development and provide the most up-to-date information. A large national, university or public library will concentrate on books and periodicals, but may be a depository library for openly available technical reports in certain subject fields. When the proportion of unpublished material is small it can be considered as a side-line and receive no special attention, but this fails to make the best use of valuable sources. As the proportion of reports increases the methods special to the unpublished material tend to become dominant and the activities of the centre become more and more attuned to its specialized requirements.

KINDS OF REPORTS

Unpublished reports are not concerned only with scientific and technical research and development in the usually understood meaning of that phrase, though they are nearly always technical in the wider sense of the word. The chapter on materials mentions a range of subjects, which may be legal, medical, economic or on any specialized subject, and there are other kinds of report, such as those on the work of committees which usually deal with technical subjects of one kind or another. Since the subjects of reports do not greatly affect the methods used in storing or retrieving the information contained in them, the different subjects are not separately considered except in some instances in which special facilities exist.

STRUCTURE OF THE MONOGRAPH

In this monograph the emphasis throughout is on the underlying principles, and immediate practical applications are in most chapters used as illustration rather than as the substance of the text.

Many of the considerations dealt with in this monograph apply more or less to other materials and some at least of them will be dealt with from a different point of view in other monographs in this series. It will be readily appreciated that many of the procedures described apply equally to both unpublished and published reports, so that reference will be made to published reports when it is considered helpful to do so.

One problem that constantly recurs is that of making one monograph equally useful to such different types of reader as the senior and junior staff of information centres, to users of these centres and to students in schools of information and library science. Although some aspects are necessarily dealt with from a particular point of view, in general the chapters aim at being useful to all readers, and it is hoped that those who read the monograph from one of these points of view will gain some insight into the interests, responsibilities and difficulties of others who are concerned with unpublished reports, and, indeed, with any source of technical information. It is assumed that the reader has some knowledge of the terms and methods common to library and information work, and it is unlikely that the complete beginner will start with this monograph.

ACKNOWLEDGEMENT

Mr Fuccillo wishes to acknowledge a personal communication from Mr Scott Adams.

References

BUSH, V. As we may think. *Atlantic Monthly*, **167**(1). July, 1945. 101–108.

NATIONAL REFERRAL CENTER FOR SCIENCE AND TECHNOLOGY. Directory of Federally supported information analysis centers. 3rd ed. Washington, Library of Congress, 1970. pp. 55. *COSATI Report 70–1*. (Available from NTIS as PB 233 582.)

PRESIDENT'S SCIENCE ADVISORY COMMITTEE. Science, government and information: the responsibilities of the technical community and the Government in the transfer of information. Washington, US GPO, 1963. pp. 60. *Report of the Panel on Science Information, Chairman, Alvin M. Weinberg.*

ROYAL SOCIETY SCIENTIFIC INFORMATION CONFERENCE, London, 1948. Report and papers submitted. London, 1948. pp. 723.

TALLMAN, J. E. The history of technical reports, 1700 BC to date, with interesting and humorous sidelights encountered on the way. Paper presented at the first annual Resources Information Symposium, North Hollywood, California, 23 Feb., 1972. pp. 15.

TALLMAN, J. E. Special types of technical publications: Part IV, Technical reports: history, sources, indexes, availability, special handling problems. *UCLA SLS*–221 (1973). pp. 22. Copies of these may be obtained from Mrs Johanna E. Tallman, Director of Libraries, California Institute of Technology, Pasadena, Calif., 91109, USA.

TAUBE, M. The cataloging of publications of corporate authors, *Library Quarterly*, **20**(1). January, 1950. 1–20.

CHAPTER I

Material

DEFINITIONS

The origin of the word 'report' tells us much about its meaning and function. It derives from the Latin word *reportare*, to bring back. But there appears to be no accepted international definition. The British Standard definition of a research and development report is: 'A document which formally states the results of, or progress made with, a research and/or development investigation, which, where appropriate, draws conclusions and makes recommendations, and which is initially submitted to the person or body for whom the work was done. A report is usually issued as one of a series and commonly carries a report number which identifies both the report and the producing, disseminating or sponsoring organization.'

This definition is given in the context of the presentation of technical reports and is not intended to cover other important aspects. It does, however, indicate the purpose of a report, and the responsibility of the originator of the work reported for any subsequent distribution of the report. Perhaps the most important aspect not covered by the definition is the speed at which reports can be produced using office duplicating equipment, which makes them a unique source of information on research in progress.

A brief definition of a technical report is: organized, factual, and objective information on a technical or scientific subject brought by a person who has experienced or accumulated or researched it, to a person or persons who need, want, or are entitled to it (Weisman).

This is not the only definition. Gray has classified reports by their subject matter and from his own experience in writing them. The behavioural scientist would stress the intent of the report and its condition of stimulus control, especially in behaviour modification (Ronco). The information scientist would stress the value of information in changing the 'decision state' of the decision-maker (Whittemore & Yovits). Other views point out the highly detailed nature of the report and its similarities to or differences from other forms of literature.

Reports are usually initially submitted to the person or body for whom the work described was done and some of them never get any further. Some are covered by restrictive markings and others are subject to controlled distribution by their originators although there may be no markings to indicate this. These restrictions may be permanent but usually they become pointless with the passage of time. There is sometimes a statement on the report giving a date when the restrictions can be removed or made less stringent. On the other hand some reports are written to be openly published and others are made publicly available at a shorter or longer period after their original production.

REPORTS AS PRIMARY DOCUMENTS

The primary-secondary controversy about reports still goes on. Whether or not a report may be considered primary or secondary literature is an important question from a legal, copyright, and priority (of scientific discovery) point of view. Gray & Rosenborg showed, in a pilot study of a hundred reports in four scientific fields in 1952, that technical reports tended to become papers in journals. Most of them do not directly become published, and one report may result in several papers spread over a period of years. Other studies have corroborated this basic fact. Editors of scientific journals generally do not consider the limited distribution of information in a report as constituting publication in the sense of precluding consideration for journal publication. They do, however, regard widely distributed, abstracted, and well-known reports from established institutions as publications for purposes of citation in bibliographies, or lists of references in articles. Within some fields, formal definitions of primary publication have been proposed. A comprehensive one in biology is: an acceptable primary publication must be the first disclosure containing sufficient information to enable experts (1) to validate observations, (2) to repeat experiments, and (3) to evaluate intellectual processes. Moreover, it must be (1) capable of sensory perception, (2) essentially permanent, (3) universally available to the scientific community, and

(4) available for regular screening by one or more of the major recognized secondary services. Not many reports could meet these criteria for biological and medical journals. In one National Science Foundation study only 38·5 per cent of 276 reports in medicine and biology were announced in abstracting publications, for example.

None of these definitions or interpretations is universally agreed to. Some persons have proposed that communication of information is much more important than the question of primacy of information. These proponents argue that publication and republication is necessary for exposure of some information to all concerned groups, especially in multi-disciplinary fields (Passman).

KINDS OF REPORTS

Internal reports

The internal or limited distribution report has also been a subject of controversy. Years before the term 'cover up' became in vogue, reports have occasionally come to light and become the subject of controversy. Many documents receive only limited distribution because they contain preliminary or negative results. Some of these results would be potentially embarrassing to their writers or the sponsors of the work. These reports range from legislative documents, to agency, commission or corporate reports. Management documents may be kept 'Secret' so that personnel will not see them; trade union or labour documents might be restricted so that managers might be unaware of them, and so on. Let us examine one laboratory's practices of setting limitations on reports. Technical documents at the Oak Ridge National Laboratory (USA) have a very interesting history, and the three basic categories of these documents are the result of trial and error, refinements, and of course the requirements of the funding agency. The laboratory has been operated by three different groups: a university from the early 1940s until mid-1945; a chemical firm from 1945 until 1948; and a large industrial company from 1948 until the present. The first type of document was originated in 1947. Distribution is the key to this type of document. It was prepared for internal use only: the immediate plant (not the whole laboratory), plants doing similar work, and the sponsor's officials. The subject matter of these reports was preliminary information of interest to laboratory personnel and material to be brought into the laboratory's accountability system. The second type of document, a technical memorandum, also contains preliminary information and is also given limited, external to the plant, distribution. The memoranda, however, may be abstracted and indexed. The third type of document has two kinds. The subject matter of one may contain summaries or be a compilation of abstracts. These are called semi-annual and annual progress reports; they receive very wide distribution. The other type of report is the topical report – a document covering specific experiments which merits wide distribution.

This laboratory has more than fifteen divisions, and the number of reports in some divisions is higher than the number of other publications. In biology the number of journal articles outstrips that of reports, but in divisions such as chemical technology, metals and ceramics, reports are more numerous than articles. Most reports of the third category are available from NTIS or the sponsoring group's information service. It is interesting to note that doctors' and masters' theses are sometimes published as technical memoranda from this laboratory.

The report should be viewed as one part of a complex information network. Many studies have placed the report's role in this network. Garvey and co-workers have recently studied scientific

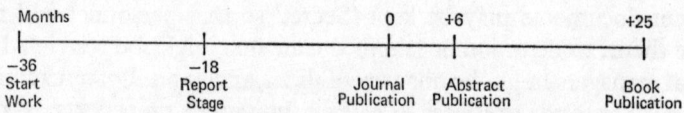

FIG. 1. Time in the dissemination of information in psychology (adapted from Garvey & Griffith).

information flow in depth and reveal the report's place at several critical junctures in the information dissemination process. The accompanying chart (Figure 1) shows part of the picture.

Various means are used for distributing reports. Of 1,001 reports in psychology, Garvey & others analysed modes of distribution. When one considers that articles sometimes are published six months to a year from submission, it can be speculated that a substantial number of reports contains the same information as articles. In a study of the ways in which technical-report and journal-article versions of the same material differed, Garvey & Griffith found the most significant differences in the length and comprehensiveness. The article was more abbreviated but contained a revised and expanded version of some material not in the report, and the article generally treated only one portion of the study. The orientation of the research presented in technical reports was mostly applied and clinical. The reasons given for presenting information in the technical-report form were principally because it was felt that the relevant audience could best be reached through that form; a second reason was that the sponsoring group required it. Garvey's work illustrates the importance that scientific communication and the report assumed in the 1960s.

Technical reports

The majority of the reports processed in an information centre will be research and development reports in numbered series, each one of which deals with the results of a particular investigation and, except when issued in parts, can bear no direct relation to adjacent numbers in the series.

Contract reports

Many organizations place contracts with industry or with other bodies such as universities or research associations for work on projects for which they may not have facilities or staff available. Government departments also place many contracts. The reports on such work are sometimes issued by the organization placing the contract in their own report series, but usually the reports are prepared by the contractor and distributed by the organization placing the contract. In the latter case the reports may either be progress or interim reports, or a final report on the work.

In the United States the contract mechanism is responsible for a large number of reports. Government contracts often specify the delivery of a report as part of the work. The sole product of some research organizations that perform work under contract to private firms or government may be the report. Outright grants, even those 'without strings attached' also result in reports to the granting organization. Contract and grant reports may never leave the filing cabinet nor receive anything more than limited distribution. But some groups have looked upon these reports as being public property or as a fine type of advertisement for the issuing body. Thus reports from grants and contracts have found their way, either systematically or sporadically, into large information centres and distribution centres. As an example, let us consider the release of government reports from a single health agency, the National Institutes of Health, Bethesda, Md. The report form has been used to communicate information to, from and within this agency for many years. Until 1964, however, the agency did not systematically disseminate or announce these reports through any national clearinghouse. In that year the Clearinghouse for Federal Scientific and Technical Information (CFSTI) was given the responsibility for distributing reports on a government-wide basis. Orr & others have summarized information output of government health research. Figure 2 is adapted from their studies. The

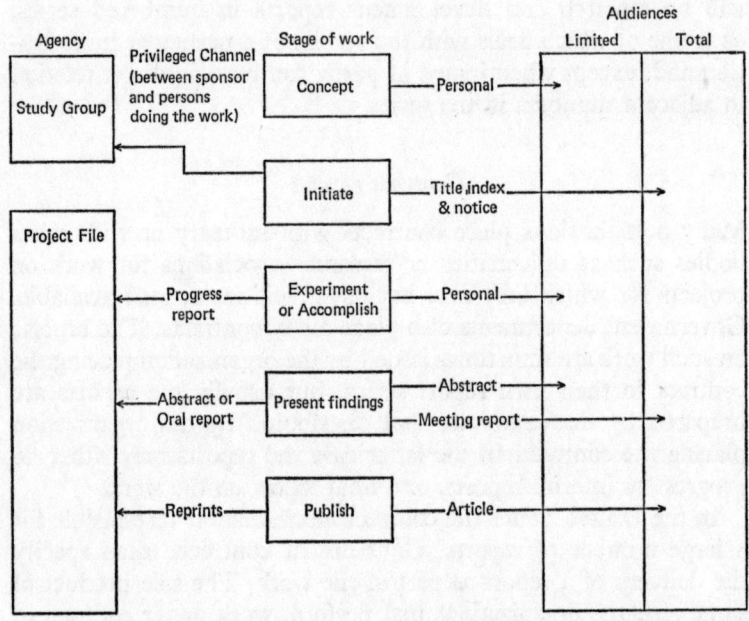

FIG. 2. Information output of US-Government-sponsored health projects (adapted from Orr and others).

place of the report appears at middle left as a 'privileged channel' and for grant-type research commonly ends up in a project file. Limited sectors of the research community receive word of this work. For the most part, informal, personal contacts are the medium of transfer of information at this, the experimentation stage of research. The emergence of contract research and development in the life sciences has changed the picture for the role of the report. Government-contract R & D is typified by large-scale activities, most of which are done at research centres geographically separated. Sometimes a similar contract in a large programme at several centres validates a result or delivers a product needed for another part of the programme. Such programmes require co-ordination and a minimum of unnecessary duplication of effort. The report is used to disseminate information on work in process throughout such a programme. Thus, in contract-sponsored work the report may be a 'privileged channel' but is more frequently an 'open channel'. With the new responsibilities of CFSTI, the health agency in our example established a channel through CFSTI for these contract reports.

The health agency policy and procedure calls for the public release of the technical report, defining it as a report obtained from a contractor as a primary objective of the contract for the development of scientific data, instruments, methodology, and information. These reports may contain, in addition to written matter, compilations of data, tables, charts, graphs, designs, blueprints, and similar materials. The reports may be acquired periodically or on a one-at-a-time basis. The agency still restricts so-called 'progress reports' and distinguishes technical reports from them. Two criteria are used: the technical report offers confirmatory evidence (positive or negative), and the work has progressed to a point where publication is desirable. It should be noted that the number of contracts funded by the agency has been on the upswing for several years, and in the two years in which reports were released to CFSTI, the number of contracts rose from 487 to 807. Within one year after the procedure was adopted, the number of reports approached 200. Some reports are still not released from this agency. The written procedure specifically excludes reports that: list only delivery of items or animals; convey primarily fiscal or administrative data; present data that within the provisions of the contract would be limited because of proprietary, security, or confidential reasons; are routinely or otherwise made publicly available; or state merely the progress of work or require no more than a simple indication that work has been done.

The project officer for the contract generally is responsible for reviewing and passing the scientific merit of a report before its release. Usually this person is a scientist doing work related to that of the contractor. Sometimes he receives materials from or collaborates with the contractor. Occasionally the contractor and the project officer may decide that information in a report may be more appropriately published in the open literature than in a report. Such information may be withheld from a report but must accompany it as part of the contract. This 'appendix' will not be released, but if within six months it has not been published the contractor is notified that it, too, will be released to CFSTI unless the contractor requests another delay in writing.

As a footnote to this example, the proponent of the CFSTI procedure disclosed two overriding reasons for releasing the reports: (1) criticism that information was not being made available to all interested persons, and (2) important negative data was not being set down where it could be used.

The idea has not been universally hailed by scientists. One complained in 1967: 'There is so much data in the journals it is almost impossible for one individual to cover his field. When I have a high index of suspicion of the technical competence of something that is circulated – reports in which details are not there or reports that are not ready for formal publication and have not gone through the review process – I am going to spend as much time reading it as material that occurs in the primary literature . . .' (statement in a discussion).

Progress reports

Progress reports will give the most up-to-date information on current work, although later reports in the series may not confirm all the results presented. Not all progress reports will have permanent value, as if there is little new to report on the technical side the report may consist only of financial and personnel details. All progress reports should, however, be processed, as they are likely to present results fully which may only be summarized in the final report, and, if the research is discontinued before the final report is prepared, they may be the only information available on the work done under the contract.

Final reports

These may be expected to summarize the work done and in particular the results obtained. Where the work has been carried out in a university, the final report may take the form of a thesis by the research student undertaking the work. Theses are dealt with more fully in a later section of this chapter (p. 35).

Committee reports

Reports on the work of committees can often be useful sources of information, especially if the committee is set up to conduct a special investigation. Specialist papers submitted to the committee are sometimes included as annexes to the committee reports. Some standing committees produce annual reports which can be a useful source of summarized information on research and development work in specialist fields, and may give references to detailed reports submitted to the committee during the year. *Ad hoc* committees usually produce a final report with recommendations. This often has no reference number and will be referred to colloquially by the name of the chairman of the committee. Care must be taken in processing such reports, so that, for instance, 'The Weinberg report' can be retrieved when requested some years later.

Annual reports of research organizations

Many research organizations, such as those funded by government, prepare annual reports for their department. Detached units of an organization may also prepare annual reports for their top management. Such reports will not be expected to contain much detailed information, but they will summarize the work of the unit and thus show whether it would be useful to scan the output of the unit in a search on a given subject. They will also be useful in giving the references to the reports and open publications emanating from the unit in the course of the year. They are very useful secondary documents and often mention some important new work not yet reported on and thus give a clue to what may be forthcoming in the future.

Conference reports

Conference proceedings are sometimes described as reports although the papers forming the proceedings may be of different types. Some may be reports of research and development work carried out, others may be state-of-the-art reports, or the reports of committees, or policy documents, or commentaries on publications appearing elsewhere, or reports of discussions taking place at the conference. Many conference reports contain a mixture of these and any research and development reports contained may be on various subjects although all bear on the theme of the conference. Some may be original publications, some may be compilations of previously available material or even full reproductions of reports produced elsewhere. Others may be preliminary drafts of papers which will later appear in recognized series. All will however have some value in a report collection, and each paper must be processed separately.

State-of-the-art reports

For some purposes this is the most valuable type of report though containing no original material. They are essentially summaries of the state of knowledge on some topic at the time of compilation, and are usually written on subjects which are at the time undergoing rapid development. It follows, of course, that they often lose much of their value fairly quickly because their contents are overtaken by later developments, but these reports are much sought after by workers who are taking on new projects. A state-of-the-art report may be a commentary on the position of work on some subject or it may be little more than a number of references with the very briefest comments on a selection of them, though the latter may be considered merely annotated bibliographies. Whatever its type it is likely to include and be based upon the collection of relevant references which have come to the notice of the compiler, so that it gives a valuable introduction to the recent literature on the subject and probably an indication of the directions in which new advances are likely to be made. Some publishers make a point of publishing serial volumes of *Recent Advances* on selected subjects which contain quantities of references, published and unpublished, on various topics with extensive discussion and comments.

Other reports

Some reports on very specialized subjects may be produced which could not be published economically because of the small potential market, and such reports are unlikely to form part of a numbered series. Reports on special investigations, e.g. of aircraft or industrial accidents, will have a considerable technical content. Staff members of an organization are usually required to write reports on visits made in connection with their work. These may not be automatically sent to the information centre, but they can contain useful technical information.

Resumés of legal proceedings are valuable to lawyers, and doctors are inundated with publicity reports on the products of pharmaceutical manufacturers. Many of these specializations have established information organizations which digest the material, which is often very bulky, and produce reports which are in effect abstract bulletins of whose existence only those immediately concerned are aware.

Theses

Theses submitted to universities in support of applications for higher degrees form a borderline class of unpublished technical reports since on the one hand the regulations often require that they should be published in deference to the universities' endeavours to make their work generally available. On the other hand it is rapidly becoming more and more difficult to secure publication of long and detailed manuscripts such as most theses are. Theses are, however, a useful source of information on new research, and the extensive bibliographies usually included are also valuable.

As a result of the publication difficulties, candidates are often required to submit a small number of typewritten copies of their theses, and at least one of these remains available for study in the university library. The universities give only limited publicity to their holdings and none to their information content. The multiplication of the number of British universities and of students in recent years has greatly increased the number of theses that are being produced and their exploitation by users is becoming an operation only undertaken as a rule in major searches by large undertakings. Further information on sources from which theses can be obtained will be found in Chapter 3 (p.72).

Bibliographies of theses. The guide for British university theses is the *Index to Theses accepted for Higher Degrees by the Universities of Great Britain and Ireland and the Council for National Academic Awards*, published annually by Aslib (3 Belgrave Square, London, SW1X 8PL). The series started with 1950/51 and the latest issue is Volume 24 for the year 1973/74 but includes some earlier and later theses. It contains brief particulars of nearly 4,500 theses arranged under twenty-nine subject headings and a number of sub-heads, with alphabetical indexes for the authors and sub-heads. There is no cumulation, so that a search may have to be extended to all twenty-four volumes.

Some 50,000 theses accepted for higher degrees in the universities of Great Britain and Ireland are to be indexed in a new bibliographical guide published by the European Bibliographical Centre – Clio Press. The *British Theses Retrospective Index* will list theses accepted for higher degrees between the early eighteenth century and 1950, covering in one source the 200-year period prior to the introduction of the Aslib index. The work will be divided into two volumes, the first to include theses titles in the social sciences and humanities, to be published in 1976, and the second to include material in science and technology, and planned for publication later.

Another and more comprehensive guide is *Dissertation Abstracts International*, formerly *Dissertation Abstracts*, which gives long abstracts averaging about 300 to 400 words of all dissertations and theses accepted in United States and Canadian universities and some others, in two sections, one dealing with the humanities and social sciences and the other with the physical sciences and technology. The entries are arranged under broad subject headings, with sub-heads; a random example, under Physics, Nuclear, runs:

THEORY OF PION INTERACTIONS WITH ATOMIC NUCLEI
AND OF HEAVY ION SCATTERING
Robert Antony CHATWIN, Ph.D.
The Florida State University, 1970
Major Professor D. Robson
Abstract

Order No. 71–13489, 134 pages

The *Abstracts* are published by University Microfilms (300 N. Zeeb Rd., Ann Arbor, Mich., USA 48106); UK address: St Johns Rd, Tylers Green, High Wycombe, Bucks.) and the order number is the identification for the microfiches of one thesis. University Microfilms also publish *American Doctoral Dissertations*, which is described as a complete listing of all doctoral dissertations accepted by American and Canadian universities. The annual volumes are arranged in subject categories, subdivided by universities, and contain an author index, but no abstracts. An entry runs:

Chemistry, New York University
FLAM, Eric. Investigation of hydrophilic composite material based upon a method of cartilage.

Masters' degree theses are generally considered unpublished in the United States and are kept in single copies in university libraries or departments. Information centres and scientific organizations also publish abstracts or title listings of selected theses and dissertations in their disciplines. Professional societies may publish lists of theses, obtained by survey, in their journals or other publications annually as a service to their members. Occasionally theses are published as technical reports from corporate bodies, especially when the work was done under a grant or contract for such a body. When the theses are published as reports they may appear in abstract journals. University Microfilms also publishes *Masters Abstracts: Abstracts of Selected Masters Theses on Microfilm*, a quarterly publication started in 1962. According to the first volume, this source was prepared in co-operation with the National Science Foundation and the Association of Research Libraries. It contains 'brief printed abstracts in journal form accompanied by publication of complete theses as positive microfilm or as xerographic copies in book form.'

Doctoral dissertations, when abstracted for *Dissertation Abstracts*

International and given a microfilm number, may be found cited in the literature sections of journal and book publications. Like Masters' theses, some are published as reports.

In recent years, there has been a tendency in the United States to accept the journal article as partial fulfilment of the doctoral degree instead of the formal dissertation. In some programmes, a dissertation or thesis is not required for conferring the degree.

For German theses there is the *Deutsche Bibliographie's Hochschulschriften-Verzeichnis*, (*Deutsche Bibliographie*, Zeppelinallee 8, 6 Frankfurt/Main, Germany [DBR]) organized under broad subject headings, in which an entry runs:

0543 [this is the entry number]
Das Konvergenverhalten von Poincareschen Reihen
1971–54 gez. B1 4
Freiburg (Breisgau) Univ Math Fak Diss
1972 (Nicht f. d. Austausch)

For theses in French there is the *Repertoire des thèses de doctorat soutenues devant les universités français* (Association des Universités partiellement ou entièrement de langue française, Centre de Documentation de la Bibliothèque, Université Laval, Québec 10, P.Q., Canada), which contains the following indexes, but no abstracts: geographical, disciplines, directors (of the studies), authors. The entries give the following bibliographical information: author, director, title, address (of the university), collation, degree awarded.

PHYSICAL FORM OF REPORTS

Reports take a number of physical forms, from a single sheet of paper to a substantial book. Because reports are not bound to any particular length they can contain much more of valuable know-how, information on other approaches explored etc., than an article published in the technical press. An average report may be of from twenty to fifty pages, perhaps bound in a manilla cover and issued in a series by the organization responsible for the work described. The series may be called *Reports*, but it may have other titles, such as *Technical Notes*, *Memoranda*, or *Notes*, perhaps qualified by some such adjective as *Research* or *Laboratory*, and in general these series titles may be taken as being in descending order of weight and value. A research establishment may produce one general series which may contain some thousands of reports on widely different topics, of widely different value and issued over a period of fifty years or more. In other organizations series are issued for the constituent units, or for different projects.

References

BRITISH STANDARDS INSTITUTION. The presentation of research and development reports. London, 1972. pp. 18. *BS* 4811.
GARVEY, W. D. *and* GRIFFITH, B. C. Scientific information exchange in psychology. *Science*, **146**(3652). 25 December, 1964. 1655–1659.
GARVEY, W. D. *and others*. The role of the technical report in the dissemination of scientific information: report of work performed under NSF Grant GN–281 (continuation of G–18494) from Office of Science Information Service of the National Science Foundation. Washington, American Psychological Association, 1965. pp. 55. *APA–PSIEP Report* no. 13.
GRAY, D. E. Technical reports I have known . . . and probably written. *Physics Today*, **13**(11). November, 1960. 24–26, 28 ff.
GRAY, D. E. *and* ROSENBORG, S. Do technical reports become published papers? *Physics Today*, **10**(6). June, 1957. 18–21.
ORR, R. H. *and others*. The biomedical complex viewed as a system. *Federation Proceedings*, **23**(5), pt. I. September/October, 1964. 1133–1145.
PASSMAN, S. The role of the technical report in scientific and technical communication. Washington, Federal Council for Science and Technology, 1968. *NTIS Report* PB 180 944.
PATERSON, G. W. *and* HARDY, J. E. Index to theses accepted for Higher Degrees by the Universities of Great Britain and Ireland and the Council for National Academic Awards. Vol. 24. London, Aslib, 1975. ISBN 0 85142 075 3. pp. 135.
RONCO, P. G. Characteristics of technical reports that affect reader behavior; a review of the literature. Medford, Mass., Institute for Psychological Research, Tufts University, 1965. *NTIS Report* PB 169 409.
WEISMAN, H. M. Basic technical writing. Columbus, Ohio, Charles E. Merrill, 1974.
WHITTEMORE, B. J. *and* YOVITS, M. C. A generalized conceptual development for the analysis and flow of information. Columbus, Ohio, Ohio State University, 1972. *NTIS Report* PB 229 260.

SELECTED BIBLIOGRAPHY

ADKINSON, B. W. *and* DUBESTER, H. J. The new challenge for university and technical libraries. *Libri*, **19**(4). 1969. 265–274.

CHAPTER 2

Production of Reports

In some organizations the information officer will be responsible for the production of research and development reports and some consideration of the subject may not be out of place. Even when he does not have this responsibility some knowledge of the subject will be helpful in extracting the information which these reports contain.

REPORT WRITING

The first problem is of course to get the author to produce his text. Many authors are more interested in doing experimental work than in writing about it, and they are only too ready to avoid writing if this is in any way possible. In particular they may regard those responsible for the production of reports as their natural enemies and resist any attempts by an information officer who may happen to be rather junior in status to urge them to write. Remedies are to point out the useful publicity and the value of the report as a possible exchange for reports from an organization in which the author is interested; also to be as helpful as possible. Many young authors have only the vaguest idea of what is required although they may have had occasion to study a number of reports, and it is a great advantage to have a plan of the finished product in mind, even if it turns out to be decidedly different from the plan. Most authors need help with some part of their work: diagrams and photographs can be nightmares to those not skilled in their production, and assistance is often welcomed in the layout of tables and the design of graphs.

There is ample literature on report writing, which should be consulted both by authors and those who may be assisting them; a selected bibliography of and references to this literature are given at the end of this chapter. Guides to the layout and reproduction of reports have been issued by various national and international organizations. In the United Kingdom the British Standard is BS 4811. In the United States the Committee on Scientific and Technical Information (COSATI) of the Federal Council for Science and Technology issued their *Guidelines* . . . in 1968. The American National Standards Institute (1430 Broadway, New York City, NY 10018) has issued (1974) *Guidelines*. Among international organizations the Advisory Group for Aerospace Research and Development (AGARD) of the North Atlantic Treaty Organization has issued a guide by Holloway (1974). This originated from a specification for AGARD's own reports, but is of much wider application and is as far as possible compatible with the practice of national report centres of the UK and USA.

In the United States the report is produced in several ways. In large organizations a department may be set up to write, edit, and publish reports. This may be a subdivision of an information section or may be a separate unit usually under management's direct control. At one large laboratory, several such units exist, with production (editing and printing) centralized. Each unit at this laboratory employs full-time writers/compilers whose job it is to put together the technical materials from the operating plant into topical or periodical reports. These drafts, after approval by the plant technical staff, are then further processed by the central editorial and printing staff. Distribution and record-keeping are also centralized, and lists of reports so produced are compiled as part of the total operation.

In some areas, such as defence work, the contractor will be responsible not only for delivery of hardware or results of testing, but for 'paper products': reports, memoranda, notes, specifications, testing plans, manuals and the like. These may be produced by the engineers and technical persons working on the project or by a writing-editing team. Temporary teams sometimes are organized, with part of the writing job 'farmed out' or contracted for at a service bureau specifically organized to write and edit. This was a popular activity on the West coast of the United States during the 1950s and early 1960s. These service companies hired writers and editors on a part-time or per-job basis to produce the documentation for certain industries. At small companies the persons doing the work write up their own results. Their literary product may not be as uniform as that done by professional writers at the large organization.

Although it is not the purpose of this chapter to present the fundamentals of technical report writing, it might be useful to review them and give some references. In the United States, the report has been the subject of numerous articles and books. An early book on the subject that is still used by senior technical writers is that by Weil, but other standard texts have been produced and are in current use (Growes & Hoffman, Nekon, Weisman). Professional writers also widely use reference books and style manuals. Style manuals exist in almost every major discipline, such as chemistry, physics, and biology; general style manuals in use include that published by the University of Chicago and the well-known US Government Printing Office *Style Manual*. For specialized uses, working specifications often are issued by the customer. The US Government, for example, has developed a number of writing guides for the preparation of manuals, handbooks, and instructional materials. Each Governmental unit has its own, and there are also many company guides.

The non-professional writer, who may be a professional scientist, may or may not have received instruction in writing, apart from a course or two as an undergraduate. He may be exposed to workshops or short courses in his professional career through his workplace or society. Since he is the source of the information, it is logical to suppose that the most efficient way to obtain reports would be for him to write them. Depending upon his ability and the encouragement he receives, the act may follow the logic. When such a writer has a vessel (a format) into which to 'pour' his information, the report may turn out well. Many style-guides are written with this premise. The objective has been uniform, clear reports.

FORM OF REPORTS

Physical production

Reports are reproduced in a variety of ways. Some are appropriately reproduced, depending on their number, method of dispatch, and size. Others are casually produced and just as casually reproduced without much thought to the economics or to the readability of published materials. In a perfect world, the large-quantity report would be typeset and printed by the offset process, and the small-quantity report might be reproduced by reprographic or spirit processes. In this same fictitious world the binding of all reports would be commensurate with their value and expected lifespan. Actually reports are found with good and bad characteristics, both in printing and in binding. Today's reports are increasingly being reproduced on film or microfiche, but more will be said about that subject later in this monograph (see p. 63).

An important point to remember when producing reports today is the world shortage of paper, which sets a limit on the number of paper copies produced. One solution to this problem is to distribute copies as microfiches. Reports should therefore be arranged so that their microfiches are easily readable and this places constraints on the positioning of references, tables and figures, and on the use of half-tone photographs. Another point to bear in mind is the increasing input of bibliographical data into computer data-bases. This can be facilitated by presenting certain data in a standard form. These points will be dealt with in more detail in the following paragraphs.

The page size of reports is now normally A4 (297mm × 210mm), and for legibility on microfiche the type-setting size should be such that in the final form of the report the main text size will not be less than 8pt. The reproduction may be from stencils, lithographic 'masters', or by photographic methods, usually photolithography.

PARTS OF A REPORT

A report normally consists of introductory material (including front cover, title-page, abstract, and list of contents), main body of the report (introduction, main text, conclusions and recommendations, tables and illustrations), and reference material.

Introductory material

The front cover should carry the report series and number at top right and parallel to the spine at top left. It is recommended in *BS* 4811 that the report number shall be an alphanumeric designation, unique within the organization producing, disseminating or sponsoring the report, which identifies the report and the organization. To facilitate computer processing the number of characters in the report number, including conventional signs and spaces, is recommended to be kept to a maximum of twelve. Examples of such report numbers are RAE TR 71177 and COSATI-70-1. The layout of the front cover will in general be governed by the house style of the organization, but should include the title of the report (which should be as informative as possible), the name and address of the organization producing the report, names of the authors and date of issue.

The title-page should carry the report number at top right. Centred on the page the following items should appear: name of the responsible organization; title of the report; name(s) of the author(s); affiliation of the author(s) if this is not the organization issuing the report.

The abstract is defined as an abbreviated, accurate representation of a document that should be published with it. An American National Standard for writing abstracts has been approved. (See also Defense Documentation Center reference.) An abstract is recommended for every formal item in journals and proceedings, and for each separately published report, pamphlet, thesis, or monograph. The abstract should be as informative as the nature of the document will permit so that readers may decide quickly and accurately whether they need to read the entire document. The purpose, methods, results, and conclusions usually are presented in summary form. The abstract is placed early in the document, and it is recommended that a full bibliographic citation should be placed on the same page so that the secondary services can use this information directly. The abstract can be placed at the foot of the title-page or on its reverse. It should normally be from fifty to 150 words in length. The list of contents should give the page number for each section. Lists of illustrations, tables and appendices should be included. If symbols and abbreviations are numerous, it is suggested that they be listed and defined separately at the end of the introductory material. If few, symbols and abbreviations should be defined where first introduced in the text.

Body of the report

The main text should be divided into sections and sub-sections and it is convenient to use a decimal notation to indicate the sections and sub-sections. To facilitate reading in microform, complete identification of references should be cited at the bottom of the page on which they first appear when this is possible. They should, however, be repeated in a List of References at the end of the report. The main text should be followed by a separate section containing any conclusions drawn from it, and new facts should not be introduced in these conclusions. Tables should be placed so as to facilitate reading in microform. They should be numbered consecutively throughout the report.

There may be a 'Background' section which sets the report in context with other work done before or in progress. It acknowledges support from sponsors, organizations, and persons. It gives the foundation or basic principles, sets the objectives and topics covered, and states the philosophical or practical consequences of the work in general.

The 'Introduction' section states the general field, the findings of others that will be challenged or developed, and the question attacked by the study. The findings of others are discussed in the introduction, showing how the present work fits in with previous work. If there are gaps in knowledge that the present work was designed to fill, these gaps are pointed out. In many reports, the introduction also gives the plan of the report itself, announcing its organization and giving brief outlines of its parts. Conclusions or recommendations may be a part of the introductions of other reports, but usually such conclusions are stated elsewhere or repeated.

Equipment, apparatus, supplies, experimental setup, and similar information is given in detail in most reports. Sometimes this section is labelled separately from 'Methods'. The list of materials may be long enough to give in an appendix. Tables of data or calibration, computations or other numerical material may be included in this section or in an appendix. The experimental design of the work, description of survey instruments, data, processing techniques, etc., will be extensively discussed in this section of the report. In architectural or construction reports, full blueprints or parts lists may be listed or referenced. The sequence of this section may be chronological, by succession of techniques, or section-subsection.

The 'Results' section is the heart of the report. It usually consists of tabular and graphical material accompanied by textual explanations of data. It may be divided into several parts, such as

Experiment 1, 2, etc., or by topical sections. It could follow the pattern of the 'Equipment and Methods' section. Tables in the 'Results' section usually contain captions, which may give the parameters of the experiments from which the data were taken. Tabular construction is covered in detail in the US GPO style manual. Tables may include footnotes explaining or stating the statistical significance of the numbers. Tables should stand alone, that is they should be able to be understood without a textual explanation. Illustrations may be found in the 'Results' section, and may consist of line drawings, mechanical or instrumental tracings, photographs, microphotographs and other graphic images (but half-tones do not copy well and should be avoided if possible). They also have captions and explanatory text, which should be informative and easily readable. Both tables and figures are designed to impart information. Intelligently and skilfully constructed tables and figures add to the value of a report; haphazardly prepared they detract from it. Colour should be avoided as it will not reproduce; cross-hatching or dots may be used instead. If few, illustrations should be placed near the first text reference made to them, but if numerous they are better placed in numerical sequence at the back of the report. Illustrations should be placed so that they can be viewed without turning the page sideways (i.e. in 'portrait' rather than 'landscape' style).

Conclusions are usually presented separately from the results in most reports. In scientific reports, these are based rigorously on the results obtained. Speculation and a discussion of the work's consequences may also be stated but should be clearly labelled. The latter may form a section: 'Recommendations for further work'.

Some reports are organized so that the 'Recommendations' section is at the beginning, so that the decision-maker can quickly act upon the results of such a study. The recommendations are based on the conclusions of the study and form the basis of setting objectives for further work, if any, to be performed. Some recommendations are written so that they actually are the design of future work by the same company or group. In a sense they are proposals for this work, and the granting agency or sponsor may place these recommendations in future contract proposals for negotiation.

AGARDograph No.178 Advisory Group for Aerospace Research and Development, NATO A GUIDE TO THE LAYOUT OF TECHNICAL PUBLICATIONS A.H.Holloway Published June 1974 24 pages Recommendations are made for the size, shape, layout and content of technical publications. Notes are included to help those responsible for writing, reproducing and handling these documents. A select bibliography and some notes for cataloguers are included. Relevant standards are listed in an appendix with some further notes on bibliographic references. P.T.O.	AGARD-AG-178 001.816:655.53 Authors Information Layout Librarianship Publications Reports Reproduction Writing	AGARDograph No.178 Advisory Group for Aerospace Research and Development, NATO A GUIDE TO THE LAYOUT OF TECHNICAL PUBLICATIONS A.H.Holloway Published June 1974 24 pages Recommendations are made for the size, shape, layout and content of technical publications. Notes are included to help those responsible for writing, reproducing and handling these documents. A select bibliography and some notes for cataloguers are included. Relevant standards are listed in an appendix with some further notes on bibliographic references. P.T.O.	AGARD-AG-178 001.816:655.53 Authors Information Layout Librarianship Publications Reports Reproduction Writing
AGARDograph No.178 Advisory Group for Aerospace Research and Development, NATO A GUIDE TO THE LAYOUT OF TECHNICAL PUBLICATIONS A.H.Holloway Published June 1974 24 pages Recommendations are made for the size, shape, layout and content of technical publications. Notes are included to help those responsible for writing, reproducing and handling these documents. A select bibliography and some notes for cataloguers are included. Relevant standards are listed in an appendix with some further notes on bibliographic references. P.T.O.	AGARD-AG-178 001.816:655.53 Authors Information Layout Librarianship Publications Reports Reproduction Writing	AGARDograph No.178 Advisory Group for Aerospace Research and Development, NATO A GUIDE TO THE LAYOUT OF TECHNICAL PUBLICATIONS A.H.Holloway Published June 1974 24 pages Recommendations are made for the size, shape, layout and content of technical publications. Notes are included to help those responsible for writing, reproducing and handling these documents. A select bibliography and some notes for cataloguers are included. Relevant standards are listed in an appendix with some further notes on bibliographic references. P.T.O.	AGARD-AG-178 001.816:655.53 Authors Information Layout Librarianship Publications Reports Reproduction Writing

FIG. 3. Layout of catalogue-card sheet for inclusion in a report.

This AGARDograph was prepared at the request of the Technical Information Panel of AGARD.	This AGARDograph was prepared at the request of the Technical Information Panel of AGARD.
This AGARDograph was prepared at the request of the Technical Information Panel of AGARD.	This AGARDograph was prepared at the request of the Technical Information Panel of AGARD.

FIG. 4. Reverse side of catalogue-card sheet (Fig. 3).

Reference material

This includes bibliographical references, appendices, distribution list, a report documentation page, and catalogue cards (Figures 3, 4 and 5). The report should contain a list of references in the order in which they appear in the text and numbered consecutively. To avoid ambiguity it is recommended that titles of periodicals should not be abbreviated. Inaccurate references are too common; they should be carefully checked. If it is desired to present references to other literature supplementary to the references cited in the text of the report, this should be presented as a separate bibliography which should indicate the principles on which it has been compiled, e.g. Comprehensive or Selected Bibliography.

Appendices give detailed explanation of methods summarized in the main text together with supplementary matter (specimen forms, flow diagrams, etc.) which it would not be appropriate to include in the main body of the text.

Unpublished reports should contain a statement of the organizations or individuals to which they have been distributed initially. This should be on a separate page.

The development of computerized information-retrieval services make it useful to include in a report a sheet on which bibliographic and other cataloguing information are collected together to form a ready-made punching document for use by a recipient organization. This sheet, termed variously a 'Document control sheet', 'Standard title-page' or 'Report documentation page' consists of numbered boxes in which the bibliographical data of the report are presented in standard form. A typical example is shown in Figure 5.

Although the use of catalogue cards has decreased, they still serve a useful purpose in many information centres, and it is helpful to include in reports a sheet of four 125mm × 75mm catalogue cards. Layout of a typical sheet is shown in Figures 3 and 4.

TECHNICAL REPORT STANDARD TITLE PAGE

1. Report No. COSATI-70-1	2. Government Accession No. PB 189 300	3. Recipient's Catalog No.	
4. Title and Subtitle Directory of Federally Supporter Information Analysis Centers January 1970		5. Report Date January 1970	
		6. Performing Organization Code	
7. Author(s)		8. Performing Organization Report No.	
9. Performing Organization Name and Address COSATI Panel on Information Analysis Centers		10. Work Unit No.	
		11. Contract or Grant No. N.A.	
		13. Type of Report and Period Covered	
12. Sponsoring Agency Name and Address COSATI Federal Council for Science and Technology			
		14. Sponsoring Agency Code	
15. Supplementary Notes Produced for COSATI by the National Referral Center for Science and Technology, Library of Congress			
16. Abstract This directory of 119 Federally supported information analysis centers is descriptive, containing information on mission, scope, and services provided by the listed centers. Included are an index of subject areas covered by the centers, an index of center directors, a list of organizations, and a list of locations. The centers are numbered serially to facilitate indexing.			
17. Key Words Information analysis centers, data, information, information services, directories	18. Distribution Statement Unlimited		
19. Security Classif. (of this report) Unclassified	20. Security Classif. (of this page) Unclassified	21. No. of Pages x, 71p	22. Price $3.00

FIG. 5. Report documentation or standard title page.

References

AMERICAN NATIONAL STANDARDS INSTITUTE. American national standard guidelines for the format and production of scientific and technical reports. New York, 1974. pp. 16. *Standard* No. Z39.18.1974.
AMERICAN NATIONAL STANDARDS INSTITUTE. American national standard for writing abstracts. New York, 1971. pp. 12. *Standard* No. Z39.14.1971.
BRITISH STANDARDS INSTITUTION. The presentation of research and development reports. London, 1972. pp. 18. *BS* 4811.
COMMITTEE ON SCIENTIFIC AND TECHNICAL INFORMATION (COSATI). Guidelines to format standards for scientific and technical reports prepared by or for the Federal Government. Washington, Federal Council for Science and Technology, 1968. pp. 18. (Available from NTIS as PB 180 600.)
DEFENSE DOCUMENTATION CENTER. Abstracting scientific and technical reports of Defense-sponsored RDT & E. Alexandria, Va., 1968. AD 667 000.
GROWES, H. F. *and* HOFFMAN, L. S. S. Report writing. Englewood Cliffs, NJ, Prentice-Hall, 1965.
HOLLOWAY, A. H. A guide to the layout of technical publications. Neuilly-sur-Seine, AGARD, 1974. pp. 24. *AGARDograph* No. 178.
NEKON, J. Writing the technical report. 3rd ed. New York, McGraw-Hill, 1952.
UNIVERSITY OF CHICAGO PRESS. A manual of style. 12th ed. Chicago and London, 1969. pp. 546.
US GOVERNMENT PRINTING OFFICE. Style manual. Rev. ed. Washington, 1973.
WEIL, B. H., *ed*. The technical report... New York, Reinhold, 1954. pp. 485.
WEISMAN, H. M. Basic technical writing. 3rd ed. Columbus, Ohio, Charles E. Merrill, 1974.
WEISMAN, H. M. Technical report writing. 2nd ed. Columbus, Ohio, Charles E. Merrill, 1974.
   An abridgement of 'Basic technical writing'.

SELECTED BIBLIOGRAPHY

BRITISH STANDARDS INSTITUTION. Proof correction and copy preparation. London, 1958. pp. 28. *BS* 1219.
BRITISH STANDARDS INSTITUTION. Bibliographical references. London, 1950. pp. 18. *BS* 1629.
BRITISH STANDARDS INSTITUTION. The abbreviation of titles of periodicals. Part 1. Principles. London, 1970. pp. 12. *BS* 4148. ISBN 0 580 08957 X.
COOPER, B. M. Writing technical reports. Harmondsworth, Mddx., Penguin, 1964. pp. 188.

GODFREY, J. W. *and* PARR, G. The technical writer. London, Chapman & Hall. 1960. pp. 340.

INTERNATIONAL ORGANIZATION FOR STANDARDIZATION (ISO). Bibliographical references, Geneva, 1968. pp. 16. *ISO R 690.*

INTERNATIONAL ORGANIZATION FOR STANDARDIZATION (ISO). Documentation international code for the abbreviation of titles of periodicals. Geneva, 1972. pp. 4. *ISO 4.*

KAPP, R. O. The presentation of technical information. London, Constable, 1948 (reprinted 1970). pp. 159.

SIMONS, E. W. The writing of English in abstracts and reports. *Aslib Proceedings*, 5(2). May, 1953. 121–127.

CHAPTER 3

Sources and Acquisition

Unpublished reports are produced by many different types of originator; some are only obtainable from their originators, but many are available from distribution centres which may hold reports of a number of originators. Many information centres have accumulated collections from which they are prepared to supply copies of single reports or groups of reports for retention or on loan, either free to users with a recognized need for the information, or on payment of a charge to cover reproduction costs and/or postage and packing. In addition certain libraries have been designated as depository libraries for special categories of reports.

National report centres where they exist are normally the best sources for obtaining reports except in very specialized fields. Such centres will collect reports not only from organizations in their own country but also from overseas sources. In this chapter some of the most important report centres in the United Kingdom and in the USA will be described first. Accounts will then be given of sources of government reports, sources in other countries, international sources, sources holding special subject collections or special types of material, specialized information centres, and miscellaneous sources.

Guides to specialized sources will be mentioned in the various sections, but information covering a wide field will be found in *AGARD Lecture Series* No. 69. *How to obtain information in different fields of science and technology – A user's guide*, and, for the United Kingdom, the *Aslib Directory* (ed. by Wilson) and the British Council's *British scientific documentation services*. The Aslib Information Department has published a guide to report literature in the UK.

GOVERNMENTS AS SOURCES

All governments produce quantities of reports of many different types. Some are intended to inform or instruct the public about government policy and some are not intended to enter the public domain at all. There are reports of commissions set up to enquire into specific questions, reports of investigations or accidents, the reports of numbers of committees, papers prepared to provide information to Parliament and other legislatures, technical reports issued by many departments and many other types.

The various types of United Kingdom official publications are described in detail in the monograph by Pemberton. Those in print can be purchased from Her Majesty's Stationery Office (HMSO), (PO Box 569, London SE1 9NH, or at Government bookshops). HMSO issues daily, monthly and annual lists of publications, and also sectional lists by Departments responsible for the publication. The UK Cabinet Office has also issued (1974) *Government research and development: a guide to sources of information*. In this booklet addresses are given under each Department's entry from which further information can be obtained. A comprehensive guide to UK government library and information services will be found in the monograph by Burkett (1974) which includes information on report sources.

For atomic energy reports produced in the United Kingdom, reference should be made to Smith's *Guide to UKAEA documents* which gives detailed information on publication, dissemination, availability and bibliographical control of the reports and other documents issued by the United Kingdom Atomic Energy Authority. UKAEA documents released for public sale can be purchased through Her Majesty's Stationery Office.

REPORT CENTRES IN THE UNITED KINGDOM

The British Library

The British Library was set up in 1973 and its resources are described in a paper by Hookway. It consists of three divisions and a central research and development department. The operational divisions are the Lending Division, the Reference Division (the former library departments of the British Museum, including

Sources and Acquisition

the National Reference Library for Science and Invention, now the Science Reference Library), and the Bibliographical Services Division (including the *British National Bibliography*). The Research and Development Department comprises the functions of OSTI (the Office of Scientific and Technical Information) extended to include work in the humanities, together with a systems team concerned with studies and development of the Library's future computing and allied requirements. The most important source of reports in the British Library is the Lending Division, but the Science Reference Library has a photocopy service although it does not lend, and the Research and Development Department supports research which leads to the production of reports. Notes on each of these are given in the following paragraphs.

British Library Lending Division (BLLD), (Boston Spa, Wetherby, Yorks LS23 7BQ) was formed in 1973 by the amalgamation of the National Lending Library for Science and Technology (NLLST) and the National Central Library. It has extensive collections of British and overseas reports which are available for unlimited distribution. The collection comprises both paper copies and reports in microform. NLLST was set up in its present location in 1961 but the basis of its report collection is of earlier date.

Of 'the older reports held, the collection includes reports produced at the end of the Second World War by the British Intelligence Objectives Subcommittee (BIOS) and Combined Intelligence Objectives Subcommittee (CIOS), and paper copies and reports on microfilm obtained from the predecessors of NTIS: the US Department of Commerce Publication Board (PB reports), subsequently the Office of Technical Services (OTS) and later the Clearinghouse for Federal Scientific and Technical Information (CFSTI). Reports issued in the USA during the Second World War were all made available to the public through OTS when they were declassified. Currently BLLD purchases all available reports in microfiche form from NTIS. These include those made openly available by the Department of Defense (reports with reference numbers in the series AD-600 000 and AD-700 000) and the US Educational Resources Information Center (ERIC). BLLD is a depository library for reports from the Rand Corporation, and also for reports from the US Atomic Energy Commission, received as paper copies up to July, 1964, but now as microfiches. BLLD also holds a large collection of NASA reports. It should be noted that the microfiches from NTIS will include some reports from overseas countries. BLLD acquires as many openly available British reports as possible, including reports from government research establishments, nationalized industries, and universities. These British reports are announced in the monthly *BLLD Announcement Bulletin* (described in Chapter 6, p. 126). The report collection of BLLD is described in the papers by Barr, and by Chillag (1970, 1973).

Since January 1973, BLLD has been designated the official depository library for documents published by the European Communities, and these include those of the Council of Ministers, the Commission, the Economic and Social Committee, the European Court, the European Parliament, the European Investment Bank, and the Statistical Office of the Communities.

BLLD also acts as a centre for microfiching, storing and disseminating lengthy tables of numerical data, computer printouts, etc. (known as Supplementary Publications) which have been submitted by various journal editors who would otherwise have to print them at great cost alongside the parent articles, despite the small proportion of their readers who might be interested in such details.

As a result of a co-operative agreement made with the Center for Research Libraries, Chicago, BLLD can arrange to borrow US Federal Government non-depository documents (those not printed by the US Government Printing Office) which are issued direct by the Federal Government and listed in the *Monthly Catalog of US Government Publications*. These are available from 1952, and requests should quote the entry in the *Monthly Catalog*.

BLLD as a source of theses will be described later in this chapter.

BLLD serves registered borrowers in the UK (libraries and other approved centres) and overseas users. British centres must submit their requests on the BLLD Loan/Photocopy forms which cost £23·00 + £1·84 VAT per unit of fifty forms each entitling the user to the loan of a single item or a photocopy of one item of up to twenty pages in length. For photocopies of items longer than twenty pages it is necessary to attach photocopy coupons to the forms. Each coupon permits an additional ten pages of original copy to be photocopied. Coupons at present cost £5·00 + 8%

VAT per book of twenty coupons. Overseas users should use prepaid international loan forms: £20 per pack of twenty forms (Europe) and £40 per pack of twenty forms (outside Europe) to obtain loans, and overseas photocopy coupons (used with forms which are free) which cost £15·00 for a book of twenty in Europe and £17·00 outside Europe to obtain photocopies. As with coupons in the UK, overseas coupons permit the copying of ten pages of original each.

BLLD's activities in the development of the UK MEDLARS service are described in Chapter 5 (p. 108).

Science Reference Library. Formerly the National Reference Library of Science and Invention, the Library has two divisions, Holborn (25 Southampton Buildings, Chancery Lane, London, WC2A 1AW) (originally the Patent Office Library) and Bayswater (10 Porchester Gardens, Queensway, London W2 4DE). The Holborn division specializes mainly in the literature of the physical sciences and of engineering and technology, the Bayswater division in the life sciences and in literature printed in less familiar languages. The main stock of reports is at the Holborn division and includes US Government-sponsored reports (AD and PB series), US Atomic Energy Commission, NASA, US Department of Agriculture, Forest Service reports, United Kingdom government reports released for unlimited distribution, research association and university reports. Atomic energy, research institute and university reports from overseas countries are also held. Many of the US AD and PB series are held on microfiche, and these, with paper copies when available, and the USAEC reports are held in the Kean Street Annexe. (A reader-printer is available.) Other reports are held in the main library of the Holborn division. Photocopies can be purchased. Report series are listed, together with other series, in *Periodical publications in the NRLSI* (1969/71).

British Library Research and Development Department (Sheraton House, Great Chapel Street, London W1V 4BH). The functions of the Office of Scientific and Technical Information (OSTI) which are included in this department include the sponsoring of research in information science. These projects have produced a number of reports all of which are available as microfiches from the British Library Lending Division. OSTI also issued a quarterly newsletter which is being continued as the *British Library Research and Development Newsletter* (from No. 1, September 1974). The *Newsletter* gives information on the progress of current projects and lists recent reports.

Defence Research Information Centre (DRIC)

This Centre was set up in 1971 within the Procurement Executive, Ministry of Defence (Orpington, Kent), by merging the defence and aerospace functions of the former Ministry of Technology, Technology Reports Centre with the Naval Scientific and Technical Information Centre. It is the central facility of the Ministry of Defence for the acquisition of unpublished scientific and technical reports from UK and overseas sources. DRIC's services are available to Government defence departments and defence contractors in industry and universities. Plate 1 shows the building housing DRIC and TRC (see below).

DRIC's holdings include UK Government defence reports, US reports from 1941 to the present day, including a nearly complete set of NACA and NASA reports, and a complete and regularly updated microfilm library of US *Military Specifications* and related *Federal Specifications* and drawings, *MIL Standards*, *MIL Handbooks*, and *Qualified Products List*.

Although DRIC's principal operations are concerned with controlled distribution documents, all reports which can be made openly available are designated 'Unlimited' and copies are passed by DRIC to the British Library Lending Division and to the Department of Industry's Technology Reports Centre (TRC).

The report input is scanned and details of technical innovations arising from the UK defence programme, e.g. new devices and gadgets, constructional techniques, processes etc. which have no security restrictions, are identified and details are passed to TRC for exploitation by British industry through the *Techlink* service.

Technology Reports Centre (TRC)

The Technology Reports Centre (Department of Industry, Orpington, Kent, BR5 3RF) is the Department of Industry's research and technical information centre. (See Plate 1.) It processes and makes available for industry and research centres exploitable and unpublished research and development reports arising from UK government programmes and those of overseas governments. The majority of non-classified technical reports produced in UK government research establishments are held. TRC receives paper copies of NASA documents and many other openly available reports from the USA and other overseas countries under exchange agreements and purchases microfiches from NTIS. It also leases the NTIS *GRA* magnetic tape. The Centre's publications include *R & D Abstracts* and *Selected Report Announcements* (for both see Chapter 6) both available on annual subscription, and the selective dissemination service *Techlink*.

Techlink is aimed particularly at those in industry concerned with research, development and design. A *Techlink* is a one-page digest containing the essentials of a new technological idea or process, with details of where further information can be obtained. Each *Techlink* is placed in one or more of forty subject categories and subscribers elect to receive only those subjects pertinent to their interests. *Techlink* is available on subscription at present only within the United Kingdom.

Other TRC services include supply of facsimile copy or microfiches of reports for the cost of reproduction and postage. Prices are advertised in *R & D Abstracts*. TRC has an on-line terminal giving access to the ESRO/SDS computer at Frascati, and will conduct searches on request. There is a charge for searches, except those for UK government departments. Leaflets describing TRC's services can be obtained on application.

REPORT CENTRES IN THE USA

One of the largest producers or sponsors of reports is the Federal Government. The two major suppliers of these documents are the US Government Printing Office for openly available reports, and the National Technical Information Service. All of the former are listed in the *Monthly Catalog of US Government Publications* (Superintendent of Documents, Government Printing Office, Washington DC 20402). The December issue of this catalogue contains an annual index. A good source book of government publications has been written by Schmeckebier & Eastin. AGARD has also issued a useful guide. Current publications of the GPO are listed in various flyers, catalogues, and secondary publications. The announcement publications of NTIS will be described later. Agencies of the government also announce and distribute reports, and official charts of the organization of the Federal agencies are kept up to date by the General Accounting Office. State and municipal agency publications are usually catalogued by a variant of GAO, such as the Budget Bureau or Finance Section. Such listings could be used as source guides to literature produced by agencies.

Other producers of reports are industrial firms (businesses, companies, plants), and individuals. Many of these reports are less systematically handled and a key to their existence will be in disciplinary divisions. References to these reports, particularly in applied areas, may be found in the business or trade literature. Industrial organizations, such as the National Conference Industrial Board, or study groups such as the Brookings Institution, may also keep listings of reports. Occasionally bibliographies are prepared in selected fields. The Special Libraries Association, the American Library Association, the Council of Planning Librarians, and other specialized groups are constantly surveying this literature. Obtaining these reports may be difficult, or expensive. Some of the internal or administrative materials may be impossible to acquire.

An important entry into sources of reports is the modern information centre or service. Many of these groups have been established. A directory of Federally sponsored information centres is updated periodically (National Referral Center).

Within the US Government a common source, collector and generator of reports is the task force. Such a group is set up sporadically to collect information and make recommendations on particular subjects. Subject specialists are brought together in teams. For example, a task force on prescription drugs might include pharmacologists, physicians, chemists, lawyers, and industrial experts. These task forces are legally charged with scanning thousands of reports and may gain access to many unpublished materials. When they finally issue recommendations to their chartering agency or to Congress, their report may contain extensive bibliographies of these reports. The reports themselves may become part of the library holdings of the agency, may be sent to the Library of Congress for cataloguing, or may become dispersed.

Sources and Acquisition 61

Occasionally task force reports are printed *in extenso* in the *Congressional Record* and will be indexed there.

In the following paragraphs are given brief outlines of the services offered by major Federal information resources in the United States. Most of the descriptions were recently updated by a personal survey in 1974: those of the Defense Documentation Center and the Library of Congress were current to about 1971. There is no limitation on the use of these services, other than DDC, by persons or organizations outside the USA, but prices are higher. Full information is available from NTIS.

National Technical Information Service (NTIS)

(5285 Port Royal Road, Springfield, Virginia 22151.) NTIS (see Plate 2) is a central source for public sale of government-sponsored research and development reports and other analyses prepared by Federal agencies, their contractors and grantees. It is also a central source for Federally generated machine-processable data files. NTIS sends out 11,500 information products daily and supplies the public with approximately 4,000,000 documents and microforms annually. The collection exceeds 800,000 titles and 100,000 titles are in current shelf stock. The service operates NTISearch, an on-line computer search service. The data-base comprises the abstracts of 360,000 reports, and an additional 180,000 abstracts from the Smithsonian Science Information Exchange are also available from NTIS. The data file is available for lease. Current summaries of new research reports and other specialized technical information are published in weekly newsletters, which are indexed. A fortnightly journal is also published, *Government Reports Abstracts*, indexed bimonthly in *Government Reports Index* (described in Chapter 6, p. 120). A standing order microfiche service (SDIM) automatically provides subscribers with full texts of research reports selected to satisfy individual requirements.

National Referral Center for Science and Technology

(Library of Congress, Washington DC 20540.) The Center deals with enquiries in the physical, biological and social sciences, engineering and related technical areas. It provides names, addresses, telephone numbers, and brief descriptions of appropriate information resources. The Center also publishes directories of information resources in a number of scientific areas.

Smithsonian Science Information Exchange, Inc.

(1730 M Street NW, Washington DC 20036.) This service has

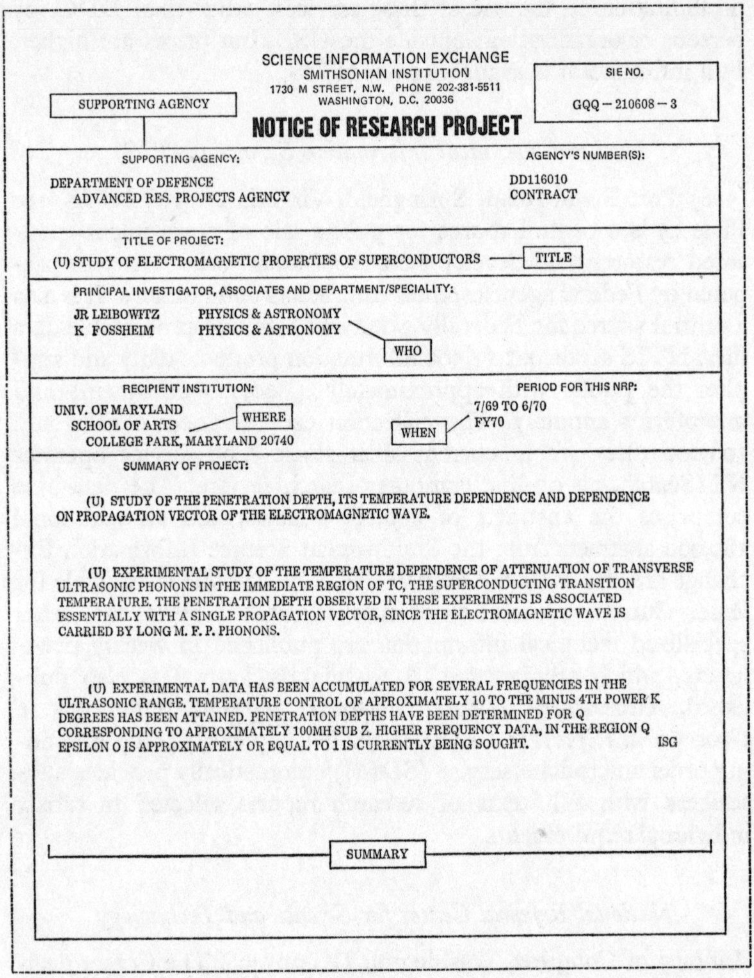

SCIENCE INFORMATION EXCHANGE
SMITHSONIAN INSTITUTION
1730 M STREET, N.W. PHONE 202-381-5511
WASHINGTON, D.C. 20036

SIE NO.
GQQ – 210608 – 3

NOTICE OF RESEARCH PROJECT

SUPPORTING AGENCY

SUPPORTING AGENCY:
DEPARTMENT OF DEFENCE
ADVANCED RES. PROJECTS AGENCY

AGENCY'S NUMBER(S):
DD116010
CONTRACT

TITLE OF PROJECT:
(U) STUDY OF ELECTROMAGNETIC PROPERTIES OF SUPERCONDUCTORS — TITLE

PRINCIPAL INVESTIGATOR, ASSOCIATES AND DEPARTMENT/SPECIALITY:
JR LEIBOWITZ PHYSICS & ASTRONOMY
K FOSSHEIM PHYSICS & ASTRONOMY
WHO

RECIPIENT INSTITUTION:
UNIV. OF MARYLAND
SCHOOL OF ARTS
COLLEGE PARK, MARYLAND 20740
WHERE

PERIOD FOR THIS NRP:
7/69 TO 6/70
FY70
WHEN

SUMMARY OF PROJECT:

(U) STUDY OF THE PENETRATION DEPTH, ITS TEMPERATURE DEPENDENCE AND DEPENDENCE ON PROPAGATION VECTOR OF THE ELECTROMAGNETIC WAVE.

(U) EXPERIMENTAL STUDY OF THE TEMPERATURE DEPENDENCE OF ATTENUATION OF TRANSVERSE ULTRASONIC PHONONS IN THE IMMEDIATE REGION OF TC, THE SUPERCONDUCTING TRANSITION TEMPERATURE. THE PENETRATION DEPTH OBSERVED IN THESE EXPERIMENTS IS ASSOCIATED ESSENTIALLY WITH A SINGLE PROPAGATION VECTOR, SINCE THE ELECTROMAGNETIC WAVE IS CARRIED BY LONG M. F. P. PHONONS.

(U) EXPERIMENTAL DATA HAS BEEN ACCUMULATED FOR SEVERAL FREQUENCIES IN THE ULTRASONIC RANGE. TEMPERATURE CONTROL OF APPROXIMATELY 10 TO THE MINUS 4TH POWER K DEGREES HAS BEEN ATTAINED. PENETRATION DEPTHS HAVE BEEN DETERMINED FOR Q CORRESPONDING TO APPROXIMATELY 100MH SUB Z. HIGHER FREQUENCY DATA, IN THE REGION Q EPSILON O IS APPROXIMATELY OR EQUAL TO 1 IS CURRENTLY BEING SOUGHT. ISG

SUMMARY

FIG. 6. A *Notice of Research Project* sheet issued by Smithsonian Science Information Exchange Inc.

been in existence for more than twenty-five years as a source of information on research in progress. It maintains and updates a data base of more than 180,000 ongoing and recently terminated projects in the life, physical, social, engineering, and behavioural sciences. Project information is gathered from more than 1,300 supporting organizations in both Federal and private sectors, indexed by professional scientists and engineers, and entered into a computerized data base. The basic record is a single-paged Notice of Research Project (Figure 6). Information is provided in a variety of formats. The *SSIE Science Newsletter* is composed of listings of research information packages on current topics. Searches are also conducted on demand. Recently a new monthly selective dissemination of information service was offered. The customer supplies SSIE with a description of his subject interests in his own terminology, a user profile is established, and the computer file is searched monthly. User profiles are modified to keep the output relevant.

Library of Congress Science and Technology Division

This division (Library of Congress, Washington DC 20540) is a central point in the Library of Congress for reference, bibliographic, and consultative service in all fields of science and technology. Clinical medicine and technical agriculture are excluded, since the National Library of Medicine and the National Agricultural Library handle these subjects. All languages are covered. The division answers reference questions, performs brief literature searches, compiles subject bibliographies on request, and offers advisory services.

National Library of Medicine (NLM)

The NLM (8600 Rockville Pike, Bethesda, Maryland, 20014) covers biomedical information for practitioners, investigators, and educators. It answers reference enquiries, provides inter-library loans and photocopies of material not readily available locally, makes collections available for on-site use, provides bibliographies on specialized subjects through the library's computer-based Medical Literature Analysis and Retrieval System (MEDLARS) and the MEDLINE (MEDLARS on-line) systems, and produces about thirty continuing bibliographies in specialized fields of biomedicine. Publications of NLM are *Index Medicus, NLM Current Catalog, Bibliography of Medical Reviews, Medical subject headings* (MeSH), *Lists of journals indexed in Index Medicus,* and *The National Library of Medicine classification.*

Defense Documentation Center (DDC)

This Center (Cameron Station, Alexandria, Virginia 22314) is the depository for documents and information generated by activities of the Department of Defense. It provides copies of documents to government agencies and to their contractors and grantees, computer-produced bibliographies of abstracts in response to user requests, and furnishes rapid bibliographies in response to teletype requests. A data-base is available on research and development work in progress. The Center publishes the *Technical Abstract Bulletin* and *Technical Abstract Bulletin Indexes*. It co-operates with NTIS and SSIE in disseminating information about its unclassified titles and research in progress.

National Agricultural Library (NAL)

(US Department of Agriculture, Beltsville, Maryland, 20705.) The library answers reference enquiries in the agricultural sciences, provides interlibrary loans and photocopy services, and makes collections available for on-site use. Cataloguing and index records are available of about 10,000 items added each month on magnetic tape. Published versions of the tape record are available through various commercial channels. The CAIN (Cataloging-Indexing) System provides comprehensive worldwide coverage of the published literature on agriculture and allied subjects. Other on-line systems currently available are MEDLINE and JURIS, the first from NLM and the second from the retrieval and enquiry system of the US Department of Justice. A Food and Nutrition Information and Educational Materials Center is located at NAL.

National Aeronautics and Space Administration (NASA)

(Scientific and Technical Information Office, Washington DC 20546.) This agency maintains at the NASA Scientific and Technical Information Facility a computer-oriented information store of more than a million publication references related to aerospace science and technology. Large collections of NASA documents are available at NASA Centers, major public and special libraries, the American Institute of Aeronautics and Astronautics, Technology Utilization Regional Dissemination Centers, and are offered for sale through NTIS. The office publishes *Scientific and Technical Aerospace Reports (STAR)* (described in Chapter 6, p. 123), *Computer Program Abstracts (CPA)*, and formal series of documents: *Technical Reports, Technical Notes, Technical Memoranda, Technical Translations*, Contractor Reports, and Special Publications. The NASA computer system is called NASA/RECON, and is operated from a remote console (see also p. 109). The data-base consists of abstracts and index terms from *STAR* and *International Aerospace Abstracts*. The user can scan subject areas and communicate with this data-base to select relevant abstracts. NASA is also willing to enter into exchange agreements (NASA Scientific and Technical Information Facility, Foreign Exchange and Acquisitions Branch, PO Box 33, College Park, Md 20740, USA).

Educational Resources Information Center (ERIC)

(National Institute of Education. Operated by Leasco Systems & Research Corp., 4833 Rugby St, Suite 303, Bethesda, Maryland 20014.) This Center was conceived in the US Office of Education in the mid-1960s as a system for providing access to educational literature. It is composed of a series of Clearinghouses specializing in different aspects of education, located throughout the country at host institutions. The Center publishes a monthly abstract journal, *Research in Education*, which announces research reports and other non-journal literature. Cumulative indexes are published by Macmillan Information, 216R Brown St, Riverside, New Jersey 08075. Reports announced in *Research in Education* can be purchased in microfiche and paper copy from the ERIC Document Reproduction Service, PO Box 190, Arlington, Virginia 22210. Major products of ERIC are bibliographies, reviews, state-of-the-art reports, monographs, and other publications. The Clearinghouses answer requests for information. A list of the sixteen Clearinghouses and other information can be obtained. The operation of

ERIC is typical of the decentralized type of information clearinghouse operations in the United States.

US Atomic Energy Commission (USAEC)

(Washington DC 20545.) About February 1975 the name of the Commission changed and its functions have been merged with those of the Energy Research and Development Administration (ERDA). It is expected that many of the information activities of USAEC will continue or even expand. Through the leadership of Dr Alvin Weinberg and others, the Commission has pioneered technical information and data centres and provided various services. At present about twenty-four centres exist. They collect, analyse, and disseminate information on nuclear science and technology to the scientific and educational communities. The USAEC also supports research and reference libraries at major laboratories to aid the scientific community, industry, and the public. Resources and services are described fully in USAEC publication *TID-4550, What's available in the atomic energy literature.*

As a result of the United Nations agreement on the peaceful uses of atomic energy, the US Atomic Energy Commission maintained a worldwide network of depository libraries from the early 1950s to 1969. The depository library system was discontinued in 1969, but many of the libraries are maintaining their collections by means of bilateral agreements or purchase. The Commission also publishes *Nuclear Science Abstracts* (described in Chapter 6, p. 124), which lists literature and reports by subject area and contains numerous indexes. Each of the information and data centres publishes various reports and literature reviews. Three technical progress reviews are currently published, *Nuclear Safety, Power Reactor Docket Information,* and *Regulatory Adjudication Issuances.*

Other centres

Other information resources abound in the United States. Two large, non-governmental sources are the Chemical Abstracts Service (CAS) and the Biological Sciences Information Services (BIOSIS) of *Biological Abstracts.* CAS is located at the Ohio State University at Columbus, Ohio, and BIOSIS is in Philadelphia, Pennsylvania. A small number of the abstracts in their abstract

Sources and Acquisition 67

journals cover the report literature. Both services offer magnetic tapes and perform automated searches by title, authors, corporate author, subject, and other identifiers.

A number of computerized data bases are becoming available throughout the United States at large university libraries and government report centres.

SOURCES IN OTHER COUNTRIES

Sources of unpublished reports on research and development in other countries include military technical information agencies, where they exist, technological laboratories in developing fields (particularly atomic energy and aerospace), universities, and documentation associations such as the Deutsche Gesellschaft für Dokumentation. National information centres are being set up in a number of countries. The military technical information agencies are unlikely to be willing to give much help to foreigners and are usually not equipped to give a service outside their own organization, though in some instances they are prepared to give a measure of help to reasonable enquirers. Because of exchange agreements, reports from atomic energy and aerospace laboratories have a high probability of being advertised in *Nuclear Science Abstracts* and the NASA *STAR* respectively, and microfiches of such reports may be available from NTIS. Where national information centres exist they will normally be anxious to help enquirers from other countries, possibly with a view to developing an exchange agreement. They will probably be able to suggest sources of supply of reports which they do not themselves hold. A list of some national centres which should be able to help in this way is given as an appendix to this monograph (see pp. 231-4). For particular countries, reference should be made to papers by Gardner (Japan), Cremer (Germany) and the monograph by Burkett (1968) (Netherlands).

Official publications of the European Economic Communities are described in a series of papers presented at a Conference organized by Aslib in April, 1974. The papers are by Vanwijngaerden (Belgium), Ejlersen (Denmark), Honoré (France), Zoller-Philips (German Federal Republic), McKenna (Republic of Ireland, and Northern Ireland), Graziani (Italy), Clement

(Luxembourg), Oltheten (Netherlands), and Holland (United Kingdom). Distribution centres are given in some cases.

SOME INTERNATIONAL SOURCES

There are several international sources which produce reports or abstract bulletins; some offer magnetic-tape services in addition. Organizations which produce reports as part of their activities include the Advisory Group for Aerospace Research and Development (AGARD) of NATO, and the European Space Research Organization (ESRO). Organizations which are primarily information services include the International Information System for the Agricultural Sciences and Technology (AGRIS), the International Food Information Service, the International Nuclear Information System (INIS), and the International Road Research Documentation (IRRD) scheme. The International Federation for Documentation, although not primarily a producer of reports, is a useful source of information.

Individual international sources

The NATO Advisory Group for Aerospace Research and Development (AGARD) (7 Rue Ancelle, 92200 Neuilly-sur-Seine, France). AGARD's mission is to bring together the leading personalities of the NATO nations in the fields of science and technology relating to aerospace to stimulate research, exchange information and provide advice. It has a number of technical panels: Aerospace Medical, Avionics, Electromagnetic Wave Propagation, Flight Mechanics, Fluid Dynamics, Guidance and Control, Propulsion and Energetics, Structures and Materials, and Technical Information. Each panel organizes an annual conference, and lecture series, both in most of the NATO countries in turn, and sponsors research. These activities result in a number of technical publications: *AGARDographs*, *AGARD reports*, *Lecture Series*, and *Conference Proceedings*. Each NATO nation has an AGARD distribution centre which distributes these documents without charge to interested organizations within their own country. The United Kingdom centre is the Defence Research Information Centre (DRIC). Microfiches are also available in the UK from BLLD and TRC and in the USA from NTIS. The annual conferences organized by the Technical Information Panel should be highlighted in that they deal with current problems and developments in information science and can be attended by invitation by any NATO national with an interest in the subject on application to AGARD. Recently such conferences have had the titles: Government Assistance for Technical Information in Industry and Simple Mechanization for Small Information Centres (Ankara, 1972): New Developments in Storage, Retrieval and Dissemination of Aerospace Information (London, 1973); National and International Networks of Libraries, Documentation and Information Centres (Brussels, 1974).

The European Space Research Organization, Space Documentation Service (ESRO SDS)* (Headquarters: Via Galileo-Galilei, 00044 Frascati, Italy. Microfiche requests: 114 Avenue Charles de Gaulle, 92 Neuilly-sur-Seine, France). The ESRO Space Documentation Service was set up in 1965 by the European Space Research Organization and the European Space Vehicle Launcher Development Organization (ELDO). From the beginning ESRO SDS has co-operated closely with NASA, and it supplies NASA with the European input to *STAR*. ESRO's own reports, some written under contract, are abstracted in *STAR* and microfiches are available in the UK from BLLD and TRC and in the USA from NTIS. ESRO SDS also runs the RECON information retrieval network described in Chapter 5 and provides SDI (selective dissemination of information) and Standard Title services described in Chapter 7. European requesters may purchase facsimile copy of microfiches of NASA and NASA-sponsored documents (those identified in *STAR* by both the symbols # and *) from ESRO/ELDO Space Documentation Service, European Space Research Organization.

International Information System for the Agricultural Sciences and Technology (AGRIS). AGRIS was set up under the auspices of the Food and Agriculture Organization of the United Nations (Via delle Terme di Caracalla, 00100 Rome, Italy). It takes input from co-operating centres which cover the literature of their own country or region, and this is processed by computer by the International Atomic Energy Authority in Vienna to prepare a monthly current awareness journal *AGRINDEX* (from January 1975). A

* Now the European Space Agency (ESA).

magnetic tape service containing all the references in *AGRINDEX* will also be offered.

International Food Information Service (UK: Commonwealth Bureau of Dairy Science and Technology, National Institute for Research in Dairying, Shinfield, Reading, RG2 9AT; USA: Institute of Food Technologists, 221N La Salle St, Chicago, Ill., 60601). This is a partnership between the Commonwealth Agricultural Bureaux in the UK, the Institut für Dokumentationswesen (IDW) in Germany, the Institute of Food Technology (IFT) in the USA and the Centrum voor Landbouwpublikation en Landbouwdocumentatie (PUDOC) in the Netherlands. An abstract bulletin, *Food Science and Technology Abstracts*, has been issued since 1971, covering journal articles, reports, standards, patents and books, the input being provided by the participating members and processed by the Zentralstelle für maschinelle Dokumentation in West Germany. About 20,000 abstracts a year are processed, and a magnetic tape version of the abstracts is produced. Computer searches are offered by IDW and an SDI service by PUDOC. The service is described in a paper by Newton.

International Nuclear Information System (INIS) (International Atomic Energy Agency, PO Box 590, A-1011 Vienna, Austria). INIS was set up under the International Atomic Energy Agency in 1970. It receives input from participating member states, either in magnetic tape form or as bibliographical data sheets which are processed in-house. An indexed announcement bulletin, *INIS Atomindex*, is produced together with a magnetic tape containing detailed bibliographical records and subject descriptors for all the announced items. Copies of the tape are available to any international organization or to the government of any member state participating in INIS. Available on subscription are abstracts on microfiche for every item on the magnetic tape, in at least one of official languages of the IAEA (English, French, Russian or Spanish). Full texts on non-conventional literature are available on microfiche, including laboratory technical reports, pre-conference papers, and theses. The services of INIS are described in the paper by Pelzer.

International Road Research Documentation (IRRD) (Transport

Sources and Acquisition

and Road Research Laboratory, Department of the Environment, Crowthorne, Berks., RG11 6AU, England). This scheme, described in a paper by Mongar, was initiated in 1965. There are three co-ordinating centres, the UK Transport and Road Research Laboratory, the Laboratoire Central des Ponts et Chaussées in Paris and the Forschungsgesellschaft für das Strassenwesen in Cologne. Other member countries are Austria, Belgium, Canada, Denmark, Ireland, the Netherlands, Norway, Portugal, Spain, Sweden and Switzerland. Some eight hundred periodicals from thirty-six countries are regularly scanned, together with technical reports, patents, conference proceedings, etc. Each IRRD member country is responsible for searching its own literature; that from non-member countries is shared. Member countries prepare abstracts in one of the three official languages, French, English and German. Keywords are selected from a three-language thesaurus. Each abstract on a standard information sheet is sent with the original document to the co-ordinating centre responsible for the language in which it is written. The centre assigns an IRRD accession number and copies of the information sheet are sent to all members on reproducible paper. Information on on-going research projects is also exchanged. Information is exchanged between IRRD and the International Road Federation which supplies abstracts of research projects from non-IRRD countries, and between IRRD and the US Highway Research Information Service. The system is suitable for retrieval using optical coincidence cards, but the Transport and Road Research Laboratory uses a System 4 computer and offers retrospective search against specific enquiries and an SDI service on a limited basis.

The International Federation for Documentation (FID) (7 Hofweg, the Hague 2001, Netherlands). FID exists to assist and develop the methods of handling technical documents and its own papers deal exclusively with such topics; the best known of them is the Universal Decimal Classification (UDC). FID is not a source of research and development reports, but its monthly information *FID News Bulletin* gives useful information on current events in the documentation world, including meetings and conferences, publications, and new sources of information.

SOURCES OF THESES AND TRANSLATIONS

Theses

In the United Kingdom the British Library Lending Division is recognized as a depository library for theses by a number of British universities. The theses are advertised for loan in the *BLLD Announcement Bulletin* (see Chapter 6), a special copyright declaration being required by the actual user. Theses are available from most UK universities from about 1972 onwards.

Virtually all dissertations listed in Section A and B of *Dissertation Abstracts International* with a 70- or later prefix are also available for loan from BLLD. As a result of the co-operative arrangements made with the Center for Research Libraries in Chicago, BLLD has access to a collection of over 600,000 foreign dissertations, mostly German, French, Dutch, Scandinavian and Swiss, about 90 per cent of them published since 1890.

In the USA, some doctoral theses are cited in *GRA* and *STAR*, but copies are not normally available from NTIS. See also *Dissertation Abstracts International*, p. 36.

Translations

A European Translations Centre (Doelenstraat 101, Delft, Netherlands) was founded by OECD in 1960 as a clearinghouse for scientific and technical translations prepared primarily from East European, Middle Eastern and Far Eastern languages into western languages especially English, French and German. ETC issues monthly a *World Index of Scientific Translations* and a list of translations notified to ETC.

In the United Kingdom, Aslib maintains the Commonwealth Index of unpublished translations, and will answer queries on the location of translations of specific papers. The Aslib Information Department has published a useful guide to translations in the United Kingdom. There are large collections of translations both at BLLD and at the Science Reference Library (Holborn Division).

In the United States the John Crerar Library, Chicago, maintains a National Translations Center which collects translations from sources in the USA and provides a photocopy service. Foreign sources of information are more highly prized in some fields than in others. Several literature searches of reports have been made in specialized fields by the US Government, its contractors, by firms, or by individuals. Translation firms are usually employed to do this work. The Joint Publications Research Service (JPRS), Washington DC for several years was active in assembling teams of translators for these projects. During the 1960s a number of Soviet language documents were translated, catalogued, and disseminated. Automatic translation of Russian and other languages became an active field for a time, and experimental translations were made available in report form.

SPECIALIZED INFORMATION CENTRES

Specialized information centres (often termed Information Analysis Centres) have developed most rapidly in the United States, given an impetus by the Weinberg report in 1963 which stated:

'We believe that the specialized information center, backed by large central depositories, might well become a dominant means for transfer of technical information. . . . Specialized information centers, to be fully effective, must be operated in closest possible contact with working scientists and engineers in the field. The activities of the most successful centres are an intrinsic part of science and technology. The centers not only disseminate and retrieve information; they create new information. . . .'

Over a hundred federally supported information analysis centres are now operating in the USA. The US Committee on Scientific and Technical Information (COSATI) has set up a panel on information-analysis centres which has defined such centres as follows:

'An information analysis center is a formally structured organizational unit specifically (but not necessarily exclusively) established for the purpose of acquiring, selecting, storing, retrieving, evaluating, analyzing, and synthesizing a body of information and/or data in a clearly defined specialized field or pertaining to a specific mission with the intent of compiling, digesting, repackaging, or otherwise organizing and presenting pertinent information and/or data in a form most authoritative, timely, and useful to a society of peers [experts] and management.'

The COSATI panel has issued a useful *Directory of Federally supported information analysis centers* (National Referral Center). Several of these centres are located at the Battelle Memorial Institute, and a paper by Murdock of the Institute discusses the concept, mission and operation of scientific and technical information analysis centres.

In the United Kingdom OSTI supported the development of five specialized information centres which are now self-supporting. Nearly all the UK centres are listed in the British Council's *British scientific documentation*.

VARIOUS KINDS OF ORGANIZATION AS SOURCES

R & D organizations

There are many other organizations which conduct research and development operations and produce reports on their work. In the United Kingdom there are the Research Associations (RAs) which cover a wide range of industries. These are supported mainly by the subscriptions of their industrial members and by sponsored work, and many of their reports are available only to their members, although some of these may be generally released on sale after a period. Most RAs produce abstract bulletins which are on public sale. Details of all the RAs will be found in *Technical services for industry*, issued (1975) by the Department of Trade and Industry (obtainable from Department of Industry, 1 Victoria Street, London, SW1 0ET). This publication also gives information on government sources and includes availability of publications.

There are also research associations in other countries, e.g. the Industrial Relations Research Association, Madison, Wis., USA, and the Forschungsvereinigung Verbrennungskraftmaschinen, Frankfurt/Main, Germany (DBR).

Statutory organizations

In addition to government departments there is a number of statutory bodies (i.e. bodies set up by laws or statutes) in the United Kingdom and elsewhere which produce reports among their other activities. Many of them make annual reports, although these seldom contain much technical information, but a number of them do produce valuable technical reports. Examples of such authorities are the British Broadcasting Corporation (whose reports are available on subscription), the Central Electricity Generating Board, the Post Office Engineering Department, and the UK Atomic Energy Authority (the latter's reports have already been mentioned). In the United States there are the Atomic Energy Commission and NASA among others, and in France the Office National des Études et Recherches Aéronautiques (ONERA).

Other organizations

There are also smaller undertakings which do not have series of reports but produce the occasional one which may well be important. It cannot be predicted where the next of these important reports will come from, but many medium-sized firms are sources of unpublished reports, usually relevant to the subjects of their interests, but occasionally of general importance.

Many large commercial organizations, such as Imperial Chemical Industries Ltd, and the major drug and oil companies, conduct considerable research operations and may be willing to release some of their reports to enquirers who make out a good case for themselves. Reference should be made to Burkett (1972) for information on firms having information departments which should be useful enquiry points. *Industrial research in Britain* also gives information on potential sources.

INFORMATION ON CURRENT RESEARCH

An information centre should keep aware of current research on topics of interest which will produce reports in due course. In the United Kingdom the Department of Education and Science publishes annually *Scientific research in British universities and colleges*. In the United States the Smithsonian Institution (for address see p. 62) operates the Smithsonian Science Information Exchange which annually collects 85,000 to 100,000 single page records of research projects currently in progress in all sciences. Extracts of this data base in the aerospace field are published in *STAR* and the Exchange will conduct subject searches of the data base and provide copies of relevant records. Each record gives a technical summary of the project and includes information on who supports the project, who performs the work, and where and when the research is performed. INSPEC is the UK exclusive agent for the Exchange in the subject areas of aerospace engineering, earth and space sciences, electronics and electrical engineering, mathematical sciences and physics, and will arrange for searches or provide 'information packs' of project records at intervals. (Information on availability and costs from INSPEC, Institution of Electrical Engineers, Savoy Place, London, WC2R 0BL). Scrutiny of US technical journals such as *Aviation Week* will also give information on contracts placed by the American government, and this can be followed up by scrutiny of the indexes to *STAR* and *Government Reports Announcements* for information on reports which have been released.

In the United States, contracts are announced in the *Commerce Business Daily*. Grants are announced in printed lists issued by agencies, such as the *Research Grants Index*, published for many years by the National Institutes of Health. The National Science Foundation, like many public and private agencies, announces its grants in annual lists. Federal agencies annually prepare detailed proposals for Congress in the above publication for Appropriations Hearings. These proposals include brief summaries of reports from grants and contracts with the agencies over the past year. The Appropriations Committee publishes the statements, edited by the agencies, in the *Congressional Record*. Although the cited reports may not be part of this record, their existence is acknowledged, and under the US *Public Information Act* (Congress) a citizen can obtain a copy of any item he can identify to an agency. Philanthropic groups, such as the Rockefeller Foundation, periodically summarize their accomplishments, list grants, and present bibliographies.

ACQUISITION

The organizations mentioned in the first part of this chapter are potential sources of reports, or of information to a reports centre wishing to build up its stock, and it is important that the centre draws up a definite acquisitions policy. This will initially be dictated by the terms of reference of the centre, which will lay down whether the centre is to specialize in a particular subject field or to cover several disciplines, and the community which is to be served. Once the fields covered, including fringe areas, have been defined, a list of likely sources can be drawn up and a decision made on which to approach for gifts, where exchanges might be negotiated, and where purchase arrangements must be made.

Methods

Acquisition by gift. A large information centre will probably be part of a larger organization which includes research establishments which produce unpublished reports. The centre may be the main channel through which these reports are distributed, but even if this is not the case, arrangements should be made for at least one copy of each report to be deposited in the centre. Where such reports are subject to control on their distribution, the centre must ensure that such controls are rigorously enforced. Smaller organizations working in the same subject area of the centre may be glad of its services to help in exploiting their reports, and will agree to arrangements for their new reports to be distributed by the centre and advertised in the centre's announcement bulletin.

Acquisition by exchange. The centre should make contact with the main report-issuing centres both at home and overseas with a view to arranging exchanges of reports. An information centre will probably have authority to supply certain of the reports in its possession to third parties, and will have its own report series, special bibliographies, state-of-the-art reports or translations which can be offered as exchange material. It is very important that no reports with restrictions on their distribution be offered as material for exchange unless the recipient organization is entitled to receive such reports.

Exchange need not necessarily be of like documents: it may be possible to arrange that an announcement bulletin which is on sale be exchanged for a supply of reports. It may in fact be very useful to have some publication which has an obvious value on public sale, as it can be used as an exchange medium for documents or other things which would not otherwise be obtainable, or as a backup or alternative to report-for-report exchanges.

Acquisition by purchase. As will be described in Chapter 6, many of the reports advertised in the US *Government Reports Announcements*, *STAR*, and *Nuclear Science Abstracts* can be purchased from NTIS as paper copies or microfiches. NTIS provides a service of Selective Dissemination of Microfiches (SDIM) whereby all available fiches in certain subject fields are supplied. A deposit account can be arranged with NTIS. US reports can also be purchased from the Government Printing Office, which also offers deposit account facilities.

In the United Kingdom, published reports can be purchased from HMSO, and announcement bulletins such as the Technology Report Centre's *R & D Abstracts*, and the *BLLD Announcement Bulletin* give addresses from which individual reports can be purchased, together with prices. Many university departments issue reports, making a charge to cover the printing cost. Some of these are advertised in the *BLLD Announcement Bulletin*. In view of the increasing cost of paper and printing, a centre must nowadays be prepared to pay for reports from such organizations, although in the past they might well have been distributed without charge.

Acquisition by special request. The centre will arrange to receive, by purchase if necessary, a number of announcement bulletins from other information centres. These should be scrutinized to identify new report-issuing organizations or new report series. These reports should be borrowed to assess their value, and consideration given to making more permanent arrangements to receive future reports, either by exchange or purchase. If a new organization is to be approached, a letter should be sent requesting the report, describing the functions of the centre, why the report is required and what use would be made of it. This is preferable to using a printed request form, and has a better chance of success. Some sources will release a document for the requester's own information, but not if there is any question of its being passed on to a third party. In such a case it may be possible to give the report limited publicity while arranging that any request arising from that publicity be passed on to the originator for him to deal with.

Whenever a report has been received from a new source it should be acknowledged and one should consider whether the connection should be developed. The first report will almost certainly contain information about others from the same source or on the same subject, and although it is unsafe to form conclusions on the first acquaintance, the balance between the amount of work involved in correspondence and the probable value of its outcome needs to be determined as soon as practicable.

Reports not in English. Foreign sources of course commonly imply reports in foreign languages for which translation facilities may or may not be available. It is comparatively easy to form some impression of the value of a report from the tables and illustrations it contains even if it does not have an abstract or other information in English, as many of them do; some Japanese documents, for example, are entirely in English although announcements may give the impression that they are in Japanese. A source of reports in foreign languages should not be neglected if the translation facilities are not adequate: there should be no difficulty in getting at least an abstract translated, and it is much better to hold a good report which cannot be read at the time than to be asked for it when it can no longer be obtained.

References

ADVISORY GROUP FOR AEROSPACE RESEARCH AND DEVELOPMENT. How to obtain information in various fields of science and technology: a user's guide. *AGARD Lecture Series* No. 69. Neuilly-sur-Seine, 1974.
ASLIB. Information Department. Report literature in the UK. *Aslib Proceedings*, 25(8). August, 1973. 320–324.
ASLIB. Information Department. Translations in the UK. *Aslib Proceedings*, 25(7). July, 1973. 264–267.
ATOMIC ENERGY COMMISSION (USA). What's available in the atomic energy literature. 6th revision. [Oak Ridge?], 1960. pp. 46. *TID*–4550.
BARR, K. P. Non-standard material at the NLL. *Aslib Proceedings*, 17(8). August, 1965. 240–245.
BRITISH COUNCIL. British scientific documentation services. London, 1974. ISBN 0 90029 15 2. pp. 72.
BURKETT, J. Special libraries and documentation centres in the Netherlands. Oxford, Pergamon Press, 1968. pp. 103.
BURKETT, J. Industrial and related library and information services in the United Kingdom. 3rd ed. Vol. 1 of Special library and information services in the United Kingdom. London, Library Association, 1972. ISBN 0 85365 086 1. pp. 273.
BURKETT, J., ed. Government and related library and information services in the United Kingdom. 3rd ed. Vol. 2 of Special library and information services in the United Kingdom. London, Library Association, 1974. ISBN 0 85365 127 2. pp. 223.
CABINET OFFICE. Government research and development: a guide to

sources of information. London, HMSO, 1974. ISBN 0 11 630127. pp. 22.
CHILLAG, J. P. Problems with reports, particularly microfiche reports. *Aslib Proceedings*, 22(5). May, 1970. 201–216.
CHILLAG, J. P. Don't be afraid of reports. *BLL Review*, 1(2). October, 1973. 39–51.
CLEMENT, L. Official publications of the Grand Duchy of Luxembourg. *Aslib Proceedings*, 26(7/8). July–August, 1974. 320–337.
CONGRESS. Public Information Act, 1966. US Code, Title 5, Section 522. Washington, US GPO, 1966.
CREMER, M. The German information scene. *Aslib Proceedings*, 23(12). December, 1971. 629–634.
DEPARTMENT OF EDUCATION AND SCIENCE. Scientific research in British universities and colleges. Vol. 1 Physical sciences, Vol. 2 Biological sciences, Vol. 3 Social sciences. London, HMSO. 1974. ISBN 0 11 270366 6* (Vol. 1); ISBN 0 11 270367 4* (Vol. 2), ISBN 0 11 270368 2* (Vol. 3).
DEPARTMENT OF INDUSTRY. Technical services for industry. London, 1975. pp. 253. (Obtainable from Research and Development Contractors Division, Department of Industry, Abell House, John Islip Street, London SW1P 4LN.)
EJLERSEN, R. Danish official publications. *Aslib Proceedings*, 26(7/8). July–August, 1974. 282–286.
GARDNER, K. S. Japanese sources of information. *Aslib Proceedings*, 11(12). December, 1959. 335–347.
GRAZIANI, A. Italian official publications. *Aslib Proceedings*, 26(7/8). July–August, 1974. 313–319.
HOLLAND, D. British official publications. *Aslib Proceedings*, 26(7/8). July–August, 1974. 272–281.
HONORÉ, S. French official publications. *Aslib Proceedings*, 26(7/8). July–August, 1974. 287–295.
HOOKWAY, H. T. The resources of the British Library. *Aslib Proceedings*. 27(1), January, 1975. 2–7.
Industrial research in Britain. 7th ed. Guernsey, Francis Hodgson Ltd., 1972. ISBN 0 85280 320 6.
MCKENNA, B. Irish official publications. *Aslib Proceedings*, 26(7/8). July–August, 1974. 304–312.
MCKENNA, B. Official publications of Northern Ireland. *Aslib Proceedings*, 26(7/8). July–August, 1974. 347–351.
MONGAR, P. E. International cooperation in abstracting services for road engineering. *Information Scientist*, 3(2). July, 1969. 51–62.
MURDOCK, J. W. Concept, mission, and operation of scientific and technical information analysis centres. *AGARD Conference Proceedings* No. 78. *Information analysis centres*. Neuilly-sur-Seine, AGARD, 1970. 1-2—1-12.
NATIONAL REFERENCE LIBRARY OF SCIENCE AND INVENTION. Periodical publications in the . . . Library . . . London, Trustees of the British Museum, 1969, 1970, 1971. 3 v.

NATIONAL REFERRAL CENTER FOR SCIENCE AND TECHNOLOGY. Directory of Federally supported information analysis centers. Washington. Library of Congress, 1970. pp. 45. *COSATI Report* 70–1 (Available from NTIS as PB 233 582.)
NEWTON, J. The International Food Information Service. *Aslib Proceedings*, 23(10). October, 1971. 544–547.
OLTHETEN, T. H. Official national publications of the Netherlands. *Aslib Proceedings*, 26(7/8). July–August, 1974. 338–346.
PELZER, C. W. The International Nuclear Information System. *Aslib Proceedings*, 24(1). January, 1972. 38–55.
PEMBERTON, J. E. British official publications. 2nd (rev.) ed. Oxford, Pergamon Press, 1974. pp. 328.
SCHMECKEBIER, L. F. *and* EASTIN, R. B. Government publications and their uses. 2nd rev. ed. Washington, Brookings Institution, 1969.
SMITH, J. R., *ed.* Guide to UKAEA documents. 5th ed. London, UKAEA, 1973. ISBN 0 8535 6025 0. pp. 48.
VANWIJNGAERDEN, F. National official publications of Belgium. *Aslib Proceedings*, 26(7/8). July–August, 1974. 267–273.
WILLIAMS, C. H., *comp.* Guide to European sources of technical information. 3rd ed. Guernsey, Francis Hodgson Ltd., 1970. ISBN 0 85280 250 1. pp. 309.
WILSON, B. J., *ed.* Aslib directory. 3rd ed. London, Aslib, 1968, 1970. ISBN 0 85142 022 1, 2. 2 v. Volume 1: Information sources in science, technology and commerce; Volume 2: Information sources in medicine, the social sciences and the humanities.
ZOLLER-PHILIPS, G. Official publications of the German Federal Republic. *Aslib Proceedings*, 26(7/8). July–August, 1974. 296–303.

SELECTED BIBLIOGRAPHY

BUCKLEY, C. Distribution of US Government publications. *Law Library Journal*, 63(1). February, 1970. 100–102.
CARTER, C., *ed.* Guide to reference sources in the computer sciences. New York, Macmillan Information, 1974. ISBN 0 02 468300 0.
HARVEY, N. Sources of information on environmental pollution. *Aslib Proceedings*, 25(8). August, 1973. 300–304.
HOUGHTON, B. Technical information sources. 2nd ed. London, Bingley, 1972. ISBN 0 85157 126 3. pp. 119.
KRUZAS, A. T., *ed.* Encyclopedia of information systems and services. 2nd ed. Ann Arbor, Michigan, Kruzas Associates, 1974. pp. 1271.
MEKEIRLE, J. O. Guide to information sources on environmental science and technology. Antwerp, Flemish Economic Association, 1974. p. 230.
MINISTRY OF DEFENCE. Guide to Government Department libraries and other libraries and information bureaux. 20th (and final) edition. London, 1971. pp. 114.
WHITE, C. M. *and others.* Sources of information in the social sciences: a guide to the literature. 2nd ed. Chicago, American Library Association, 1973. ISBN 0 8389 0134 4. pp. 720.

CHAPTER 4

Report Processing and Abstracting

The catalogues and subject indexes of an information centre are to enable the staff to identify documents which contain needed information, no matter how they may be described in the requests received. If this intention could be converted into achievement the work of information centres would be simplified, but in fact it is impossible to predict how information will be asked for, and practical considerations limit the completeness of catalogues and indexes.

Requests reach information centres in so many forms that if the centres aim to satisfy as many of the users' requests as possible they need to maintain a considerable variety of catalogues and indexes. It is unlikely that any centre maintains an index that can deal successfully with the sort of request that comes somewhat in the form 'I was looking at a report two or three years ago which contained a method for measuring such-and-such a parameter; I remember that it had a green cover, with a tea-stain on it. Can you find it for me?' There is very little exaggeration in this description, and in any case it is better than the far more common form in which the description appears to be exact, but is wrong. Such requests are not beyond being satisfied by the memories of the staff, and the memories of the staff can be the most valuable of indexes. They must, however, not be allowed to take the place of adequate records which are not subject to sickness or retirement.

PHYSICAL FORM OF CATALOGUES AND INDEXES

The physical form of the catalogues and indexes is less important than the information recorded in them, but it is important in that it places a limit on the variety and number of clues which they contain and that variety is also limited by the money and effort which can be devoted to identifying the cataloguing entries and reproducing and maintaining the catalogue. Even if the cataloguers use the entries in a selected announcement bulletin with a minimum of modification to suit the centre's needs – and this may be no more than adding the centre's accession number – some effort is needed to make this slight addition and to organize the information for entry into the catalogues and indexes.

There is much discussion about the relative advantages of bookform indexing and card catalogues. A study by Heinritz compared use of *Engineering Index* produced on catalogue cards and in book form. His conclusion was that although searching costs using cards were less, overall the book form of the *Index* was much cheaper than the card form. Bookform indexes are essentially a by-product of mechanized methods and since they can so easily be produced when access to a computer is available it is a fairly general rule that computerized centres will produce indexes for issue to their users, often at a price to defray the considerable cost of doing so. Manually operated centres, on the other hand, will as a rule use card catalogues or sheaf indexes, i.e. entries on standard sheets in a ring binder, and provide their users with announcement bulletins which are seldom cumulated or indexed. If the smaller centres are able to find the effort necessary to produce annual indexes, these are commonly of title and author only.

CATALOGUING

The amount of reports catalogued by conventional libraries is comparatively small (Sargent). In general, the rules and practices in cataloguing report literature are less rigorously followed than those for ordinary books. Traditional librarians have felt that the report represents ephemeral material, and that it will be published in a different form later. The usual procedure is not to catalogue it, but to send it to the library's 'document collection', where it is filed. Another reason for this casual treatment is because reports are produced casually, compared to the book literature. There is no consistency in format or in entry of the material. For example, the issuing agency may be reporting to an organization that has changed its name years ago; yet the reporter may still use the old name. The conventional cataloguer would have difficulty in tying down such material to related material. Thus cataloguing of report literature is difficult. A third reason reports are not always catalogued is because of expense and the backlog owing to a shortage of cataloguers. Recently, the National Library of Medicine has been cataloguing technical reports using the COSATI Rules: (Committee for Scientific and Technical Information). Subject headings are taken from *Medical subject headings (MeSH)*, published by the (US) National Library of Medicine) and the reports are listed in *Current Catalog*, which is available on magnetic tapes.

Problems

Report material presents special problems in cataloguing, particularly because of the many varieties of originating organization and report reference numbers. The various codes of cataloguing rules naturally concentrate on the more conventional types of library material, but it is useful to study the *Anglo-American Cataloguing Rules*, as some of them can be helpful in standardizing cataloguing practice among information centres. A monograph by Bakewell gives a useful discussion of cataloguing problems, and has a chapter on cataloguing special materials in which government publications are dealt with in some detail. In the USA COSATI (1966) has issued a standard for descriptive cataloguing of government scientific and technical reports.

It should be borne in mind that in large report centres cataloguing is often done by non-professional staff; any rules adopted must therefore be uncomplicated with the minimum of exceptions. They should be written down in the form of desk instructions and issued to every staff member involved in the cataloguing process.

Assembling cataloguing data

Most information centres will use printed forms (process sheets) on which the cataloguing information and movement of the report through the various stages are recorded. The layout of the process sheet will be essentially the same as that used for the centre's announcement bulletins and catalogue cards. (The layout of announcement bulletins will be discussed in Chapter 6.) The process sheet should have numbered boxes for each item of information to be recorded. This assists in standardization, and is essential if the information is to be transferred to machine-readable form for computer processing. It is often possible to cut down on clerical work

Report Processing and Abstracting

by marking the relevant data on the report cover or title-page with the appropriate box number on the process sheet. Spaces for 'house-keeping' information, such as date of receipt, numbers of copies, restrictions on dissemination, etc., should also be included on the sheet. The sheet is started as soon as the report has been checked for novelty and an accession number assigned. It will be securely attached to the master copy of the report if multiple copies have been received, the other copies being stamped with the accession number and put aside until the master copy has gone through all the processing procedures. A volume of conference proceedings should be given an accession number and recorded as a complete entity, then split into individual papers which are given successive accession numbers and processed separately. This is most easily done if at least two copies are available.

If the centre maintains card catalogues, a temporary card is made out for the new acquisition, and filed in the most appropriate catalogue, usually that for the corporate author. If a further copy of the report is received while the original copy is being processed, it can then be identified as a duplicate. If the centre relies almost entirely on bookform indexes it is worth maintaining one card catalogue of corporate authors for the sole purpose of preventing duplicate processing. In such a case the 'temporary' cards become permanent.

The various clues on a report which help to identify it include the following: (1) corporate author, i.e. the organization which carried out the research and produced the report; (2) agency, i.e. the organization which sponsored the work, usually under contract, of the corporate author; (3) reference number(s) assigned by the corporate author; (4) reference number assigned by the agency; (5) accession number assigned by a report distribution centre; (6) title of the report; (7) personal author(s), i.e. the individual(s) who wrote the report; (8) contract number, i.e. the reference number assigned by the agency to the contract under which the work was conducted; (9) project name or number; (10) date. Each report will present some of these clues, but few will have all of them.

Kinds of entry

Corporate author and agency. These are the most difficult to catalogue. Changes of name are a particular problem: industrial firms merge, government departments change their names, and government research establishments are transferred from one department to another. Another problem is the existence of subdivisions within organizations, e.g. departments within universities, and specialized divisions of large firms, each of which can be the source of distinct series of reports.

A decision has to be made as to how much is recorded to avoid too many changes with the passage of time. A useful guide is the COSATI *Corporate author headings* (1970) which lists some 50,000 corporate authors with the preferred headings in bold type. Former names and acronyms are also included with extensive cross-referencing. The preferred headings for government research establishments, for instance, give the name of the establishment and location. Heading changes due to government reorganizations are thus minimized.

In general the corporate author should be recorded as stated on the report in sufficient detail to identify the source unequivocally, but eliminating redundancies. If the name of the organization contains part of the location, this is not repeated in the entry. Thus: Cambridge University Cavendish Lab., UK, but Brunel University, Uxbridge, Mddx, UK.

A register should be maintained of the corporate author headings used, so that they are recorded in standardized form. Abbreviations can be employed for words such as Research, Department, Division, except when forming the first word of the entry as in Research Triangle Institute or Department of the Environment. For computer processing, a numerical code should be assigned to each entry (the COSATI guide mentioned above uses an eight-digit code). It is best if the responsibility for maintaining the corporate author register is assigned to one member of the staff to ensure consistency of the entries.

Report reference numbers. The corporate author reference numbers can be of various types. In some cases the reference is an alphanumeric code identifying the organization, e.g. a typical report from the Atomic Energy Research Establishment, Harwell, has the reference AERE-R-7001. Agency references are usually self-identifying in this way, e.g. a typical NASA-sponsored report has the agency reference NASA-CR-2401. Other corporate author references may give no indication of their source and be either a report number such as TR-250, or an alphanumeric code which does not identify the source. An example of this is a report reference ORC-74-4, from California University, Berkeley.

An example to show the multiplicity of reference numbers which can be assigned to a single report is the following, taken from an entry in *STAR*:

N74-28491 Aeronautical Research Council, London, England
A PARAMETRIC STUDY OF THE USE OF NOSE BLUNTING TO REDUCE THE SUPERSONIC WAVE DRAG OF FOREBODIES
P. G. Pugh and L. C. Ward
Supersedes NPL-Aero-SR-043, ARC-32284
(ARC-CP-1271, NPL-Aero-043, ARC-32284)

Of these numbers: N74-28491 is the accession number assigned by NASA; NPL-Aero-SR-043 and NPL-Aero-043 are numbers assigned by the corporate author, the Aerodynamics Division of the National Physical Laboratory; ARC-32284 is the accession number assigned by the Aeronautical Research Council; ARC-CP-1271 is the number assigned by the Aeronautical Research Council when it published the report in its *Current Paper (CP)* series through HMSO.

A helpful guide through the maze of report numbers is Godfrey & Redman's *Dictionary of report series codes*. This contains two computer-produced sections: (i) report series codes with related agencies, and (ii) corporate entries with related report series codes. Also included are useful reference notes explaining series designations.

Title. This is normally straightforward but it is usual to disregard the definite or indefinite article at the start of the title when filing. Titles in foreign languages should be translated, and both foreign language and translation recorded. Titles in Cyrillic scripts must be transliterated using an accepted system such as *British Standard* 2979 or *ISO* R9. For contract reports it is useful to include the period covered by the report after the title.

Personal authors. Names should be recorded surname first with initials of fore-names. Most centres will limit the number recorded to two or three to cut down on the number of entries, the remainder being indicated by 'et al.' or 'and others'. The filing order of hyphenated or prefixed names needs care, and a 'letter-by-letter' arrangement, i.e. one in which arrangement ignores spaces, and is alphabetical according to the letters of the heading, regardless of whether or not they form complete words, minimizes the number of rules necessary. M' and Mc are filed as Mac. Typical entries using this system would run:

Davis, A.	King, C.	Mabon, G.	Vanderplaats, P.
De Bono, E.	King-Hele, D.	Macdonald, R.	Van der Pol, C.
Debruyne, F.	Kingston, J.	McTavish, I.	Van Loon, H.
Dumas, A.		Macy, Y.	Vogt, R.
Dumaurier, G.			Von Karman, T.
			Vonnegut, D.

Contract number. This should be recorded as given on the report, but for computer processing it may be necessary to 'zero-fill' in order that the entries appear in the correct order, e.g.:

NONR-0401 not NONR-401

so that this entry appears before NONR-1234. An abbreviated period reference indicating e.g. quarterly report (QR) or final report (FR) can also be included.

Project name or number. The project name or number can be a useful retrieval tool and should be recorded if computer processing is available. Effort expended in maintaining a complete card catalogue of project names and numbers is probably not justified. It is useful, however, for technical staff to keep a small card catalogue of project names with some explanatory notes on the purpose of the project to which they will add the accession numbers of relevant reports, as this is helpful in subject retrieval.

Other data

Date. Although not a filing point, the date is important when a request limits a subject search to a specific period, say the last five years.

The collation, i.e. number of pages and references, should also be recorded, as this information is useful in assessing the value of a report as a source of reference to other documents.

Most of the cataloguing information will be found on the 'Report

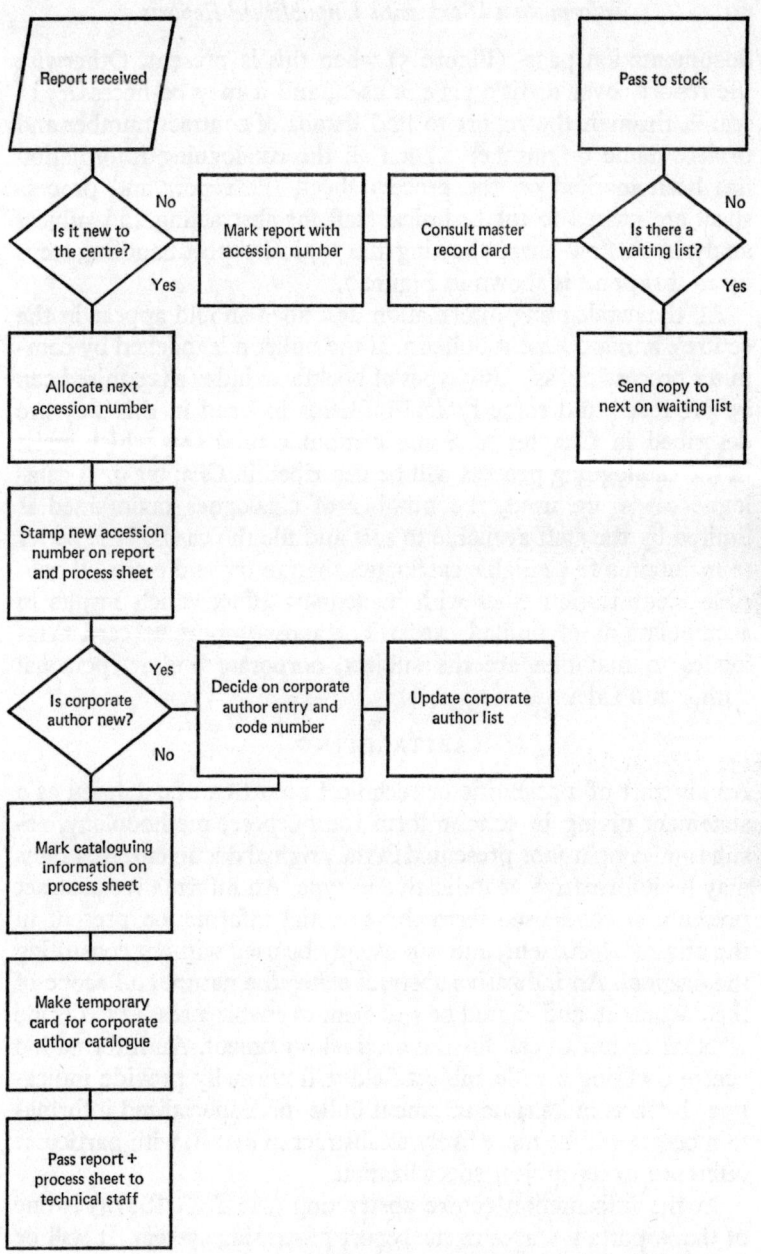

FIG. 7. A flow-chart for report processing.

documentation page' (Figure 5) when this is present. Otherwise the report cover or title page is used, and it may be necessary to search through the report to find details of contract number and project name or number. When all the cataloguing information has been marked on the process sheet, the report and process sheet are passed to the technical staff for abstracting and subject analysis. A flow-chart showing the typical report handling steps up to this point is shown in Figure 7.

All the cataloguing information described should appear in the centre's announcement bulletin. If the bulletin is indexed by computer processing, as many types of bookform index as required can be produced and some typical bulletins indexed in this way are described in Chapter 6. Some computer programs which assist in the cataloguing process will be described in Chapter 9. If catalogue cards are used, the number of catalogues maintained is limited by the staff available to sort and file the cards. It is better to maintain a few reliable catalogues than to try and cover all possible identification clues with inadequate effort which results in accumulations of unfiled cards. The most important card catalogues to maintain are the subject, corporate author, personal author and title.

ABSTRACTING

An abstract of a scientific or technical report can be defined as a statement giving in concise form the purpose, methodology, results and conclusions presented in the original document. Abstracts may be informative or indicative in type. An informative abstract presents in condensed form the essential information present in the original document, and can usually be used without consulting the original. An indicative abstract states the nature and scope of the document, and should be sufficient to enable a reader to decide whether or not to call for the original document. An information centre covering a wide subject field will normally provide indicative abstracts in its announcement bulletin. A specialized information centre will be more likely to abstract in depth, with particular reference to its subject specialization.

In the information centre abstracting (see *ISO* R 214) is one of the important stages in the report processing system. It will be one of the tasks assigned to the technical staff, and reports will usually be allocated to them according to their subject specialization. When the number of reports being processed is very large, it will not be possible for the abstractors to read every report from cover to cover, and short cuts must be taken. Many reports will have abstracts provided by their authors. These abstracts can often be used as they stand, or shortened if necessary. If no abstract is provided, information can often be taken from the introduction and conclusions.

When a complete abstract has to be written, it is useful to adopt the guidelines summarized by Ashworth (1967). The requirements are that an ideal abstract requires statement of: the leading subject of the text, the type of study covered (e.g. an experimental survey, product development, evaluation, or theoretical), the nature of the problem investigated and the methods and conditions of its solution, particularly if novel; the conclusions reached and the justifications advanced for them.

An abstract should be written concisely in good English. It should be a single paragraph, with unusual acronyms spelled out in parentheses. It is unnecessary to repeat information given in the title, which will have been read by the user before scanning the abstract. Good style facilitates use of an announcement bulletin and enhances the reputation of the information centre.

It is important that abstracting should not be regarded as a chore by the abstractors. It is the best method of improving their subject specialization and keeping them up to date with developments. Ashworth (1973) discusses abstracting as a fine art, and if this attitude can be inculcated in the abstractors, it will result in the best possible abstracts.

The cost of abstracting has led to the investigation of automatic abstracting by computer by Luhn (1957, 1958) and others. This involves computer processing of machine-readable text to count significant words. For each sentence a 'significance factor' is derived which reflects the number of significant words in a sentence and their relationship. One or more of the highest ranking sentences are printed out as the 'auto-abstract'. Until optical character recognition systems become more generally available, the cost of converting the whole text of a report into machine-readable form will be considerably more than that of a human abstractor, but the process remains an interesting possibility for the future.

ACKNOWLEDGEMENT

Mr Fuccillo wishes to acknowledge a personal communication from Miss Emilie Wiggins, National Library of Medicine.

References

ANGLO-AMERICAN CATALOG(U)ING RULES; prepared by the American Library Association, the Library of Congress, the Library Association and the Canadian Library Association. British text: London, Library Association, 1967. pp. 422. North American text: Chicago, American Library Association, 1967. pp. 422.

ASHWORTH, W. Abstracting. *Ashworth, W., ed. Handbook of special librarianship and information work.* 3rd ed. London, Aslib, 1967. 453–481.

ASHWORTH, W. Abstracting as a fine art. *Information Scientist,* 7(2). June, 1973. 43–53.

BAKEWELL, K. B. A manual of cataloguing practice. Oxford, Pergamon Press, 1972. ISBN 0 08 016697 0. pp. 298.

BRITISH STANDARDS INSTITUTION. Transliteration of Cyrillic and Greek characters. London, 1958. pp. 23. *BS* 2979.

COMMITTEE ON SCIENTIFIC AND TECHNICAL INFORMATION (COSATI). COSATI standards for descriptive cataloging of government scientific and technical reports. Washington, 1966. (Available from NTIS as AD 641 092.)

COMMITTEE ON SCIENTIFIC AND TECHNICAL INFORMATION (COSATI). Corporate author headings. Washington, 1970. *COSATI Report* 70–7. (Available from NTIS as PB 198 275.)

GODFREY, L. E. *and* REDMAN, H. F., *ed.* Dictionary of report series codes. 2nd ed. New York, Special Libraries Association, 1973. ISBN 0 87111 209 4. pp. 645.

HEINRITZ, F. Book versus card catalog costs. *Library Resources and Technical Services,* 7(3). Summer, 1963. 229–236.

INTERNATIONAL ORGANIZATION FOR STANDARDIZATION (ISO). Abstracts and synopses, Geneva, 1961. pp. 4. *ISO R* 214.

INTERNATIONAL ORGANIZATION FOR STANDARDIZATION (ISO). International system for the transliteration of Slavic Cyrillic characters. 2nd ed. Geneva, 1968. pp. 8. *ISO R* 9.

LUHN, H. P. A statistical approach to mechanized encoding and searching of information. *IBM Journal of Research and Development,* 1(4). October, 1957. 309–317.

LUHN, H. P. Automatic creation of literature abstracts. *IBM Journal of Research and Development,* 2(2). April, 1958. 159–165.

SARGENT, C. W. Handling technical reports in the medical library. *Bulletin of the Medical Library Association,* 57(1). January, 1969. 41–46.

CHAPTER 5

Subject Analysis and Information Retrieval

The subject analysis of reports is a most important operation since it perhaps demands more skilled effort than any other task in an information centre, and the success or failure of later information retrieval operations depends on how well the original subject analysis was done. The method of subject analysis will be dictated to some extent by the retrieval system used by the centre, and because of this the systems will be discussed first. Bourne and others have summarized methods of information handling. The methods are changing as advances are made in indexing, thesaurus construction, cataloguing, retrieval and language.

INDEXING SYSTEMS

Indexing systems may be divided into pre-co-ordinate and post-co-ordinate systems according as to whether the co-ordination of the indexing terms to form the concepts required for retrieval takes place at the indexing stage or at the retrieval stage.

Pre-co-ordinate systems

A commonly used pre-co-ordinate system is the Universal Decimal Classification which has been used successfully for the subject indexing of reports. The UDC is issued under the authority of the International Federation for Documentation (FID) (7 Hofweg, the Hague, Netherlands) and the English-language version is published by the British Standards Institution as separate parts of *BS* 1000. The UDC is very suitable for a subject index based on standard catalogue cards, but several cards may have to be produced if the number of concepts covered in the report is large. The disadvantage of UDC is the slowness with which it is revised, so that users may adopt home-made extensions in areas in which they have most accessions in order to avoid having too many cards behind each tab card in their own index drawers. Pre-co-ordinated systems are seldom used in information retrieval by computer, especially in the large computerized systems in the USA (e.g. DDC, MEDLARS, NASA). Work has, however, been reported on the application of UDC to machine searching including papers by Caless & Kirk, for seismological literature, by Rigby, on computerizing the UDC meteorology schedules, and by Freeman & Atherton on the American Institute of Physics' Project AUDACIOUS (Automatic Direct Access to Information with On-line UDC System).

It is interesting to note, also, that pre-co-ordinated subject headings are used in many computer-produced bookform subject indexes to increase their usefulness for information retrieval, although when computer searching the magnetic tapes used to produce the indexes a post-co-ordinate system is employed.

Post-co-ordinate systems

In such systems the combination of terms takes place at the retrieval stage. One of the first widely used post-co-ordinate systems was the Uniterm system introduced by Mortimer Taube. In this system the documents are given an accession number and the subject of each document is broken down, as far as possible, into a series of single words, combinations of words being called 'bound terms'. The terms are used as headings on cards ruled into ten columns numbered 0–9. The accession numbers of the documents are entered (posted) in the column corresponding with their *last* digit. When information on a complex subject is to be retrieved, the appropriate cards for the single terms which by co-ordination define this subject are extracted from the index and visually compared. The numbers common to all the cards are the accession numbers of the documents dealing with the subject. Advantages of post-co-ordinate systems include faster indexing, because there is no need to decide on a citation order for the various elements of a complex subject and then assign a class number; savings in space because of the number of documents which can be posted on one card, and the ease in which the system can be adapted to computer retrieval. Disadvantages include the necessity for translating the accession number into meaningful bibliographical data before the relevance of the report to the request can be assessed, and the problem of false co-ordinations or retrieval of irrelevant information (sometimes called 'noise').

The thesaurus. The basis of post-co-ordinate indexing usually is the list of subject indexing terms (in this context usually known as 'descriptors') called a 'thesaurus'. Many thesauri have been published in particular subject fields, such as the NASA thesaurus for aerospace and the Euratom thesaurus in the field of atomic energy. For a wide subject coverage the best-known is probably the *Thesaurus of engineering and scientific terms (TEST)* issued in the USA in 1967 by the Engineers' Joint Council (EJC) in association with the Department of Defense. *TEST* resulted from the merging of a project (Project LEX) of the US Office of Naval Research with an EJC project to update the first EJC thesaurus issued in 1964. *TEST* contains 17,800 descriptors. The thesaurus of terms is an alphabetical list in letter-by-letter arrangement, each main term being associated with the appropriate COSATI subject category field and group and followed by USE FOR (U.F.) terms, if applicable, and a series of Broader Terms (B.T.), Narrower Terms (N.T.) and Related Terms (R.T.). Where the term is not an approved term there is a USE reference, e.g.

    Chalks
     USE Calcium carbonates

    Cheese antennas
     USE Cylindrical antennas
     and Directional antennas
     and Parabolic antennas

A typical approved term is set out as follows:

    Medical services 1505 0605
     U.F. Outpatient services
     B.T. Services
     N.T. Hospitalizing
     R.T. Casualties
      —Contracted services
     Dental services

Field hospitals
_Hospitals
Logistics operations
_Medical equipment
_Medical supplies
Preventive medicine

The symbol _ directs the user to see the descriptor referred to for narrower terms. In addition to the alphabetical list of terms there is a permuted index which is a computer-generated display of all terms in the thesaurus permuted according to each significant word in the single and multi-word terms, arranged in alphabetical order on the permuted words; a subject category index, in which the descriptors are grouped alphabetically by subject under the COSATI subject category field and group numbers, and a hierarchical index which displays descriptor families based on the Broader Term-Narrower Term references in the *Thesaurus of . . . terms*. Certain kinds of terms are not included in the thesaurus although they may be useful in indexing. These include project names, military nomenclature, geopolitical names, units of measurement, and proper names. Such terms, usually known as 'identifiers' can be assigned by users at their discretion, and it is up to the user to ensure consistency of their entries.

TEST is widely used for indexing report collections covering a broad field, and the descriptors included in the entries in NTIS *Government Report Announcements* are in general compatible with *TEST*. Centres which obtain a considerable input of *GRA*-listed reports thus have considerable inducement to use *TEST*. Unfortunately *TEST* is unlikely to be updated, as the US Defense Documentation Center is intending to use machine-aided indexing and a natural language data-base which will be described later in this chapter.

An interesting project was the preparation of the *Medical and health related sciences thesaurus* (Department of Health, Education and Welfare). This thesaurus is extensive – more than five hundred pages of small print. It is used to index in depth all research grants of the National Institutes of Health, whose annual budget exceeds $1,500,000,000. This thesaurus is continually updated. An annual index of grants is produced by use of the thesaurus, and the index words are part of a retrieval system for the grant

1. Station Square House, St Mary Cray, Kent, which houses DRIC and TRC.

2. The National Technical Information Service (NTIS), US Department of Commerce, is located in Springfield, Virginia. The agency has more than 400 employees. It is housed in two buildings, occupying more than 100,000 square feet.

3. RECON terminal at Technology Reports Centre.

4. A newly developed XEROX Micro-Enlarger Processor is used at the NTIS to produce a printed report from microfiche. The new machine is capable of printing up to forty-five pages per minute.

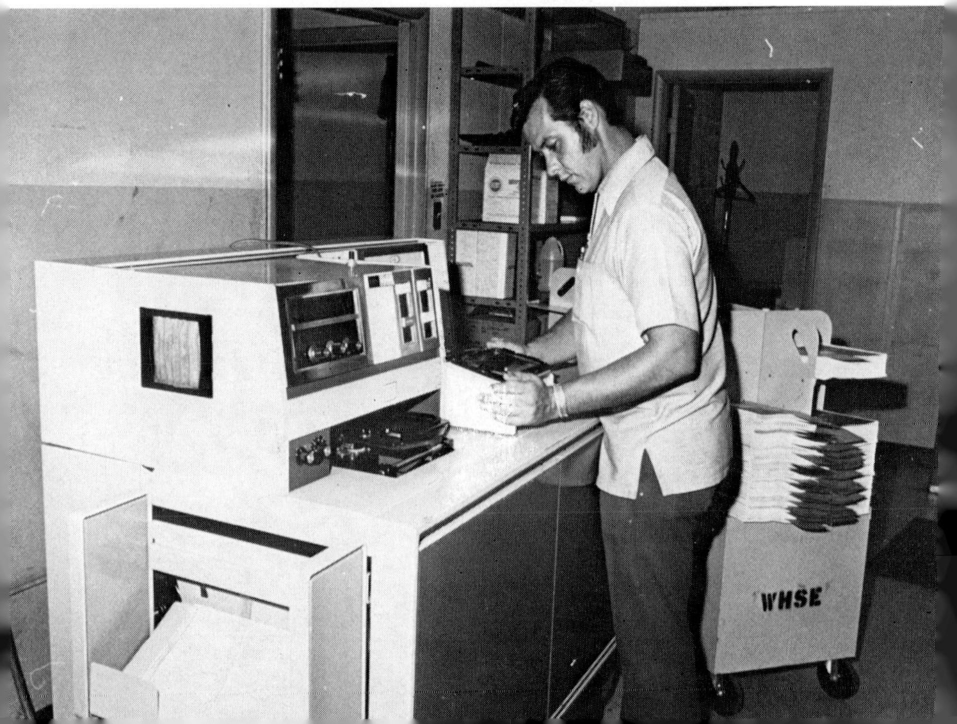

documents. As part of this system, the financial and management information is filed. Cumulations of document titles, dollar figures, publications, and other data are compiled periodically with this system. This example is given to alert the reader to the contributions of management-information systems to cataloguing, indexing, and thesaurus construction. Although considered a special field, management information work has provided stimulus to documentation. Managers and business persons have been interested in their own information (Blagden 1969), Vernon & Lang) as well as that of the firms for which they work (Meltzer).

With so much work going on in retrieval, inevitably problems of compatibility of equipment and techniques occur. Henderson & others have summarized some of these problems. A continuing effort is being carried out at the National Bureau of Standards to dovetail at least government information systems.

Thesaurus construction. Specialized information centres may find TEST too general, and will want to construct their own thesaurus which covers their speciality in depth. For this a good deal of preparation, both mental and physical, is essential. Some proponents assert that only a very small number of terms (a few hundred) need be used for any collection of papers, but this argument is unlikely to be acceptable in any large information centre. On the other hand physical and memory considerations are likely to set an upper limit to the number of terms used, and these considerations are reinforced by using a comparatively small thesaurus. A collection of a few thousand terms seems a reasonable compromise, as the indexers can carry a large proportion in their memory and the need for artificial conventions is minimized. Care must be taken to avoid the inclusion of synonyms or of terms which could be taken as such.

The thesaurus will contain numbers of 'bound terms' (e.g. Tropical tests) and very general terms will be avoided. It is useful to have a compulsory division of terms which involve measurement in scales, e.g. 100–200°C, 200–400°C; generous provision of scope notes is highly desirable, and the hierarchical relations of terms should be displayed. A 'dummy run' is almost essential before any thesaurus, whether home-made, adapted or adopted, is taken into regular use, particularly when a conversion from classification to keyword indexing is being made. This familiarizes the staff with the techniques they will have to acquire and the general advantages and disadvantages of the method, quite apart from its usefulness in bringing to light the inevitable weaknesses in the construction of the thesaurus and in its application.

No thesaurus is proof against the passage of time: unsuspected errors will be found, some terms turn out to be hardly ever used while others are so frequently used as to be useless for retrieval purposes. The concepts represented by these latter terms need to be broken down into more detailed keywords. Amendments are essential from time to time, though this necessity becomes less frequent and less onerous as experience and expertise increase; the usual problem, however, arises when amendments are made: are they to be retrospective or only applicable from a stated accession number? The answer must depend upon local circumstances.

The possibility of computer assistance in thesaurus construction is examined in the paper by Pickford (1968). This system was developed as part of the UK Medical Research Council's Project FAIR (Fast Access Information Retrieval). An Atlas computer was programmed to select the basis of a thesaurus from descriptors allotted by part-time indexers to a representative cross-section of the literature of biomedical engineering, but the method is independent of the subject.

A useful literature review on thesaurus compilation methods has been published by Blagden (1968), and for a detailed description of various thesauri, methods of construction and evaluation, and the role of the thesaurus in searching, reference should be made to the monograph by Gilchrist. A practical manual on thesaurus construction has been written by Aitchison & Gilchrist.

Subject analysis

Intellectual. As defined by Vickery, the process involves three stages:

(1) The text is scanned to select a set of words, phrases or sentences which collectively represents its subject.
(2) A decision is taken as to which of these subject descriptions are worth recording as being relevant to the purpose of the retrieval system.
(3) The relevant subject descriptions are transferred into the standard descriptor language used in the system.

It is arguable whether the subject analyst needs to scan the whole report, or whether he can obtain sufficient clues from the title and abstract. A paper by Scheffler & others reports an investigation at the Aerospace Materials Information Center, University of Dayton Research Institute, on the significance of titles, abstracts and other portions of technical documents as sources of indexing information from the point of view of cost-effectiveness of the indexing process.

Whether a pre- or a post-co-ordinate system is used, it is necessary to determine how specific the indexing is to be, bearing in mind the need for a balance between recall and precision at the searching (information retrieval) stage. Recall may be defined as the proportion of total relevant references retrieved during a search, relative to the total number of relevant references contained in the data-base. Precision may be defined as the proportion of relevant references retrieved during a search, relative to the total number of references retrieved. High recall may be achieved if many broad generic terms are included at the input (indexing) stage, at the risk of swamping the requester with too many citations, some of which are only marginally relevant. High precision may be achieved by indexing with only the most narrow descriptors. However, excessive specificity at this stage can result in partially relevant, and even key, documents being excluded from the output. In a manual card catalogue, it is possible to browse through the cards and find more general or more specific references, but in a post-co-ordinate system the output is usually in the form of accession numbers, and it is not possible to browse. It is therefore more important in a post-co-ordinate system to include generic as well as specific terms, and to be generous in the number of descriptors allotted.

The amount of effort to be given at the subject analysis stage is determined to some extent by the amount the data-base is to be subsequently used for retrieval. Fast retrieval is facilitated by good subject analysis, but if it is never necessary to retrieve a large proportion of the reports in the system, very detailed subject analysis is uneconomic, and extra time can be given to developing the search strategies in the limited number of information retrieval operations that take place.

In natural language. One facet of subject analysis which has attracted attention in recent years is the use of what is sometimes referred to as natural language or free text in subject indexing; this amounts to the use as descriptors of words extracted from the title and abstract, or sometimes the full text of a document. This has advantages provided that the author of the text is not too addicted either to the invention of new words as labels for his concepts, or to the excessive use of 'elegant variations', or, worse, to the misuse of existing words for his meanings. The process of automatic abstracting referred to in Chapter 4 can be used to print out the most significant and frequently used words in a text, which could then be used as descriptors. However most of the work so far reported has been done by human scanning of titles and abstracts.

INDEXING BY COMPUTER

An early form of computer-produced index which has proved to be of lasting value is the KWIC (Key Word In Context) introduced by Luhn and used by the American Chemical Society in *Chemical Titles*. After being supplied with a 'stop list' of non-significant words the computer will sort titles so that each significant word appears in the centre of a column in alphabetical order surrounded by the words in the title preceding and following it. Variations on KWIC are KWOC (Key Word Out of Context) or KWAC (Key Word And Context) in which the significant word appears as a catalogue heading to the titles containing it. KWIC and KWOC indexes are produced with the minimum of human effort and are popular with users, but they depend on informative titles to be of use in retrieval. The heading of one article on helicopters, 'Anything a horse can do', will hardly produce a useful KWIC entry.

One of the first investigations in the use of natural language subject indexing formed part of the Cranfield project on factors determining the performance of indexing systems, and was reported by Cleverdon (1966). The tests simulated a mechanized system and compared the effects of indexing different numbers of terms and then retrieving by combinations of different numbers of these indexed terms. It was found that in the conditions of these tests the use of natural language was, on the whole, more effective than that of the controlled terms found in a thesaurus. The advantage of natural language was dependent on the use of a comparatively large number of indexing terms, and with a small number of indexing terms the advantage would be with the controlled vocabulary. Others (e.g. Salton, and Keen & Digger) have come to similar conclusions.

An investigation, first reported in two papers by Aitchison & others, and Aitchison & Tracey, and summarized in a paper by Barlow, was made when setting up the INSPEC system, entitled the DEVIL project (Direct Evaluation of Index Languages). The result showed the thesaurus-based language to be the most effective, with free indexing second. Since it was considered impracticable to use the thesaurus-based language for input which might be provided internationally and since it was believed that a method could be developed for raising the effectiveness of free-indexing to match it, it was decided to adopt the free indexing system. Studies by Hersey & others, Olive & others, Bhattacharyya and other authors have been made on the subject.

More than ten years ago, a report was made to the US Senate of activities in documentation, indexing and retrieval of scientific information (Senate). Many of these activities have been expanded, modernized, and continued. For instance, in May, 1960, the National Library of Medicine submitted to the study staff a copy of the first issue of *Index Medicus*, which had been produced by a partially mechanized process. Today's NLM operates an extensive network with on-line computer access to *Index Medicus*. During the past twenty years the Department of Defense as well as civilian agencies and private organizations have supported work in the fields affecting retrieval of information. If adequate support is continued, especially in fundamental work, the whole enterprise will move ahead. A project of long-standing interest should be mentioned here. The Defense Documentation Center (DDC) has persisted in work on machine-aided indexing and in the construction of a natural-language data-base (Klingbiel, all references). The system is described as a partial syntactic analysis technique for indexing text. The text (data-base) is comprised of titles and abstracts of reports. These words are entered into DDC computers and a recognition dictionary is built up from the words. A programme selects only 'unique' words for this dictionary, and noun-clusters and other combinations of words are formed from the dictionary. Incoming text is now being indexed by use of this dictionary and syntactic analysis of the context of text. Successful indexing by this method depends upon the idea that the number of 'unique' words will be manageable. At least for DDC documents, this idea seems likely. At the million word level, a dictionary of 21,463 words was generated. Now at the two-million-word level, the dictionary has grown only to 26,500 unique words. The workers predict a peak of 75,000 unique words at ten million words of text.

Computer-aided indexing

KWIC and KWOC indexes require the minimum of intellectual effort, but give no subject analysis of the documents other than title words. Two systems are reported in which the computer is used to generate indexing terms from titles and abstracts, and the human indexer can intervene to approve or discard these terms. In the United Kingdom, Imperial Chemical Industries Ltd Agricultural Division has developed the ASSASSIN system (Agricultural System for Storage And Subsequent Selection of INformation) (see also p. 106).

Sharp describes a type of indexing he devised and entitled SLIC (Selective Listing In Combination) in which permuted indexing terms (normally up to five) selected by the subject analyst are printed out against document accession number. This in effect computerizes the operation of retrieval by co-ordinating feature cards.

Another approach to computer-aided indexing is suggested in the article by Gray & Harley, in which the principle of citation indexing (see p. 103) is used. The method analyses the index terms assigned to the references cited by the new document. This produces a list of index terms weighted according to their expected correlation with the subject matter of the new document so that the indexer is presented with a weighted list of proposed indexing terms as an aid. Tests of the technique with a trial set of documents already indexed for the MEDLARS system gave encouraging results.

A different type of computer-aided indexing, in which the intellectual effort precedes the computer operation is exemplified by the PRECIS system (PREserved Context Index System) developed by the *British National Bibliography* to generate subject index headings for MARC tape entries. The system is described in the article by Austin, and in a PRECIS manual *(British National Bibliography)*.

A state-of-the-art review of semi-automatic indexing by Fangmeyer has recently been published by AGARD. This includes discussion of both the KWIC-type and the keyword or descriptor type of indexing. A state-of-the-art review on automatic indexing has also been prepared by Sparck-Jones and issued as an OSTI report.

A useful guide to computer-produced indexes, including KWIC, KWOC and SLIC types, is given in the report by Campey. The information presented includes type of computer, programming information and cost data.

Mention should also be made of citation indexing, exemplified by *Science Citation Index* published by the Institute of Scientific Information. In this index all citations of a previously published paper are computer-sorted alphabetically under the name of the cited author. In addition to the index by cited author, *Science Citation Index* has a source index arranged by author and containing detailed information about the citing articles, and a 'permuterm' subject index, produced from the title input to the main index.

There does not at present appear to be a clear-cut answer to the problem of retrieval. Perhaps the best advice is given in the paper on natural language information retrieval systems by Townley. She concludes:

> 'stick to what you know – human indexing and a controlled vocabulary – unless either someone is making natural text available to you at no more cost than you would have to face if you were inputting citation plus indexing terms; or you know so little about the collection or your users' needs that you cannot anticipate by drawing up a controlled vocabulary'.

EVALUATION OF INDEXING SYSTEMS

Pioneer work in comparing the efficiency of indexing systems was carried out in the United Kingdom at the College of Aeronautics, Cranfield (now the Cranfield Institute of Technology) as the Aslib Cranfield Project under the direction of C. W. Cleverdon and with the support of the US National Science Foundation. The first part of the project (Cranfield I) reported by Cleverdon (1960, 1962) compared four indexing methods (UDC, a faceted classification, alphabetical subject headings, and Uniterm post-co-ordinate indexing for a collection of 18,000 documents (half journal articles and half reports). Four hundred questions were put to the indexed collection. Little difference was found in the recall ratios of the four systems. The Cranfield methodology was also used to test the index of metallurgical literature at Western Reserve University, Ohio, and the results reported by Aitchison & Cleverdon. Cranfield II (Factors determining the performance of indexing systems) has already been discussed in the section on indexing in natural language.

The College of Librarianship Wales, Aberystwyth, began an investigation into indexing systems in 1968 using a data-base of reports and journal articles in library and information science. A recent report on the project by Keen & Digger on tests in which three post-co-ordinate and two pre-co-ordinate index language systems were used for 800 documents showed no really large differences in retrieval effectiveness and efficiency.

Both the Cranfield and Aberystwyth experiments took place in a research environment. In the production situation of an information centre the cost of the indexing process must also be taken into account. In connection with work on developing rules for human, machine, and man-machine indexing, Schultz describes how measures of cost and of effectiveness can be considered jointly in deciding how to reduce cost of indexing at a given level of effectiveness. Cost-effectiveness also was the primary measurement in the work by Scheffler & others already cited in connection with the significance of titles, abstracts, and other portions of technical documents for information retrieval.

INFORMATION RETRIEVAL

Intellectual systems

Information retrieval with pre-co-ordinated manual systems is the simple visual operation of scanning cards in a card catalogue or subject heading entries in a bookform index. The intellectual effort required is that to formulate the search strategy, and the fact that the results can be immediately verified by reading the bibliographical data provided on the card or under the printed index entry enables the strategy to be quickly modified if required.

With post-co-ordination using the Uniterm system, columns of report numbers have to be scanned in parallel to identify coincidences. This can be time-consuming in a complicated search in which several terms are co-ordinated, and the process has been considerably facilitated by the development of optical-coincidence or 'feature' cards. In these systems large cards are supplied commercially printed with a numbered grid of up to 20,000 or more squares which are converted into holes by punching the appropriate numbers for the relevant report accession numbers. Co-ordination is observed by aligning the cards and holding them up to the light. Passage of light through the coincident holes immediately identifies the 'hits', and the accession numbers of the reports required are read from the grid.

A cheap method of preparing feature cards is another by-product of Project FAIR and is described by Pickford (1969). This method employs standard 80-column cards which can be punched by computer and reproduced in quantity using an 80-column card reproducer for dissemination to users. It is suggested that such a system is suitable for an annual input of up to 5,000 items.

The paper by Johnson & Baker gives a useful discussion of the practical considerations of operating an optical-coincidence card system.

Machine systems

For information retrieval by computer the bibliographical data and descriptors for each report must be input to the computer in machine-readable form, either by punched cards, punched paper tape or magnetic tape. The data must be structured into 'fields' so that the same type of data always appears in the same field. The fields can be terminated by any special symbol which the computer can recognize. For information retrieval the field to be particularly considered is that for the descriptors. Within this field the descriptors can be separated by any desired symbol, provided this symbol does not appear in the same field with another connotation. For a small data-base the computer can be programmed to search for single descriptors in the descriptor field of each item in serial order, to match against the descriptors of the search equation.

A subject search will co-ordinate descriptors as in manual post-co-ordinate systems, and in computer retrieval this is normally by using the Boolean operators 'and', 'or', and 'not'. (Further discussion of such search strategies will be found in the section on SDI in Chapter 7.) For large data-bases, the best method of search is to use the same type of inverted file arrangement as is used in optical-coincidence cards. The computer is programmed to take off the descriptor data from the original serial file and construct a file in which each descriptor is followed by the document identification numbers (either the document accession number or an equivalent computer-generated number) in ascending order, of all reports to which this descriptor has been allocated. This inverted file is the one used to search against the Boolean search equation. The document numbers which meet the requirements of the Boolean equation are matched against the serial file and the bibliographical data printed out for each document number as the answer to the search. It can be arranged that the number of documents meeting the equation is printed out before the final data printout, so that the search question can be broadened or narrowed to give a reasonable number of 'hits'.

There are some computer program packages developed for information retrieval using an inverted file which are offered to other users on terms to be negotiated. Examples are the ASSASSIN system, INFIRS (Inverted File Information Retrieval System) developed by UKCIS, and IBM's IRMS (Information Retrieval and Management System). The International Labour Office has designed ISIS (Integrated Scientific Information System).

ASSASSIN (Agricultural System for Storage And Subsequent Selection of INformation) is an information retrieval package developed by Imperial Chemical Industries Ltd, Agricultural Division for operation on an IBM 360/65 computer with a data-base of 50,000 to 70,000 documents. From a single paper tape input containing bibliographical data, abstract, and added terms, SDI and KWOC listings are produced and the inverted file updated. The retrospective search facility uses weighted terms, searches being batched. Programmes for producing a structured thesaurus are part of the package. The system is described in papers by Clough & Bramwell and Clough & others.

INFIRS is a document search system offering a comprehensive range of search facilities. It can handle both free-text and con-

Subject Analysis and Information Retrieval

trolled data-bases both for retrospective search and SDI. It is described in the report by McCracken & others.

IRMS is a programme package designed to run on a small IBM 360 computer. The system comprises a thesaurus of index terms, an inverted search file and a bibliographic file. Its use is described in the paper by Abbot & Simkins who applied IRMS to an index of chemical structures and to index laboratory experiments.

ISIS described in the manual by Schieber, is an inverted-file disc-based information retrieval system which can be used for batch or on-line processing. It is designed for small- to medium-sized computers, and has been implemented on an IBM 360. New records can be input from on-line terminals.

Commercial batch-information-retrieval systems

In the United Kingdom searches can be made on some large data-bases, which are operated on a commercial basis. The best-known of these services are UKCIS and the UK MEDLARS service.

UKCIS (United Kingdom Chemical Information Service) (Service Department, UKCIS, The University, Nottingham, NG7 2RD) offers retrospective search services on the Chemical Abstracts Service tapes *Chemical Titles* (1962 to date), *Chemical-Biological Activities* (1965 to date) and *Chemical Abstracts Condensates* (1965 to date). Searches may be restricted to any specified period of one or more years. A new data-base, C. A. Reviews, currently consisting of all references to reviews contained in the *Chemical Abstracts Condensates* data-base during the period January 1972 to December 1974 can also be searched. This data-base will be updated every six months until a five-year period has been covered, and will then be maintained to cover the five most recent years.

UK MEDLARS. MEDLARS (Medical Literature Analysis and Retrieval System) (British Library Lending Division, Boston Spa, Wetherby, West Yorkshire, LS23 7BQ) is a computer-based system set up by the National Library of Medicine in the USA. The data-base consists of the contents of *Index Medicus*, indexed by descriptors from *Medical subject headings* (MeSH). Search strategies are currently formulated by staff of the UK MEDLARS Service at BLLD and the searches are processed on the ICL 4/50 computer at UKCIS. Searches can now be transmitted to the computer via an ICL Termiprinter at BLLD. The searches are stored on disc at the computer, batches processed weekly and a charge made for each request processed. A monthly SDI service can also be purchased. Since autumn 1968, the greater part of the British medical periodical literature has been indexed at BLLD for input to the system. On-line searching of the MEDLARS database is also available as an experimental system, MEDUSA, and this is described in a later section.

On-line information-retrieval systems

In large centres with their own computers operating in a multi-programming mode, it is possible to have terminals distributed throughout the centre and interrogate the computer directly. Lancaster & Fayen describe a number of on-line retrieval systems in the USA and the UK, and give information on equipment, searching, file design, performance criteria and effectiveness evaluation. With an on-line system the user can interact with the computer, and systems are usually designed to display the number of documents indexed under a given descriptor, and the number of documents which meets the requirements of a Boolean logical equation. If this latter number is very large, the user can make his search more specific by including narrower terms or, if the logical equation produces very few references, the search can be broadened. UK 'in-house' on-line systems described in the literature include OVID (Patten), QUOBIRD and QUODAMP (Carville & others) and RIOT (Negus, Negus & Hall, and Hall & others). Remote on-line systems available by networking will be described in the next section.

The benefit of an on-line system for information retrieval will increase with the size of the centre's data-base. It is possible to augment this by leasing commercial magnetic tapes, e.g. that of the US *Government Reports Announcements* (this topic is also discussed in the context of SDI in Chapter 7). Problems in using such tapes for retrospective search are discussed in papers by Rowlands and Robinson. If the difficulties of using external tapes in one's own system outweigh the advantages, the answer may lie in obtaining access to large magnetic-tape data-bases by means of a terminal in an information retrieval network.

Information retrieval networks. Most of the commercial magnetic-tape data-bases are available on computers accessed by remote terminals. Such a terminal can be installed in the information centre with either a leased line to the computer or a 'dial up' facility. The efficiency of the system is, of course, very much dependent on the efficiency of the telecommunication system.

The AGARD Technical Information Panel held a conference on National and International Networks of Libraries, Documentation and Information Centres in 1974, and the papers presented have been published as AGARD *Conference Proceedings* No. 158. (Advisory Group . . .) At this conference a paper by Holmes described the British Library's research programme for the development of a future library and information network in the United Kingdom, and Van Velze & Davies described the network for scientific and technical information being developed for the European communities.

SCISEARCH, the data-base operated by Cybernet Timesharing Ltd, holds the most recent four weeks' input of source references to the *Science Citation Index*. 'Dial-up' access is via a Teletype terminal, and search terms are matched against words appearing in the titles of references. A terminal is available for use in the Science Reference Library at 25 Southampton Buildings, London WC1, and this can be operated by users of the library at a charge based on connect time and amount of computer central processing unit time.

RECON (REmote CONsole) is an on-line information retrieval network operated by the European Space Organization Space Documentation Service from a single-use IBM 360/50 computer in Frascati, Italy. The system was developed for NASA by Lockheed Aircraft Company based on Lockheed's Dialog system and an inverted-file structure is employed. The system is fully interactive, each remote terminal having a visual display unit (VDU) and a keyboard for transmitting messages to the computer, these and the computer's responses being displayed on the VDU. Various keys on the keyboard initiate commands to the computer, and it is possible to display sections of the thesaurus and select relevant descriptors, and also to display related terms. Each descriptor in the display also shows against it the number of citations in which it was used. The search is made by formulating a logical equation using the Boolean operators 'and', 'or' and 'not'. The number of citations which meets the requirements of the logical equation is displayed, and it is also possible to display one by one the actual citations. As these latter show the descriptors assigned, it is possible to select further descriptors to broaden the search. Printouts resulting from a search are printed at the computer on a high-speed printer and mailed to the recipient, but individual citations can also be printed on a local printer at the terminal.

RECON started with one data-base, that of the contents of the NASA *STAR* and *International Aerospace Abstracts*, from 1962 onwards, but additional data-bases have now been added as follows, some on an experimental basis: *Metals Abstracts* (METADEX), from 1969; *Engineering Index* (COMPENDEX), from 1969; *Government Reports Announcements*, from 1970; *Nuclear Science Abstracts*, from 1968; INSPEC, from 1971; Environmental Science, from 1971; MARC (BNB), test file; Earth resources, CA Condensates, (restricted access). There is also an Electronic Components Databank which contains information on physical, performance, and reliability characteristics of electronic components.

Each bibliographic data-base has its own thesaurus, but the method of search is broadly similar for each. In addition to subject searches, in the *STAR*/AIAA data-base it is possible to search on personal and corporate authors, and in the INSPEC and Environmental Science data-bases on personal authors.

RECON terminals are available in twelve European cities and towns. Of the terminals in the United Kingdom, that at the Defence Research Information Centre is for the use of the UK Ministry of Defence and its contractors only, but TRC will carry out searches for a charge for requesters outside government departments. The terminal at the British Library (Science Reference Library, 25 Southampton Buildings, Chancery Lane, WC2A 1AW) has only recently (November 1974) been installed, and enquiries on its use should be made at the Library. The TRC RECON terminal is shown in Plate 3.

The development of RECON is fully described in papers by Isotta (1970, 1972, 1973 October and November).

Economics and effectiveness of on-line searching. On-line searching is convenient to the user in that searches can be refined or broadened while the user is at the terminal, and the results are available immediately, in contrast to batch processing. In considering the cost-benefit of such systems, however, an analysis of the costs is required. Robertson & Datta report a method developed during an investigation carried out by the Aslib Research and Development Department to discover the major determinants of the costs of searching the SCISEARCH system. The method should make it possible with this system to predict the computer time required to search a given profile, on the basis of a small number of characteristics of the profile. Katzer reports an investigation of the cost-performance of the SUPARS (Syracuse University Psychological Abstracts Retrieval Service) system, an on-line free-text bibliographic retrieval system. It was found that queries to the system employing simple Boolean operators ('and', 'or') had better cost-performance characteristics than queries using more elegant searching operators, that on-demand access to the index or dictionary improved the cost-performance of the system, and that differences between expert searchers must be taken into account in designing on-line systems with improved cost-performance. Effectiveness of another US on-line system is reported by Lancaster & others. The system is EARS (Epilepsy Abstracts Retrieval System) a magnetic tape data-base from *Epilepsy Abstracts*. EARS permits free-text searching of about 8,000 abstracts. Comparison of parallel searches by different neurologists showed that recall failures were attributable almost exclusively to quality of the search strategies. Recommendations for improvement include better instruction of users and provision of aids to the searcher at the terminal.

It is clear that time spent in operator training is well worth while when an on-line system is introduced, and systems should include user aids such as training routines and thesaurus displays.

References

ABBOT, M. T. J. *and* SIMKINS, M. A. Experience with the IRMS information retrieval package. *Information Scientist*, 6(4). December, 1972. 149–159.

ADVISORY GROUP FOR AEROSPACE RESEARCH AND DEVELOPMENT. National and international networks of libraries, documentation and information centres. Neuilly-sur-Seine, 1975. Var. pag. *AGARD Conference Proceedings* No. 158.

AITCHISON, J. *and* CLEVERDON, C. W. A report on a test on the index of metallurgical literature of Western Reserve University. Cranfield, Beds., College of Aeronautics, 1963. pp. 282.

AITCHISON, J. *and* GILCHRIST, A. Thesaurus construction: a practical manual. London, Aslib, 1972. ISBN 0 85142 042 7. pp. 95.

AITCHISON, T. M. *and others*. Comparative evaluation of index languages. Part 2. Results. London, Institution of Electrical Engineers, 1969. *INSPEC Report* No. R70/2.

AITCHISON, T. M. *and* TRACY, J. M. Comparative evaluation of index languages. Part 1. Design. London, Institution of Electrical Engineers, 1969. *INSPEC Report* No. R70/1.

AUSTIN, D. PRECIS indexing. *Information Scientist*, 5(3). September, 1971. 95–114.

BARLOW, D. H. Serving six user areas from the INSPEC data-base – some of the collection and indexing problems involved. *EUROPEAN CONGRESS ON DOCUMENTATION SYSTEMS AND NETWORKS, 1st, Luxemburg, 1973.* 24–46. Brussels, Council of the European Communities, [1973?] EUR 5058 d.e.f.

BHATTACHARYYA, K. Effectiveness of natural language in science indexing and retrieval. *Journal of Documentation*, 30(3). September, 1974. 235–254.

BLAGDEN, J. Management information retrieval: a new indexing language. London, British Institute of Management, 1969. pp. 153.

BLAGDEN, J. F. Thesaurus compilation methods: a literature review. *Aslib Proceedings*, 20(8). August, 1968. 345–359.

BOURNE, C. P. Methods of information handling. New York, Wiley, 1963. pp. 241.

BRITISH NATIONAL BIBLIOGRAPHY. PRECIS Manual. London, British Library, 1974. pp. 561. (Available British Library, Store Street, London WC1E 7DG.)

CALESS, T. W. *and* KIRK, D. B. An application of UDC to machine searching. *Journal of Documentation*, 23(3). September, 1967. 208–215.

CAMPEY, L. H. Generating and printing indexes by computer. London, Aslib, 1972. ISBN 0 85142 047 8. pp. 103. *Aslib Occasional Publication* No. 11.

CARVILLE, M. *and others*. Interactive reference retrieval in large files. *Information Storage and Retrieval*, 7(5). December, 1971. 205–210.

CLEVERDON, C. W. Report on the first stage of an investigation into the comparative efficiency of indexing systems. Cranfield, Beds., (England), College of Aeronautics, 1960. pp. 175.

CLEVERDON, C. W. Interim report on the test programme of an investigation into the comparative efficiency of indexing systems. Cranfield, Beds., [College of Aeronautics], 1962. pp. 311.

CLEVERDON, C. W. *and others*. Factors determining the performance of indexing systems. Vol. 1. Design (Part 1, Text; Part 2, Appendices).

Vol. 2. Test results. Cranfield, Beds., College of Aeronautics, 1966. 2v. in 3.

CLOUGH, C. R. *and* BRAMWELL, K. M. A single computer-based system for both current awareness and retrospective search; operating experience with ASSASSIN. *Journal of Documentation*, 27(4). December, 1971. 243-253.

CLOUGH, C. R. *and others*. ASSASSIN – a system capable of serving local retrieval needs and inter-company networks. *EUROPEAN CONGRESS ON DOCUMENTATION SYSTEMS AND NETWORKS. 1st, Luxembourg, 1973.* 90–104. Brussels, Council of the European Communities, [1973?] EUR 5058 d.e.f.

DEPARTMENT OF HEALTH, EDUCATION AND WELFARE. Public Health Service. Medical and health related sciences thesaurus. Rev. ed. Bethesda, Md, National Institutes of Health, 1970. pp. 379. *Public Health Service Publication* No. 1031.

ENGINEERS JOINT COUNCIL. Thesaurus of engineering and scientific terms. New York, Engineers Joint Council. 2nd printing, 1969. pp. 690.

EUROPEAN ATOMIC ENERGY COMMUNITIES. Euratom thesaurus. Part 1. Indexing terms used within Euratom's nuclear documentation system. Part 2. Terminology charts used in Euratom's nuclear documentation system. Brussels, Euratom, 1966, 1967. 2v. EUR 500e.

FANGMEYER, H. Semi-automatic indexing: state of the art. Neuilly-sur-Seine, AGARD, 1974. *AGARDograph* No. 179.

FREEMAN, R. R. *and* ATHERTON, P. AUDACIOUS: an experiment with an on-line, inter-active retrieval system using UDC as the index language in the field of nuclear science. [New York], American Institute of Physics, 1968. *American Institute of Physics Report* No. AIP/UDC-7.

GILCHRIST, A. The thesaurus in retrieval. London, Aslib, 1971. ISBN 0 85142 036 2. pp. 184.

GRAY, W. A. *and* HARLEY, A. J. Computer assisted indexing. *Information Storage and Retrieval*, 7(4). November, 1971. 167–174.

HALL, J. L. *and others*. On-line information retrieval. A method of query formulation using a video terminal. *Program*, 6(3). July, 1972. 175–186.

HENDERSON, M. M. *and others*. Cooperation, convertibility and compatibility among information systems: a literature review. Washington, National Bureau of Standards, 1966. *NBS Miscellaneous Papers*, 276.

HERSEY, D. F. *and others*. Free text word retrieval and scientist indexing: performance profiles and costs. *Journal of Documentation*, 27(3). September, 1971. 167–183.

HOLMES, P. L. An approach to the development of library and information networks with special reference to the United Kingdom. *AGARD Conference Proceedings* No. 158. *National and international networks of libraries, documentation and information centres.* 6–1 – 6–3. Neuilly-sur-Seine, AGARD, 1975.

ISOTTA, N. E. C. Europe's first information retrieval network. *ESRO/ELDO Bulletin*, no. 9. April, 1970. 9–17.

ISOTTA, N. E. C. International information networks. 1. The ESRO system. *Aslib Proceedings*, 24(1). January, 1972. 31–37.

ISOTTA, N. E. C. Aerospace information services – progress with the ESRO/ELDO computerized information network. *AGARD Conference Proceedings* No. 136. *New developments in storage, retrieval and dissemination of aerospace information.* Neuilly-sur-Seine, AGARD, 1973. 3-1 – 3-15.

ISOTTA, N. E. C. The Space Documentation Service – a progress report. *ESRO/ELDO Bulletin*, no. 23. November, 1973. 2-8.

JOHNSON, A. and BAKER, K. J. Practical considerations in establishing and operating an optical coincidence card system. *Information Scientist*, 4(1). March, 1970. 11-25.

KATZER, J. The cost-performance of an on-line, free-text bibliographic retrieval system. *Information Storage and Retrieval*, 9(6). June, 1973. 321-329.

KEEN, E. M. The Aberystwyth index languages test. *Journal of Documentation*, 29(1). March, 1973. 1-35.

KEEN, E. M. *and* DIGGER, J. A. Report of an information science index languages test. Part 1, Text; Part 2, Tables. Aberystwyth, College of Librarianship Wales, 1972. 2v.

KLINGBIEL, P. H. Machine-aided indexing. Alexandria, Va., Defense Documentation Center, 1971. *NTIS Report* No. AD 721 875.

KLINGBIEL, P. H. Machine-aided indexing of technical literature. *Information Storage and Retrieval*, 9(2). February, 1973. 79-84.

KLINGBIEL, P. H. A technique for machine-aided indexing. *Information Storage and Retrieval*, 9(9). September, 1973. 477-494.

KLINGBIEL, P. H. The use of natural language for automated indexing. *Quarterly Bulletin of the International Association of Agricultural Librarians and Documentalists*, 18(3). 1973. 148-180.

LANCASTER, F. W. and FAYEN, E. G. Information retrieval on line. Los Angeles, Melville Publishing Co., 1973. ISBN 0 471 51235 4. pp. 597.

LANCASTER, F. W. *and others*. Evaluating the effectiveness of an on-line, natural language retrieval system. *Information Storage and Retrieval*, 8(5). October, 1972. 223-245.

LUHN, H. P. Keyword in context index for technical literature. New York, IBM, 1959. pp. 16. *IBM Advanced Systems Development Division Report* RC-127.

MCCRACKEN, I. B. *and others*. INFIRS – Inverted file information retrieval system. Nottingham, UKCIS, [1973]. *UKCIS Research Report* No. 3. (Available UKCIS Service Department, Nottingham University.)

MELTZER, M. F. The information center: management's hidden asset. New York, American Management Association, 1967. pp. 160.

NATIONAL AERONAUTICS AND SPACE ADMINISTRATION. NASA Thesaurus-alphabetical update. Washington, NASA, 1971. pp. 610. *NASA* SP-7040.

NEGUS, A. E. A real time interactive reference retrieval system. *Information Scientist*, 5(1). March, 1971. 29-44.

NEGUS, A. E. *and* HALL, J. L. Towards an effective on-line reference

retrieval system. *Information Storage and Retrieval*, 7(6). December, 1971. 249–270.
OLIVE, G. and others. Studies to compare retrieval using titles with that using index terms: SDI from *Nuclear Science Abstracts*. *Journal of Documentation*, 29(2). June, 1973. 169–171.
PATTEN, M. N. Experiences with an in-house mechanized information system. *Aslib Proceedings*, 26(5). May, 1974. 189–209.
PICKFORD, A. G. A. An objective method for the generation of an information retrieval language. *Information Scientist*, 2(1). March, 1968. 17–37.
PICKFORD, A. G. A. 80-column cards as feature cards. *Information Scientist*, 3(2). July, 1969. 69–79.
RIGBY, M. Experiments in mechanized control of meteorological and geoastrophysical literature and the UDC schedules in these fields. *Revue Internationale de la Documentation*, 31(3). August, 1964. 103–106.
ROBERTSON, S. E. and DATTA, S. Analysis of on-line searching costs. *Information Scientist*, 7(1). March, 1973. 9–13.
ROBINSON, F. External services in retrospective searching. *Aslib Proceedings*, 24(12). December, 1972. 686–695.
ROWLANDS, D. G. Exploitation of literature on tape. *Information Scientist*, 5(2). June, 1971. 51–65.
SALTON, G. The SMART retrieval system: experiments in automatic document processing. Englewood Cliffs, N.J., Prentice-Hall, 1971. pp. 575.
SCHEFFLER, F. L. and others. The significance of titles, abstracts, and other portions of technical documents for information retrieval. *I.E.E.E. Transactions on Professional Communication*, PC-17(1). March, 1974. 1–8.
SCHIEBER, W. D. Technical manual on ISIS: a generalized information storage and retrieval system designed at the International Labour Office. Stockholm, Statskontoret, 1972. pp. 74.
SCHULTZ, C. K. Cost-effectiveness as a guide in developing indexing rules. *Information Storage and Retrieval*, 6(4). October, 1970. 335–340.
SENATE. Documentation, indexing, and retrieval of scientific information: a study of Federal and non-Federal science information processing and retrieval programs, prepared by the staff of Committee on Government Operations, US Senate. Washington, US GPO, 1961. pp. 283. *86th Congress, second session, Document no. 113.*
SHARP, J. R. Some fundamentals of information retrieval. London, Deutsch, 1965. pp. 224.
SPARCK-JONES, K. Automatic indexing 1974 – a state of the art review. Cambridge, University Computer Laboratory, 1974. *OSTI Report* No. 5193. (Available BLLD.)
TOWNLEY, H. M. A look at natural language IR systems. *Information Scientist*, 5(1). March, 1971. 3–15.
VAN VELZE, P. L. and DAVIES, G. W. P. International networking: information retrieval requirements. *AGARD Conference Proceedings* No.

158. *National and international networks of libraries, documentation and information centres.* Neuilly-sur-Seine, AGARD, 1975. 8–1 – 8–7.

VERNON, K. D. C., *and* LANG, V. The London classification of business studies. London, London Graduate School of Business Studies, 1970. ISBN 0 902583 005 X. pp. 132.

VICKERY, B. C. On retrieval system theory. 2nd ed. London, Butterworths, 1965. p. 203.

For the cited reports by C. W. Cleverdon and co-workers, apply to the Library, Cranfield Institute of Technology (formerly the College of Aeronautics), Cranfield, Beds., England.

SELECTED BIBLIOGRAPHY

FISHER, M. The KWIC index concept – a retrospective view. *American Documentation,* **17**(2). April, 1966. 57–70.

JONES, K. P. Basic structures for thesaural systems. *Aslib Proceedings,* **23**(11). November, 1971. 577–590.

MATTHEWS, F. W. *and* SHILLINGFORD, A. D. Variations on KWIC. *Aslib Proceedings,* **25**(4). April, 1973. 140–152.

MEETHAM, R. Information retrieval: the essential technology. London, Aldus Books Ltd., 1969. ISBN 0 490 00133 5 (hard cover); ISBN 0 490 00134 3 (paperback).

NEVILLE, H. H. Thesaurus reconciliation. *Aslib Proceedings,* **24**(11). November, 1972. 620–626.

THOMAS, P. A. Some problems in compiling a thesaurus of transportation terms. *Aslib Proceedings,* **23**(11). November, 1971. 595–606.

WALKLEY, J. *and* FAY, B. An annotated list of thesauri held in the Aslib Library. *Aslib Proceedings,* **23**(6). June, 1971. 292–300.

CHAPTER 6

Announcement

Information officers will have two different views of announcement bulletins, i.e. what they expect in the bulletins they receive from other report sources and use as tools in the acquisition process, and what they provide in the bulletin(s) they prepare from their own acquisitions and issue to their customers. Comparison of these two approaches should lead to the design of an ideal bulletin, in which maximum information is provided in the most useful form, at minimum cost.

The working scientist in the university does not have extensive knowledge of the information field. The information centre or library can do a number of things for this person, who is primarily profession- or discipline-oriented. The library can provide new information through what may be considered fortuitous browsing. The scientist would not come upon this information by chance if everything was systematized, with indexing, abstracting, and the provision of a completely mechanical, ideally compartmentalized system. In other words, the library could supply copies of reports and place them where the scientist will see them. When the scientist browses, he is really seeking accidental discoveries.

Many working scientists are not aware of reports as sources of literature information. They depend on the scientific journal and book. Government documents are sometimes kept in separate parts of the library or in other buildings. Of course this does not apply to all scientific and technical persons. Engineers and physicists, for example, will use these documents extensively if they are involved in project work. Another deterrent to some users of documents is the common practice of putting a fence around them. This stems from their security and proprietary values. The unclassified and classified documents often are kept behind the same fence. In announcing reports, the unclassified, unrestricted nature of them should be especially noted.

The working scientist may receive many announcement bulletins, but that does not mean that he will act on them. For example, one US national laboratory publishes a weekly reading list. The list contains many titles of unpublished or soon-to-be-published reports. The titles are followed by the usual cryptic symbols such as ACRH or CEX, symbols that mean little or nothing to the average scientist.

BULLETINS

Production of bulletins

When planning an announcement bulletin, it is important first to consider the types of user for which it is intended. If the bulletin is sent to other centres and libraries in large organizations, it is to be expected that the recipients will scan the bulletin with their own users' interests in mind. A comprehensive bulletin is then the answer. If the bulletin is sent to individual research workers, each one will be interested in his subject specialization, and he may resent the time necessary to skim through a comprehensive bulletin containing subjects of no interest to him. It must be considered whether specialist users would not be better served by a selective dissemination of information (SDI) service (see Chapter 7). However, large centres usually have many types of customer, and a compromise solution has to be reached. If an extended SDI service is too expensive, the solution can be to issue a general bulletin, and reprint separately special subject sections of the bulletin for the specialist user.

The information provided in an announcement bulletin will normally be the bibliographical details for the reports processed by the centre, i.e. cataloguing data, subject analysis and abstract. This information is used by the centre in its day-to-day operations, and is a vital product of the centre's activities. The cost of producing the bulletin can therefore be minimized if its production can be harmonized with products used in the centre.

If the centre uses catalogue cards in its operations, the bulletin items can be typed in card format on wax stencils. After running off the bulletin pages, a separate run is made on card stock and the card pages are guillotined into individual cards. The guillotining must be accurately done to ensure uniformity in the cards produced, and there can be some delay in card availability. Alternatively the cards can be typed first, then assembled into pages, photoreduced and the pages duplicated by offset lithography. This system is used in the High Temperature Processes Information Centre at Leeds University, and is described in the paper by Brain & others. Both of these systems have the disadvantage that indexes to the bulletins can only be produced by an extra and laborious process.

If a tape-typewriter is used to prepare punched-paper tapes of the bibliographical data for each report, the paper tapes can be assembled into the subject arrangement for the bulletin, and electronically 'read' through the tape-typewriter typing offset-litho masters automatically and simultaneously producing a second-generation punched-paper tape which can be computer processed to produce indexes to the bulletin. Such a system is described in the papers by Vessey and Schuler. In this system a computer bureau was used to process the tapes, and the computer printout of the various indexes was photoreduced and the pages duplicated by offset lithography.

If a computer is available in the centre, the whole bulletin can be computer-produced, either by using an upper-and-lower-case printer or by computer typesetting. It is then feasible to extract data from exchange magnetic tapes such as those available on lease from the US National Technical Information Service for the *Government Reports Announcements*. The tapes are normally received in the United Kingdom six weeks in advance of microfiches of the reports announced in the corresponding issue of *Government Reports Announcements*.

An important consideration in compiling announcement bulletins of reports is to ensure that no entry contains information which cannot be made available to all recipients. Thus, if the bulletin is available to the public it must not contain references to reports which are not openly available. These reports may be those available only to members of a particular organization or reports subject to security or proprietary information restrictions. If reports are subject to such restrictions it is necessary to omit them from the general bulletin and to announce them in a separate bulletin which is supplied only to appropriate recipients. This avoids the embarrassment of having to refuse requests and it also protects reports the knowledge of whose existence may have to be kept within a restricted circle.

It is important that announcement bulletins should be produced as quickly as possible. While a bulletin is in preparation the availability of the reports cited is known only to those who have received copies by selective dissemination or because of previous requests. It is an important responsibility of management to keep this 'dead period' as short as possible by ensuring a smooth flow of work through the various cataloguing, subject analysis and abstracting stages in the centre.

Lay-out of bulletins

Lay-out has in the past been largely a matter of individual choice, but the increase in computer processing is leading towards standardization. Centres which use a computer for bulletin production will probably arrange exchange of their magnetic tapes with other computer-based centres. In such cases the processing of tapes is facilitated if a standard format is employed. In the United Kingdom the British Standards Institution has issued *BS 4748 Specification for bibliographic information interchange format for magnetic tape*, and this is compatible with *International Standard ISO 2709*, (1973). European centres are co-operating in further developments in standardization through the European Association of Scientific Information Dissemination Centres (EUSIDIC) (the UK secretary is Dr A. Kent, UKCIS, the University, Nottingham, NG7 2RD).

Some important bulletins

In this section the more important announcement bulletins are described in some detail.

Government Reports Announcements (GRA) is produced by the US National Technical Information Service (see p. 61) twice monthly, and an issue contains particulars of well over a thousand reports, with a good deal of cross-indexing. The reports include all those released by the US Department of Defense for public sale (i.e. reports carrying reference numbers in the AD–600 000 and AD–700 000 series), reports sponsored by the US Atomic Energy Commission, NASA documents, translations from various sources, and a number of reports from countries outside the USA. *GRA* is arranged in the twenty-two subject fields and sub-groups developed by the Committee on Scientific and Technical Information of the Federal Council on Science and Technology (COSATI).

Field 1, Aeronautics; Field 2, Agriculture; Field 3, Astronomy and Astrophysics; Field 4, Atmospheric Sciences; Field 5, Behavioral and Social Sciences; Field 6, Biological and Medical Sciences; Field 7, Chemistry; Field 8, Earth Sciences and Oceanography; Field 9, Electronics and Electrical Engineering; Field 10, Energy Conversion (non-propulsive); Field 11, Materials; Field 12, Mathematical Sciences; Field 13, Mechanical, Industrial, Civil and Marine Engineering; Field 14, Methods and Equipment; Field 15, Military Sciences; Field 16, Missile Technology; Field 17, Navigation, Communications, Detection and Countermeasures; Field 18, Nuclear Science and Technology; Field 19, Ordnance; Field 20, Physics; Field 21, Propulsion and Fuels; Field 22, Space Technology.

Some entries are shown in Figure 8. Most of the reports are publicly available either as microfiche or paper copy from NTIS, prices being $2·25 (domestic) and $3·75 (foreign) for microfiche, and according to report length for paper copy. Certain entries are not available on microfiche; these include reprints and published papers, patents, and university theses. Paper copies of reports printed by the US Government Printing Office are obtainable from that office at Washington, DC 20402 and not from NTIS. All reports purchasable as microfiches from NTIS are received in the UK at the British Library Lending Division and a good proportion of them at the Technology Reports Centre.

Each issue of *GRA* contains a single index arranged alphanumerically by accession number. The COSATI field and group where the report citation can be located in the journal precede the accession number. There is a separate twice-monthly index publication, *Government Reports Index*,* priced separately, which contains indexes to corporate author, subject, personal author, contract number, and accession/report number of the citations in the corresponding issue of *GRA*. The indexes are cumulated annually, the accession/report number index including the document price. NTIS has agencies in a number of countries outside the USA. In the United Kingdom it is Thompson, Henry Ltd, The Bear

* As from April 1975 *GRA* and *GRI* were combined into *Government Reports Announcements and Index (GRAI)*.

5I. Personnel Selection, Training, and Evaluation

AD-A011 752/3GA   PC$3.25/MF$2.25
Naval Health Research Center San Diego Calif
Prediction of SCUBA Training Performance,
Robert J. Biersner, and David H. Ryman. 27 Aug 73, 5p Rept no. 73-54
Availability: Pub. in Jnl. of Applied Psychology, v59 n4 p519-521 1974.

Descriptors: *Scuba divers, *Mathematical prediction, *Performance(Human), *Naval training, Selection, Underwater, Hazards, Work, Attitudes(Psychology), Reprints.
Identifiers: Hazardous occupation.

The predictive relationship of demographic, health and attitude measures with success in U.S. Navy SCUBA training was investigated. A multiple regression equation consisting of two health scales, two attitude scales and three demographic items was significantly associated with the pass-fail criterion on a validation sample, and was also significantly related to training success in a cross-validation sample. Those scales dealing with general mental health and concern about training were the most significant and reliable predictors of training success. These findings emphasize the importance of perceived health and attitudes in predicting the performance of those involved in training for extremely hazardous occupations.

AD-A011 819/0GA   PC$6.25/MF$2.25
Naval Training Equipment Center Orlando Fla
Holographic Heads-Up Display for Naval Aviation Training.
Final rept. Jul 72-Dec 74,
Alfred H. Rodemann, Denis R. Breglia, and Windell N. Mohon. May 75, 165p Rept no. NAVTRAEQUIPC-IH-229

Descriptors: *Naval training, *Naval aviation, *Holography, Display systems, Head up displays, Technology, Transfer, Flight simulators, Theory, Systems engineering, Computer applications, Chemical properties, Lenses, Optical properties, Performance tests, Optical images.

This report summarizes the results of an effort to apply the technology of high efficiency holographic lens design and fabrication to the specific case of a heads-up display system for use in visual simulators for aviation training. Design methods are developed. Materials research is described. Holographic lens elements are evaluated.

AD-A011 846/3GA   PC$4.75/MF$2.25
Honeywell Inc Minneapolis Minn Systems and Research Center
The Feasibility of Generalized Acoustic Sensor Operator Training.
Final rept. Feb 74-Feb 75,
Richard W. Daniels, and David G. Alden. May 75, 79p NAVTRAEQUIPC-74-C-0067-1
Contract N61339-74-C-0067

AD-A011 986/7GA   PC$3.75/MF$2.25
Air Force Human Resources Lab Brooks AFB Tex
Simulating Maintenance Manning for New Weapon Systems. Volume I. Maintenance Manpower Management During Weapon System Development.
Final rept. 1 May 71-31 Oct 74,
Frank A. Maher, and Michael L. York. Dec 74, 34p Rept no. AFHRL-TR-74-97(I)
See also Volume 2, AD-A011 987.

Descriptors: *Maintenance personnel, *Maintenance management, *Weapon systems, *Logistics planning, *Computerized simulation, Air Force planning; Air Force procurement, Military aircraft, Attack bombers, Trade off analyses, Predictions, Estimates, Manpower, Requirements, Central processing units, Factor analysis, Air Force Systems Command, Logistics support, Management information systems.
Identifiers: Life cycle costing, *Logistics management, A-10 aircraft, CDC 6600 computers, LCOM computer program.

There is a need for a more responsive method for predicting maintenance manpower requirements for aircraft systems during development. This method should provide early estimates for use in trade offs and evaluations, and should be sensitive to the ways in which the new aircraft will be employed. A maintenance manpower simulation model was developed. In using the model, early estimates of maintenance task data for the new aircraft are based on Air Force experience with comparable subsystems and equipment on existing aircraft, factored for the new design and environment. These data are meshed with a detailed operations scenario and support concept assumptions in a model run on the Logistics Composite Model (LCOM) simulation program. The simulation output is iterated and analyzed in post-processor programs whose final output is a complete basic manning authorization document. This approach was evaluated by applying it to the A-10 Weapon System. The entire effort is reported in a five volume technical report.

AD-A011 987/5GA   PC$5.75/MF$2.25
Air Force Human Resources Lab Brooks AFB Tex
Simulating Maintenance Manning for New Weapon Systems. Volume II. Building and Operating a Simulation Model.
Final rept. Jul 71-May 74,
Donald C. Tetmeyer, and William D. Moody. Dec 74, 139p Rept no. AFHRL-TR-74-97(II)
See also Volume 1, AD-A011 986 and Volume 3, AD-A011 988.

Descriptors: *Maintenance personnel, *Maintenance management, *Weapon systems, *Logistics planning, *Computerized simulation, Air Force planning, Air Force procurement, Military aircraft, Attack bombers, Trade off analyses, Predictions, Estimates, Manpower, Requirements, Central processing units, Factor analysis, Air Force Systems Command, Lo-

FIG. 8. Typical entries from *Government Reports Announcements*.

House, London Road, Windlesham, Surrey, GU20 6LQ, and they hold stocks of *GRA, GRI, GRAI* and the annual indexes.

Scientific and Technical Aerospace Reports (STAR). This, which is not confined, as might be thought from the title, to a narrow subject field, covers the very wide range of supporting projects which surround the American space programme and which have attracted support only second to the defence programme. Like *GRA, STAR* is issued twice a month, and contains entries for a great number of reports which overlap to a certain extent with

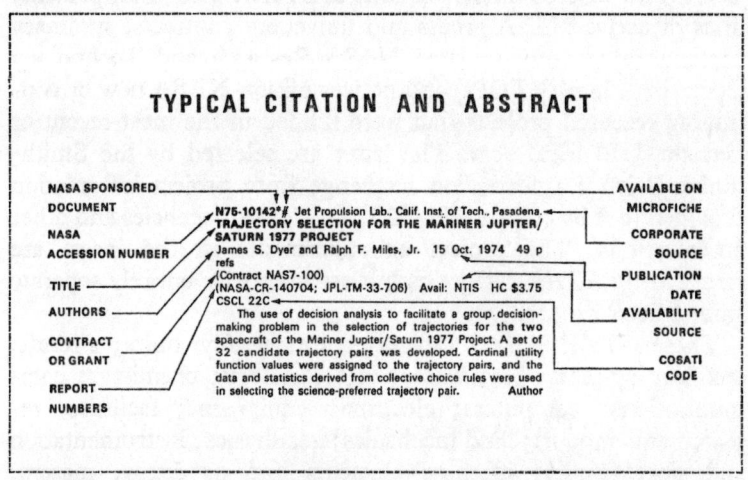

FIG. 9. A typical entry from *Scientific and Technical and Aerospace Reports (STAR)*.

GRA. A typical citation and abstract in *STAR* are shown in Figure 9. Entries in *STAR* which are collections of documents, such as conference proceedings, are followed by entries and abstracts for each of the individual papers. The entries are backed by a comprehensive series of indexes bound in with each issue, and the indexes are cumulated at semi-annual and annual intervals. The indexes are: subject (arranged by subject heading without subheadings) which includes expanded titles (referred to as 'title extension'), report numbers and NASA accession numbers, personal author index (surname and initials, and NASA accession number), corporate source index (corporate source, report title, report number, and NASA accession number), contract number (contract or project number and NASA accession number), and report/accession number index. The last-named indicates if a microfiche is available. Each copy of *STAR* contains adequate information about its contents and the availability in the United States and Europe of the documents listed. (See also Chapter 3, pp. 63-4.)

By arrangement between NASA and the Smithsonian Science Information Exchange (SSIE), a separate section of information on newly initiated and on-going aerospace-related research projects is now inserted into each issue of *STAR*. The insert presents titles of active NASA grants and university contracts, summary portions of recently updated NASA Research and Technology Operating Plans (RTOPs) and notices of non-NASA new or continuing research projects that were funded in the most recent or current (US) fiscal year. The latter are selected by the Smithsonian Science Information Exchange from project information provided to it by co-operating US Government agencies and other organizations. The project announcements in the insert are arranged by *STAR* categories but are otherwise entirely separate from *STAR* proper.

These *STAR* subject categories are: aerodynamics; aircraft; auxiliary systems; biosciences; biotechnology; chemistry; communications; computers; electronic equipment; facilities, research and support; fluid mechanics; geophysics; instrumentation and photography; machine elements and processes; masers; materials, metallic; materials, nonmetallic; mathematics; meteorology; navigation; nuclear engineering; physics, general; physics, atomic, molecular and nuclear; physics, plasma; physics, solid-state; propellants; propulsion systems; space radiation; space sciences; space vehicles; structural mechanics; thermodynamics and combustion; general.

Nuclear Science Abstracts (*NSA*)* covers a very wide field in

* From June 1976 *NSA* is replaced by *ERDA Research Abstracts* (*ERA*) which will abstract and index all literature of ERDA (Energy Research and Development Administration) origin as well as non-nuclear energy information from foreign countries with which ERDA has co-operative agreements. The world's nuclear literature will be covered by *Atomindex*, to be published by the International Nuclear Information System (*INIS*) (see p. 70).

addition to the obviously related subjects. Conference papers are abstracted and indexed separately. Each issue contains corporate author, personal author, subject and report number indexes and these are cumulated quarterly, semiannually and annually; the volumes up to No. 15 (for 1961) were cumulated. Those items available at NTIS are indicated with price. The *NSA* subject categories are: chemistry; controlled thermonuclear research; engineering; environmental and earth sciences; instrumentation; isotope and radiation source technology; life sciences; materials; nuclear materials and waste management; particle accelerators; physics (astrophysics and cosmology); physics (atmospheric); physics (atomic and molecular); physics (electrofluid and magnetofluid); physics (high-energy); physics (low-temperature); physics (nuclear); physics (radiation and shielding); physics (theoretical); reactor technology and regulation; and general.

R & D Abstracts. In the United Kingdom the Department of Industry's Technology Reports Centre (TRC) (see p. 58), produces twice monthly an announcement bulletin entitled *R & D Abstracts* which is on public sale. Two volumes are issued each year. A typical issue contains notices of about three hundred reports arranged under the twenty-two COSATI fields with their sub-groups. The entries give essentially similar information to *GRA* but are somewhat differently arranged. The availability of each item is indicated, i.e. whether it is held by TRC or whether application must be made to another source. A list of addresses is included in each issue. Abstracts are included of British reports of industrial interest received by the British Library Lending Division and included in the *BLLD Announcement Bulletin* (see next section) without abstracts. Like *GRA*, *R & D Abstracts* contains information on its contents and how to obtain the reports cited, together with a guide to the layout which is reproduced in Figure 12. *R & D Abstracts* is produced by computer-controlled typesetting and each issue contains computer-produced indexes for accession number/locator (COSATI group), subject, personal author, and report/accession number. Computer-compiled cumulated indexes are issued for each volume. These give the TRC accession number and location reference in the *Abstracts* for each citation. The indexes are: (1) subject, by up to five descriptors per report; this index also gives titles; (2) personal author, by the first two authors only; this index also gives titles; (3) corporate author; this index also gives the corporate author's reference and the first words of the title; (4) translations, by the periodical or other source from which the translation was made; this index also gives the reference to the periodical, the country in which it was published and the translated title; (5) report number; (6) contract number; (7) title; (8) conference papers, by the name of the conference; this index also gives the place and date of the conference and the author(s) and title of each paper.

Part of a specimen page of *R & D Abstracts* is reproduced in Figure 10. In addition TRC publishes *Selected Report Announcements (SRAs) in Aerospace Technology; Electronics and Communications; Materials, Manufacturing Methods and Design;* and *Physics*, with further titles in preparation. *SRAs* contain relevant material extracted from *R & D Abstracts* and the NTIS *Government Reports Announcements*. They contain bibliographic data and abstracts.

TRC purchases microfiches from NTIS and leases the NTIS magnetic tapes. Report citations from *GRA* tapes are not reproduced in *R & D Abstracts*.

BLLD Announcement Bulletin. Another important British announcement bulletin is that issued monthly by the British Library Lending Division (see p. 55). It first appeared (as *British Research and Development Reports*) in 1966 so that it cannot be used for acquisitions much before that date. A typical issue contains entries for about five hundred reports from sources in the United Kingdom, all of which are available on loan to registered borrowers in the UK, and photocopies of most can be supplied to any organization, both in the UK and overseas, through the BLLD Photocopy Service. The entries are much briefer than those in the bulletins described earlier and do not include any abstracts or subject analysis, but they are arranged in the twenty-two COSATI subject fields. (As mentioned in the preceding section, by arrangement between BLLD and TRC, abstracts of some of the reports appear in *R & D Abstracts*.) In addition to reports the entries include translations and a number of doctoral theses. In the case of British doctoral theses a special copyright declaration is required, signed by the actual user. Retention copies of some items can be obtained only from their originators, whose addresses,

Group 08I Page 27
Soil mechanics/Earthwork/Calcium carbonates//08I/13B/08M/07D/50D/99F/64 /

08J Physical Oceanography

T76-0109   CERC-TM-52   3301
Coastal Engineering Res.Center,Fort Belvoir,Va.,USA
SALT MARSH ESTABLISHMENT AND DEVELOPMENT
Garbisch,E.W.   Woller,P.B.   06.1975   114pp
TRC £2.90

The establishment and development of seedling transplants for shoreline erosion abatement are reported for Spartina alterniflora within the intertidal zones and for Spartina patens, Spartina cynosuroides, Distichlis spicata, and Ammophila breviligulata within the supratidal zones, of a dredged-material site and three sandy shore sites in the mid-Chesapeake Bay region. This report is published to assist coastal engineers in shore stabilization or shoreline erosion abatement by the establishment and development of vegetation on salt marshes and dredged materials.

*Shore protection/*Beach nourishment/Beach erosion/Coastal engineering/ Benthos/Erosion//08J/47C/

T76-0111   CERC-TM-54   3301
Coastal Engineering Res.Center,Fort Belvoir,Va.,USA
GEOMORPHOLOGY, SHALLOW STRUCTURE, AND SEDIMENTS OF THE FLORIDA INNER CONTINENTAL SHELF, CAPE CANAVERAL TO GEORGIA
Meisburger,E.P.   Field,M.E.   07.1975   124pp 108ref
TRC £3.10

The inner Continental Shelf off eastern Florida between Cape Canaveral and Georgia was surveyed to obtain information on bottom morphology and sediments, subbottom structure , and sand deposits (borrow sites) suitable for restoration and nourishment of nearby beaches. Primary survey data consist of 1,153 statute miles of high resolution seismic reflection surveys and 197 sediment cores. This report is one of a continuing series which describes results of the Inner Continental Shelf Sediment and Structure (ICONS) study. One aspect of the ICONS study is locating and delineating offshore sand and gravel deposits suitable for beach nourishment and restoration.

*Continental shelves/*Geomorphology/Shallow water/Geological sedimentation/ Sedimentology/+Florida//08J/47C/

T76-0131   MAI-REP-05-75-001   3301
MAR Associates Inc.,Rockville,Md.,USA
CONCEPTUAL STUDY OF THE FACTORS INVOLVED IN INSTALLATION, OPERATION, AND RECOVERY OF MOORS WITH ATTACHED BOTTOM-MOUNTED SENSORS
Gay,S.M.   07.1975   97pp 19ref
N-00014-74-C-0310   NR294-032   UL-1962
TRC £2.50

A conceptual study is reported of potential failure mechanisms associated with installation, operation and recovery of deep-sea buoy moors with attached bottom-mounted sensors. The study is directed to the "anchor-last" mode of installation. The effects considered include, among others, initial launch geometry, stability characteristics of the components (including torsional characteristics of the cables, both internally and externally generated), relation of the outlying instrument leads to the mooring riser, spin-stability of objects suspended by multiple lines and hydrodynamic effects such as strum and component rotation. The length of the instrument leads in relation to the depth is identified as an important parameter. The utility of modelling and the status of algorithms useful in the design of deep-sea mooring installations are discussed. A

FIG. 10. Part of a page from *R & D Abstracts*.

together with other relevant information, are listed in an 'Addresses and Notes' section. This applies particularly to priced publications. The layout of a typical entry is:

R
HELICOPTER BELL 47Da G–ASJW. REPORT ON THE ACCIDENT I MILE NORTHWEST OF SAXILBY, LINCOLNSHIRE ON 19 JULY 1971

*Civil Aircraft Accident Report
*CAAR 10/73 (BLLD 3268.79)
Department of Trade & Industry
Accidents Investigation Branch (HMSO)
June 1973 pp. 22 £0·39

(The asterisk denotes information required by BLLD when the item is requested.)

Other BLLD publications. BLLD also issues a monthly *Index of Conference Proceedings* received by the BLLD. The index is prepared automatically from internal records with no additional editing or checking. It lists the details of conferences indexed under subject keywords as follows: title of conference proceedings; conference number; place and date of conference; filing position at BLLD. It is available on annual subscription. The *BLL Conference Index 1964–1973* and an annual cumulation for 1974 provides information about the 55,000 conferences indexed in previous years at the BLLD. Individual papers are not listed. All items can be borrowed from the BLLD.

The *BLLD Review* contains informative articles and news of developments in BLLD services. Each issue also includes details of recent translations published by the library and prints the list of the thirteen cover-to-cover translations of Russian journals sponsored by the BLLD. *Current serials received by the BLLD March 1974* lists 43,000 current titles including the many report series received at the BLLD from over a hundred countries.

All the above publications are obtainable from: BLLD Publications Department, Boston Spa, Wetherby, West Yorkshire LS23 7BQ.

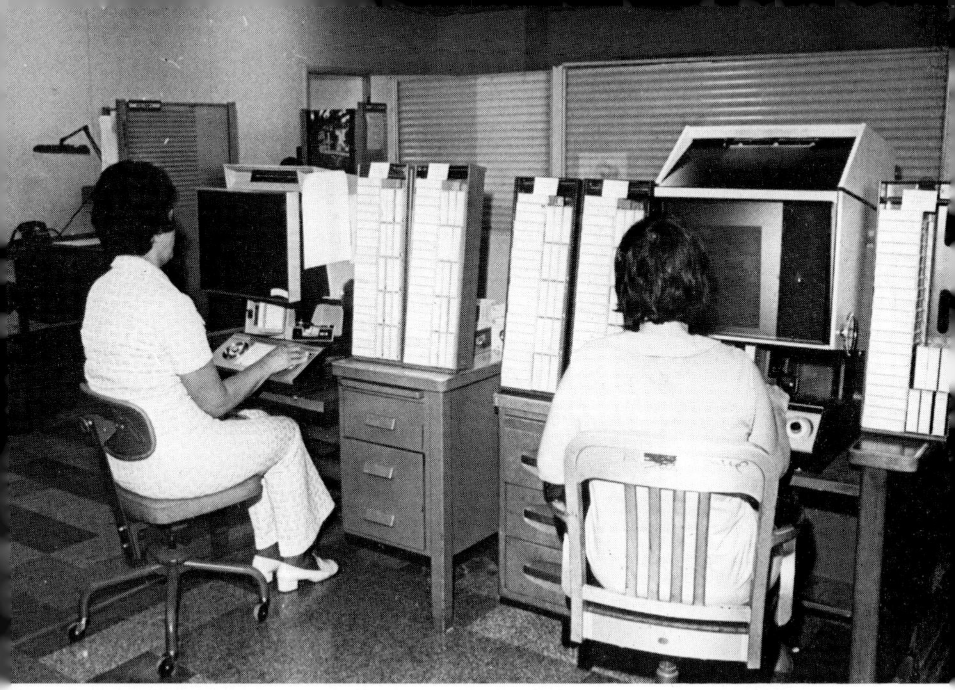

5. The National Technical Information Service uses many applications of Computer Output Microfilm to support the document distribution system. The history on 60,000 orders can be stored on one reel of 16mm microfilm. This shows two reading stations.

6. The Computer Facility at the National Technical Information Service supports all of the agency's requirements. Major applications are text processing and inventory control.

7. Storage of reports at the Defence Research Information Centre.

Indexes to bulletins

There are many other announcement bulletins, large and small, but enough have been described to show, with those mentioned in the section on theses (Chapter 1) the wide range of subjects and treatments which exist, and to suggest what wide limits might bound any new bulletin produced by an information centre. The better the indexing which is provided, the more help the bulletin gives to the user and the better the reputation of the organization producing the bulletin. Again, if a good range of indexes is provided with adequate cumulation it enables a centre to take a strong stand in asking that its accession number be quoted in any request for the reports it lists. The centre which does not issue indexes, on the other hand, has to accept a much larger proportion of requests which require more work by its staff to identify. This is another example of the dilemma which confronts many information centres, or at least those which have computer services available, whether to issue bulky and quite costly announcement bulletins with equally bulky indexes, or to face the expenditure of effort at a later stage. The balance is between the certainty of a predictable requirement at known intervals and the probability of more work whose incidence cannot be predicted. In most cases, however, the contents of the bulletin have to be prepared for the centre's own use, and the indexes are used in the centre. The main extra cost is then that for paper and printing, packaging and despatch. In some cases it is possible to recover these costs by charging an economic price to recipients of the bulletin.

The future of bulletins

The growth of SDI services such as those described in Chapter 7 might suggest that scientists' needs are better met by a personal SDI service, and that announcement bulletins have had their day. Before deciding to stop a bulletin, however, a careful investigation must be made of its distribution and of the use made of it by the centre's customers. Librarians and information scientists in other centres will probably want to retain the bulletin, especially if adequately indexed, for retrospective searches. Whitehall reports the results of an investigation of this type in which a questionnaire was sent to 150 special libraries, about a hundred replies being received. The results indicated that although SDI services were being used increasingly, they were not always available in the specialist areas required, and that custom-made bulletins from the information sections of research associations and other specialist information centres could replace in-house scanning in medium-sized information units. A survey by Hall of the use of INSPEC services also indicates the great value of *Science Abstracts* for retrospective searches, especially the author and subject indexes. It can be concluded that announcement bulletins have a future, at least at the two extremes of the spectrum: the bulletins issued by very specialized centres and those issued by large report handling organizations covering a wide field. In the latter case the bulletin must be very well indexed, and computer processing is essential for the indexes to be prepared at minimum cost.

References

BRAIN, M. E. and others. A specialized information centre for high temperature processes. *Aslib Proceedings*, 25(5). May, 1973. 186–190.

BRITISH STANDARDS INSTITUTION. Bibliographical information interchange on magnetic tape. London, 1971. *BS* 4748. ISBN 0 580 06562 6.

HALL, A. M. Comparative use and value of INSPEC services. London, INSPEC, 1972. pp. 52. *INSPEC Report* No. R 72/19.

INTERNATIONAL ORGANIZATION FOR STANDARDIZATION (ISO). Documentation format for bibliographic information interchange on magnetic tape. Geneva, 1973. pp. 4. *ISO* 2709.

SCHULER, S. C. Mintech [Ministry of Technology] Reports Centre services and mechanization programme. *Information Scientist*, 4(2). June, 1970. 47–64.

VESSEY, H. F. Mechanization in documentation: the Ministry of Aviation Technical Information and Library Services. *Aslib Proceedings*, 16(11). November, 1964. 341–354.

WHITEHALL, T. A future for the bulletin? The results of an enquiry into how bulletins are used in today's special library. *Aslib Proceeedings*, 25(2). February, 1973. 34–45.

CHAPTER 7

Selective Dissemination of Information, Other Services and User Needs

SDI

Selective dissemination of information (SDI) is a service in which documents, or information about them, are sent to those interested in the subjects of the documents. An SDI service is usually more appreciated by scientists and technologists than is an announcement bulletin, in that if properly organized it brings to their notice all important reports in their field without their having to scan a large number of document citations only a few of which are of interest. Simple systems can be operated manually, but most present-day systems are based on computer processing.

Manual systems

An information centre will usually operate some kind of distribution service for new reports. For instance it will probably be the channel for distributing the reports of its parent organization, to a list supplied by the author, the head of his department, or other responsible authority within the organization. This will be mainly a clerical task, but the information centre may be charged with the task of obtaining clearances necessary before details can be released, from patent and other departments within the organization, and it will then be necessary to organize a 'bring-forward' system so that unnecessary delays do not occur. Another type of dissemination service is that for new reports coming into the centre from other organizations. At its simplest this can be done by each abstractor suggesting a distribution from his own experience for each report he abstracts.

Any information scientist should know the subject interests of the people he serves. This may mean no more than making a mental note of new or lapsed interests. Or workers may keep a personal card index of users' subject interests, and little may be done to co-ordinate or update these indexes. It is far preferable to put the process on a more business-like footing and compile a register of fields of interest ('interest profiles') of the users of the centre. Such a register is normally organized on a subject basis using e.g. the COSATI subject headings, or the subject headings may be arranged in alphabetical order. It can be started by sending out a circular inviting recipients to complete a printed form stating their broad subject interests, and whether they prefer microfiche or paper copy. The centre then codes the replies and enters each code against the appropriate subject heading. The code should preferably be mnemonic, e.g. acronyms for names of organizations, branches of the organization, research establishments and their divisions, etc. Reference to the register under the subject of the report to be distributed then gives the distribution directly. An 'Interest Register' of this type is described in the paper by Wright. It is used in the Royal Aircraft Establishment to facilitate the distribution of incoming information, especially external research reports, to the appropriate people in the establishment, and to enable enquiries from outside the RAE to be referred to subject experts in RAE departments. An interest register requires frequent updating; some users will provide feedback but it will probably be necessary to circulate a request for updated information annually. The interest register should be reproduced in sufficient numbers for a copy to be issued to each of the professional staff.

Such manual systems can only work on a broad subject heading approach and unless multiple copies of reports are received, the number of recipients under each subject heading must be kept fairly small. If the distribution is large, extra copies of the report will have to be made to ensure that the recipients do not have a long wait before a copy is available, as this would eliminate the benefit of selective dissemination.

Computerized SDI

When a computer is available it is possible to provide a service in which individual users' interests are matched, and such systems

Selective Dissemination of Information

usually provide a computer printout of reports meeting his interests or 'profile' from which he can select the reports he actually wishes to see, the documents being sent only on request.

The first step is to send the user a form which gives the various subjects for which the centre caters in as much detail as possible and which provides ample space for the user's own explanations and comments; the form needs to be accompanied by an adequate explanation and advocacy of the service. Even so interviews may be needed. When the 'interest profile' has been completed, it is translated by one of the professional staff into a 'search profile' which is the interest profile translated into a descriptor language compatible with the indexing and searching procedure used in the computerized system. The descriptors, e.g. from the TEST thesaurus, are co-ordinated using Boolean logic operators. There are three of these operators, viz.:

Operator	Symbol	Example of use	Meaning
OR	+	(1+2)	Select reports indexed under either term 1 or under term 2.
AND	*	(1*2)	Select only reports that are indexed under both terms.
NOT	−	(1−2)	Select reports indexed under term 1 but discard any indexed also under term 2.

The logical equations are matched against the data-base in the computer, and the output is a printout of the bibliographical data of reports whose descriptors satisfy the logical equations.

Computer programs for SDI often incorporate additional features, thus author names can be used as descriptors, and searches can incorporate right- or left-hand truncation of descriptors. Right-hand truncation is exemplified by 'powder?' or 'powder . . .'. Such a descriptor input would involve a search on all terms beginning with 'powder', which in TEST are:

> powder (particles)
> powder alloys
> powder bags

> powder cutting
> powder metallurgy
> powder metals
> powder testing

This facility has to be used with caution, as it can cause false co-ordinations or 'false drops'. In the above example 'powder bags' is an ammunition term unrelated to powder metallurgy. Left-hand truncation e.g. '. . . aircraft' would mean that all the terms ending in 'aircraft' would be searched. Truncation can result in considerable economy in profile compilation if caution is exercised.

When the results of an SDI run are first submitted to the users, assessment forms should accompany the printouts so that the user can indicate the number of relevant, possibly relevant, and irrelevant references. His profile should be modified accordingly. This should continue until the number of irrelevant references is reduced to an acceptable level. With SDI it is more important to have high recall than high precision in the response to the profile. A profile with low precision is likely to retrieve reports which the user would not find for himself but which are useful while a high precision profile might only retrieve reports already known to the user. Profiles should be kept under constant review, and the recipients asked to notify any changes in their requirements. SDI printouts can also incorporate a returnable portion on which requests can be submitted for the full reports.

Compiling and maintaining profiles is a labour-intensive task for the professional staff of an information centre, and if it is intended to embark on a full-scale SDI service, each user should be encouraged to help compile his own profile. A standard profile form with explanatory notes should be prepared and sent to each user who wishes to receive the service. The report by Adams describes in detail how the UK Department of Industry's Technology Reports Centre operates such a scheme. Burton describes the SDI service operated by the US Department of Agriculture in which more than 6,000 profiles are operated with minimum staff, each user developing and modifying his own profile, helped by a *User's guide*.

Some centres recover part of the cost of an SDI service by making a charge, and this can be a useful indication of the value the users set on the service. Such a charge should only be levied

Selective Dissemination of Information 135

after a period of experimental running to prove the system. Some services operate entirely on a commercial basis, and some examples of these will be given in a later section of this chapter.

The experience of centres which have already developed SDI services should be carefully studied before setting up a new system. The paper by Kerr-Waller describes an experimental SDI service in electronics at the Standard Telecommunication Laboratories Ltd. This project called AIDS (Automated Information Dissemination System) involved creation of a thesaurus of about 6,000 terms and searching 10,000 abstracts from *Science Abstracts, Section B*, 150 research and development reports and about a hundred abridged patents. Anthony & others describe the system developed at the United Kingdom Atomic Energy Authority's Culham Laboratory, based on a KDF 9 computer. This is interesting in that a thesaurus was not employed, but the users' profiles were matched against terms occurring in the document titles. It was found in this respect that report titles were less informative than journal-article titles, and additional descriptors were added to report titles. The descriptors were allocated from terms occurring in the 'glossary of major words' produced by the computer program from the users' profiles. Goom describes a computer-based system developed at the Guest, Keen & Nettlefold Group Technological Centre, Wolverhampton (England), which produces both SDI output and a conventional monthly abstract bulletin as a by-product. The system was designed for an IBM 360/30 computer, and involved compiling a new thesaurus of about 3,000 terms.

Some commercial SDI services

A few commercial SDI services available to users in Europe will be described. These can enable a centre to augment its own services in certain fields. The computer-based services usually offer both output to meet individual profiles, and output to meet 'standard profiles', which are subjects of wide interest in the subject field covered.

Institution of Electrical Engineers (London), International Information Services in Physics, Electrotechnology, Computers and Control (INSPEC), (Marketing Manager, INSPEC, Institution of Electrical Engineers, Savoy Place, London WC2R 0BL). The INSPEC service is based on three computer data-bases containing bibliographical details and abstracts of journal articles, openly available reports, etc., in (1) physics, (2) electrical engineering and electronics, and (3) computers and control. Requesters submit their profiles in plain language and these are translated by INSPEC information scientists into free text and INSPEC thesaurus terms. The personal profiles can also include names of authors and editors, and language of the citations. Output is provided weekly on 150 × 100 mm catalogue cards. In addition, standard profiles, entitled 'Topics', are provided weekly on 150 × 100 mm cards in seventy-three subject fields.

An *INSPEC SDI User Manual* is available, and forms are provided for subscribers to send returns showing relevance of documents selected. These are used to monitor profiles and amend them as necessary.

United Kingdom Chemical Information Service (UKCIS), (The University, Nottingham NG7 2RD). This provides a current-awareness service using the Chemical Abstracts Service (CAS) products *Chemical Titles* (CT), *Chemical-Biological Activities* (CBAC), *CA-Condensates* (CAC), and a subset of CAC, 'UKCIS Macromolecular Chemistry' (MACMOL). Searches may be made for specific words, word fragments or phrases, in titles and other text, including author names, registry numbers, and molecular formulae, and for journal Coden (a code representation of the journal name) in a variety of combinations constituting the search profile. A UKCIS search manual is available, which assists users in the formulation of profiles. The output is provided fortnightly on 150 × 100 mm cards. UKCIS also provides *Macroprofiles*, or bulletins providing current awareness in specific subject areas. The output is supplied fortnightly in the form of a pocket-size bulletin.

European Space Research Organization Space Documentation Service (ESRO SDS),* (Via Galileo Galilei, 00044 Frascati, Italy). This provides an SDI service to individual profiles based on the magnetic tape data-base of the NASA *STAR* and *AIAA* [American Institute of Aeronautics and Astronautics] *Abstracts*. It also issues monthly about 130 *Standard Titles* from the same data-

* ESRO is now the European Space Agency (ESA).

base. The computer printout (in upper and lower case) is reduced to A5 size and bound in standard covers.

REQUESTS

The primary source of requests to the information centre is the centre's announcement bulletin, and requests so generated will be easy to fulfil if instructions on how to make requests are given in the introduction to the bulletin, stressing the importance of quoting the centre's accession number in the requests. A centre with large report holdings will also receive requests for reports which the requester hopes will be available but for which he does not know the centre's accession number. He may have seen the report quoted as a reference in a report he holds, or in a bibliography, or it may have been recommended by a colleague. He may not then quote adequate details for positive identification. An information centre must always make as sure as is possible exactly what it is that users want. This is much more easily done if the user appears in person or even if he asks on the telephone, but most large centres do much of their work by correspondence. Handling requests by correspondence in the centre is facilitated if a standard request form is used, and pads of such forms supplied to regular users.

Request forms

The form should be designed so that it contains numbered boxes for all the information the centre may need to identify the report and the requester. This information is: name of requester and his organization, centre's accession number (if known), title and reference number of report requested, personal author(s), corporate author of the report, and where the report reference was quoted. If the centre deals with security-controlled information, space should be provided for the reason the report is required, i.e. the 'need to know'. This can be a contract number for work which the requester's organization is conducting for a government department. The requester should be given alternative choices for the form in which his request should be supplied, i.e. paper copy or microfiche. Explanatory notes can also be printed on the form. It will not be necessary for the requester always to complete every box, and if the report was cited in the centre's accession list, the requester's name and address with the centre's accession number is sufficient provided he quotes the number correctly. There is thus a good case for giving a second means of identifying what is wanted so that the staff at the centre will be able to check that no error has been made. It may appear to users that unnecessary information is wanted, but the centre will require alternative approaches to identify unusual reports. The forms can be supplied in multiple copies interleaved with carbon paper so that the user can retain a copy, and they should be numbered serially with a record kept of the serial numbers sent to each user. The requester then only has to quote the serial number of his request in any subsequent enquiries to the centre. He can use his copy for recording the later stages of the transaction from his own point of view.

A leaflet explaining the use of the request form should be written and sent to all users when the form is first introduced. This will explain why the form requires so much information and stress that it is needed to help the centre identify requests for reports where the requester does not know the centre's accession number. A stock of the leaflets should be held in the centre so that new users can be sent a copy on their first approach to the centre.

Unless the centre insists firmly on one form being used for each item requested the regular users may well group their requests; some may ask for fifty reports at a time. In such cases it should be made clear to the requester that this will slow down the action on his request, and that a little extra work on his part in completing a separate form for each request will mean that he will receive what he wants much more quickly.

A different form should be designed and supplied to users who require subject searches. This can allot much more space to the subject of the request so that the requester can give background information and indicate what data-base he requires to be searched, and the period of time he requires to be covered.

Handling of requests

On first receipt in the centre, requests should be subjected to an initial screening to separate out subject enquiries and those which ask for information. These are immediately passed to the professional staff. Requests for reports quoting the centre's accession number can also be isolated and dealt with by junior staff. The requests remaining will be those for reports which have some bibliographical details quoted and which will have to be identified from the various card catalogues and printed indexes, and these will be dealt with by the more experienced clerical staff. When the request can be identified as a report held in the centre, the centre's accession number is written on the request form which is then passed to the junior staff to complete the action. If all copies of the report requested are out on loan the borrower's name goes on to a waiting list. If any borrower has had a copy for an unreasonably long time he will be asked to return it and a decision may have to be made as to whether a reproduction should be made at the first opportunity; if a report is held only as a microfiche it is better to make a copy of the fiche if the requester can use this form than send out the only copy. If a reproduction of a paper copy has to be made consideration should always be given to making a microfiche rather than a paper copy, as apart from the convenience of storage and cheaper postage, except for very short reports it will be cheaper to make a microfiche.

When request forms are used the centre can use a simplified recording process when it gets the request and can use space on the form for recording its own action in identifying the reports required. When this has been done it can use another pack of multiple stationery, the top copy of which is a note to the user giving the list of reports sent and the conditions of supply (period of loan, etc.) in the form of alternatives, the inappropriate items being crossed out. Successive copies of the form can be laid out for different purposes such as a receipt form for the requester to return, one or two copies for hastening return from loan, and a further copy can be used as a token left in the place of the report when it is taken from storage. If the last-named device is used, it must not replace the primary evidence of the loan, which is the record on the master movement card for the report. Such a scheme eliminates letter writing for the great majority of request work, but in other cases letters cannot be avoided, and efforts to eliminate them should not be pushed too far.

Requesters have a chance to say that their job is particularly urgent, and they should give a reason for this; the centre will soon learn to recognize users whose requests are always urgent and draw its own conclusions, but when the urgency is accepted another borrower may have to be asked to return the copy he has on loan. Popular reports will probably have to be copied in the centre. It is seldom possible to procure further copies of reports from the source, especially if they are old ones, as most reports are produced only in short runs, and originators have storage problems which usually involve weeding surplus stocks.

Requests for reports which are not held by the centre may be dealt with by asking for copies from likely sources. The catch about this method is that it often takes a long time to get the reports, especially if they have to be procured from overseas, and the requester may then have lost interest. If another centre is known to have a copy the request may be passed on to it, perhaps in parallel with a request to the source for a copy if the subject is relevant to the centre's interests; a request for a report on a subject quite outside the centre's interest will be passed on to another promising centre or returned with an explanation. In any case of a request being passed on or of its being put on to a waiting list the requester should be informed of what is being done, not only out of courtesy but also to divert possible hasteners to the right place. Passing requests on to another more likely source is much more helpful to users than returning them and does not involve much more work; pressure of work, however, may cause a centre to reject out of hand any requests that it cannot satisfy.

Requests by subject

To the searcher endeavouring to respond to a request, the size of the needle becomes invisible as the haystack becomes monumental. It is important to heed the good advice of Marcus Rosenblum:

(1) allow enough time; (2) verify, verify, verify; (3) sharpen the question; (4) know your sources; (5) 'eye' the index (scan it so that you understand how it is constructed); (6) discriminate; (7) give up in time; (8) create a useful product.

Subject requests will normally be dealt with by the technical staff, as far as possible by the same subject specialists who do the abstracting and subject analysis. This gives them more variety of work than they would otherwise have, and not only do they achieve results more quickly and more certainly than others would, since they are familiar with and can repeat the trains of thought they used in the original subject analysis, but also it brings to their notice ways in which their subject analysis could be improved. The results of searches can be supplied to the requester in various ways. If only a few reports are found, these can be sent to the requester. If the search produces a large number of references it is preferable to make photocopies of the abstracts and send them to the requester so that he can select those most relevant and request them from the centre.

Requests which call for information rather than for reports present a more serious problem. Sometimes it may be extracted from reports or from reference books without difficulty and at other times such a request may result in prolonged work for the professional staff. Because of this information centres are cautious about laying themselves open to such requests without providing for the possible consequences. If major jobs can be the subjects of negotiated contracts, this solves the problem provided that someone suitable can be found to do the work, or a standing job could be put out to contract while internal staff attend to the information enquiries. It could be that a request which amounts to asking for a state-of-the-art review coincides with a realization that one is needed on the subject and staff can be found to do the work, or it may be that an existing review can be brought up to date with comparatively little effort. If there is no prospect of the effort being found for some major request, then the requester, who may not be aware of the work it entails, has to be informed, just as he has to be given an approximate period if his request can be met but the work must take a considerable time.

Subject requests for documents are part of the everyday business of an information centre, but a fairly strict line has to be drawn between the one which can be answered quickly and the one which involves a major operation; in a good many cases it is difficult to draw such a line, and a request which appears at first sight to be an easy one may turn out to be quite otherwise. One way of dealing with this problem is to refer to senior staff anything which cannot be answered quickly with certainty, while starting operations on the easy ones without delay: if the search is not completed within a set period – say half an hour – it is stopped and a note made of what has been done and the query referred to the senior staff. It is important that junior staff, whether technical or not, should not embark on lengthy operations without the knowledge of their seniors.

It is important to keep records of all subject searches, with a note of the time taken and the references supplied. It frequently happens that a topic mentioned in the scientific press will generate several similar enquiries. Work is then saved by supplying the same material to all enquirers.

When many subject enquiries are received, it may be necessary to establish an order of priority according to the terms of reference of the information centre. If the centre is set up to serve the public, then requests can be dealt with on a first-come, first-served basis. If the centre has a particular responsibility to certain organizations or registered users, then requests from them take priority over those received from outside. Any system of priorities must be clearly laid down by the head of the centre and followed by all the staff dealing with subject requests.

SPECIAL BIBLIOGRAPHIES

Requests for information which recur indicate a continuing interest in the subject. In such cases it is worthwhile to reproduce the bibliographical details and abstracts of the reports retrieved as a formal bibliography and distribute copies more widely. The bibliography should include an author index, and its title should include the period covered in the search. For topics of particular interest, continuing bibliographies can be issued at regular intervals, such publications resembling the 'standard profiles' mentioned in the section on SDI, although they can be compiled by manual methods. Special bibliographies should be issued in a regular series, with a distinctive cover.

STATE-OF-THE-ART REPORTS

As mentioned in Chapter 1, state-of-the-art reports, in which recent progress in a specialized field is summarized, usually with many references, to the relevant reports and other publications, are a very useful source of information. There is a great demand for these reviews, particularly in fields in which most rapid progress is being made, and state-of-the-art reports based on unpublished material will be particularly valuable, published reviews usually being based on published material and thus less up to date. For a specialized information centre, compilation of such reviews should be a regular commitment, and one or more of the technical staff assigned to the task. An information centre covering a very wide field is unlikely to be able to produce state-of-the-art reports in all the fields it covers in view of the amount of staff time which would be taken up by the task; such centres seldom produce this type of publication. In centres which can undertake the task preparation of a state-of-the-art report may result from a specific request, but intelligent anticipation of the needs of users in a rapidly developing field will stimulate the production of others.

The method of compiling state-of-the-art reports in an information centre is well summarized in the paper by Geary. Such work is a useful exercise for technical staff in increasing their expertise, but if the centre does not have the effort available, it is a task which could be carried out extra-murally, perhaps by a former member of the centre's staff who would be provided with the necessary reports. Payment may be made either for the job or on the time the worker reports he has spent on it. Either method is open to some criticism but the payment may be a much less important consideration than getting the job done, and although the centre may not have direct authority to spend money, provision can be made in its budget for such purposes, just as is often done for outside translators. For state-of-the-art reviews and similar projects, time is not usually of the first importance, and the time taken to get a contract agreed may not matter much.

State-of-the-art reports should be produced in a regular series with a distinctive cover. Considerable thought should be devoted to their layout and production, and apart from satisfying the specialist users, they can be good exchange material for obtaining reports from other sources.

TRANSLATIONS

Some centres will give a service in translating technical papers from foreign languages. The centre may have a small team of specialist translators or some of the information staff may have competence in one or more foreign languages. These internal facilities are unlikely to be enough to cope with the load, which is notoriously unpredictable in its incidence. The balance is then maintained by sending work out either to an agency or to a panel of outside translators who are paid at an agreed rate of so much per thousand words, the rate varying with the assumed difficulty and rarity of knowledge of the language. The advantage of using such a panel lies in the control which can be exercised: agencies may give quicker results, but it may be found that their translations are made by people who are expert in the language but who do not understand the subject or terminology of the work they are translating. Before recruiting to the panel a specimen translation should be commissioned from the candidate, and only if this is satisfactory should he be offered further work. Translations received from the panel should be edited within the centre, to ensure standard presentation. Technical staff within the centre's own organization who will undertake translation work in their spare time are more likely to do so for the satisfaction of exercising their skill than for the money they earn, welcome as that is, but it is undesirable to allow the staff of the information centre to undertake translating in their own time for pay, as this can easily lead to abuse. When a centre has a team of internal translators it is useful to have about half the load done by them and the other half by the outside panel, as this enables the centre to keep the internal staff fully occupied while giving the panel enough work to keep them interested.

The centre's translations should be issued in a separate series, with a distinctive cover, and these can also be a useful source of exchange material. However, if it is proposed to disseminate translations outside the centre, it is important that permission to make the translation is first obtained from the holder of the copyright in the original article.

USERS

Large national information centres have a wide range of users, but most of their work is with a small number of different classes which vary according to the centre's terms of reference. Normally users are firstly, the units of the organization—usually a government department—which is responsible for the information centre, secondly, other organizations to which the centre has obligations, such as contractors, and thirdly, other information centres and other potential users. The last-named category has greater or lesser importance according to whether the centre is set up to disseminate openly available information or confines its activities mainly to controlled-distribution reports.

A large centre finds that its work is greatly facilitated if it can deal with other information centres rather than with individuals. The ultimate users are of course individuals, but if their requirements can be channelled through information centres their requests will come to the supplying centre in a form suited to its methods, and many of the enquiries will have been filtered out either because they can be met locally or because they were being directed to the wrong centre. The great majority of the request work for specific reports in large centres is done by clerical staff who cannot be expected to have any great understanding of the meaning of loosely expressed requests, and the professional staff are kept too busy with internal work or with subject enquiries to filter out any which can be dealt with without their intervention or which are too vague to be satisfied or even too frivolous to justify time being spent on them.

Proper completion of the centre's request forms mentioned earlier facilitates the handling of requests in the centre and the forms are more likely to be completed accurately by the staff of the requester's local information centre who will be aware of the problems of tracing reports from inadequate data. Professional staff are often able to find material which satisfies very vague requests but the users would be well advised not to rely upon this facility: it is obvious that the more useful information given in a request, the greater chance there is of getting what is wanted. There is also the obvious fact that the more time that is taken in hunting out obscure clues the fewer requests can be dealt with, and if there has to be a choice between a number of requests, the vague enquiry is going to be at a disadvantage.

Obviously, also, the more work that is involved in answering a request, the longer it will take to satisfy. This particularly applies to subject enquiries or to requests that require information to be extracted from reports. Some centres protect themselves by letting it be known that they will not accept subject enquiries from other than registered users, and many more will not undertake to extract information for casual enquirers. This is natural enough since such work is very time-consuming and usually requires a high degree of expertise.

Self-help by users

Users, by framing their enquiries carefully, can and should help the centre and themselves. It may seem that spending a little time in giving specific data that enable a request to be satisfied quickly by clerical staff assists only the centre at the cost of more effort by the user, but in fact any slowing of the operations of the centre delays the satisfaction of all the many enquiries that come into it and every avoidable call upon the efforts of the professional staff has its effect in delaying the production of the secondary information which the users require. The user can also help himself by passing his requests through his own information centre, if he has one, or by finding one which is prepared to act for him. Some information centres, in fact, only accept requests on their own printed forms, and only supply these forms to information centres and libraries, although they will sometimes deal with out-of-channel requests if they appear to merit it.

All users should of course state clearly what they want, and that should be as far as possible what they know the information centre is equipped to supply. If the centre normally supplies photocopies quickly, there is not likely to be any advantage in asking for a loan as against a copy for retention, but if photocopies take a considerable time the information centre may be having problems with its equipment and may be happy to have the choice between loan and retention. Of course with bulky documents it is very unlikely that there would be a copy, whether paper or photocopy, available for retention, or that the centre would be prepared to make a photocopy unless the user could specify that he needed some particular section only, or was prepared to pay the cost. If the enquirer is unable to use some particular form of document such as microfiche, he should say so, but it is an advantage to leave the information centre the widest possible choice of forms in which an enquiry can be satisfied.

One way in which users can be particularly helpful when making a subject request is to make it clear whether they want one good report, half a dozen, or whether they want all that can be found. It also saves trouble if they define any limitations, such as reports from a particular source or a particular country, or whether they want reports later than some specified date or covering a particular period (when forms are used, these questions should be included).

These limitations are particularly important with subject requests as searches may produce a mass of paper, much of which is neither wanted nor useful.

Foreign users

Some of the potential users of a large centre will be situated in other countries, and special consideration has to be given to their requests. If they ask for a report which is known or reasonably supposed to be available in their own country they would be advised to apply to their own national centre. If a controlled-distribution report is asked for special precautions must be taken: a 'need to know' has to be established and in general for such requests there will be a single government centre in any country which will authorize or refuse any request for such protected documents to be supplied to another country and lay down the procedures to be followed. Two general principles are that one government deals with another government in such matters and that protected information received from one country is not supplied to a third country. This means that any non-government organization requiring government-sponsored information from an overseas country must make the initial approach through the appropriate government department in its own country. This of course does not apply to reports advertised as available for purchase from a recognized centre such as the US National Technical Information Service.

Requests from other countries also raise the question of whether there is a reasonable expectation of a loan being returned, as there are seldom any penalties which can be applied. A unique copy should only be lent in quite exceptional circumstances and, in general, if a request is to be complied with it should be by supplying a paper copy or microfiche for retention. No report, except those approved for unlimited distribution, should be sent overseas unless the centre has been authorized to do so by the originator of the document or other responsible authority. In the case of reports supplied to the centre from an overseas source, a requester from a third country should be told to apply to the originator or to an agent of the originator in the requester's own country.

User needs

If the user is to be expected to help the information centre by properly framing his requests, the centre is also under an obligation to ensure that his needs are being satisfied. It is also important that users are kept informed of changes that may be planned in the centre's operations and products. It is useful if the centre can produce a periodic news bulletin which is distributed to users to keep them informed. Descriptive leaflets for each main service should also be prepared and distributed. Topics for leaflets might include the centre's announcement bulletin, how to submit subject requests, the translations service if one is provided, reprographic services, and computer services if available. One or more of the professional staff in the centre should also be charged, as part of their duties, with looking after customer relations. This could involve arranging visits to the centre and presentations of films or lectures on the work of the centre to interested groups. Occasional surveys by means of questionnaires can produce useful information if the questionnaires are carefully prepared. The paper by Wood gives useful advice on this point.

References

ADAMS, H. C. Guide to Technology Reports Centre selective dissemination of information service. St Mary Cray, Kent, Department of Industry, Technology Reports Centre, 1974.

ANTHONY, L. J. *and others.* Selective dissemination of information using a KDF 9 computer. *Aslib Proceedings*, 20(1). January, 1968. 40–64.

BURTON, H. D. A user-dependent SDI system. *Special Libraries*, 64(12). December, 1973. 541–544.

GEARY, P. J. Compilation of state-of-the-art surveys. *Bulletin of the Institute of Information Scientists*, 3(1). January, 1964. 4–12.

GOOM, H. H. A computer-based current awareness system producing both SDI output and conventional abstract bulletin. *Aslib Proceedings*, 26(3). March, 1974. 98–108.

KERR-WALLER, R. D. Automated Information Dissemination System (AIDS): technical evaluation. *Information Scientist*, 1(2). September, 1967. 51–72.

ROSENBLUM, M. Principles and practices in searching the scientific literature. *WOODFORD, F. P., ed. Writing for graduate students.* New York, Rockefeller University Press, 1968.

WOOD, D. N. Discovering the user and his information needs. *Aslib Proceedings*, 21(7). July, 1969. 262–270.

WRIGHT, R. C. Library and information services at the Royal Aircraft Establishment: some problems and their present solutions. *AGARD Conference Proceedings* No. 117, *Government assistance for technical information in industry and simple mechanization for small information centres*. Neuilly-sur-Seine, AGARD, 1972. 2-1 – 2-7.

CHAPTER 8

Photo- and Microcopying

ADVANTAGES

Several of the problems of large information centres may be minimized by satisfying requests for reports by the supply of photocopies of them, made on the spot as needed. This means that perhaps only a single copy of the original document need be held, and with security-classified reports there are fewer copies to be controlled. For unclassified reports this avoids the problems associated with securing the safe return of a unique original. Paperwork associated with a request is eased, for sometimes there is no need to make any record of a loan, though it is occasionally useful to be able to answer a request in the form that a copy of the report asked for was sent for retention on a given date: the record must then provide protection against the possible rejoinder that it was also returned on such another date. Except for very bulky reports it is easier, cheaper and more convenient to supply photocopies of requested unclassified reports without delving into the records of past transactions. It must be emphasized that copies of security-classified documents, or of parts of them, must be controlled as strictly as the original, and permission of the supplier is usually required before security-classified reports can be copied. The advantages of supplying photocopies are multiplied (to the supplier) if microfiches replace photocopies. Microfiches are cheaper to reproduce and the savings in packing and postal charges are considerable. The advantages are not always so apparent to the recipient, and the user's problems with microfiches will be discussed in a later section.

COPYRIGHT

One consideration that has always to be borne in mind is that of copyright. Every document which is published, and that includes every one which is distributed in any way to more than one or two persons, may not be copied (with certain exceptions) without the permission of the copyright holder, who may be the author or the publisher or both (since the typographical arrangement also carries copyright). Most publications now carry the copyright symbol © and name the copyright holder, but the absence of this does not mean that the document is not copyright.

The exceptions mentioned, in United Kingdom law, are when a single copy is made for individual study or research or by way of fair comment. The law is, of course, far more complicated than these brief quotations suggest, but they will suffice to indicate the principles which concern the information scientist. Many libraries and information centres run photocopying services on behalf of their users, and they usually (in the UK) require an undertaking that the copies will be used only for permitted purposes and that a copy of the same material has not previously been supplied: they also make a charge to cover the cost of the service. Some centres take a stricter view of the conditions than others, and some operate their service informally by exhibiting a notice conspicuously near the machine, which is operated by the user himself by a coin in a slot. An example of a more serious approach is shown in Figures 11 and 12. Any centre which contemplates setting up a new service should make a study of its legal obligations, for the UK *Copyright Act* (1956) was not drafted with the use of technical information in mind, and it covers much more than printed material. Copinger & Skone James should be consulted for a detailed discussion of UK law. A useful survey of photocopying practices in the UK is given by Barker. This was carried out for Unesco and the United International Bureaux for the Protection of Intellectual Property. The review includes an exposition of current UK copyright law and its interpretation in this area, an analysis of current photographic reproduction practices, and considerations to be borne in mind when evaluating the effect of these practices.

In general the United States Government does not claim copyright in its publications which concern the information scientist: for example *Government Reports Announcements (GRA)* contains a notice which reads, 'Contents may be quoted freely. Mention of source will be appreciated. . . .'

NATIONAL REFERENCE LIBRARY OF SCIENCE AND INVENTION
APPLICATION FOR PHOTOCOPIES

LIB no.

Photocopies are produced by Xerography. This normally gives good legibility. If for any reason better quality, particularly of half-tones, is required other methods of photocopying are available on request.

1. Except when the material to be copied is:—
   (a) a United Kingdom or foreign Patent Office publication, e.g., a Patent Specification; or
   (b) a document which has been lodged in connection with a Patent, Trade Mark or Design application,

   One of the declarations overleaf must be completed. The signature must be the personal signature of the person making the request. A stamped or typewritten signature or the signature of an agent is not sufficient.

2. The Library reserve the right to ask for further enquiries to be made or to refuse to make copies in any particular case. In particular, copies of Stationery Office publications should normally be obtained from H.M.S.O. or through a bookseller and only in exceptional circumstances will be supplied by the Library.

3. The supply of material under this application does not imply any freedom to make further copies. It may be an infringement of copyright to do so.

Customer's reference _____

Name _____

Address _____

_____ _____

Telephone number _____

Full particulars of publications or documents to be copied
(Volume, page numbers and date to be given, where applicable)

Title (not abbreviated): Country & Number (if a Foreign Patent)	Date	Volume	Part	Pages	Number of copies of each publication

Please sign one of the copyright declarations overleaf, if applicable

LIB. 23

10411/1021L. D.832145 50M 12/72 T.P. Gp.794

FIG. 11. Request for photocopies (to illustrate copyright declaration).

COPYRIGHT DECLARATIONS

I   FOR A single copy of an article from a copyright periodical.
(If more than one copy of an article is required, copyright owner's written consent must be obtained and then Declaration II will apply.)

I hereby request you to make and supply to me a reproduction of the item(s), mentioned overleaf, being an article in a periodical publication, which I require for the purposes of research or private study.
I have not previously been supplied with a copy of the said article(s) by any Librarian.
I undertake that if a copy is supplied to me in compliance with this request I will not use it except for the purposes of research or private study.

Signature.. Date........................

II   FOR One or more copies from any publication for which copyright owner's written consent has been obtained.
I hereby request you to make and supply to me..reproduction(s) of the publication(s) mentioned overleaf which I undertake to use strictly for the purpose for which the Copyright Owner's written consent, attached, has been given.

Signature.. Date........................

III   FOR A single copy of part of a textbook or pamphlet where the copyright owner could not be traced.
I hereby request you to make and supply to me a reproduction of the publication mentioned overleaf, being a part of a work other than an article in a periodical publication, which I require for the purpose of research or private study.
I have not previously been supplied with a copy of the said publication by any Librarian.
I undertake that if a copy is supplied to me in compliance with this request I will not use it except for the purposes of research or private study.
I do not know and have been unable to ascertain the name and address of the person entitled to authorise the copying and I attach hereto copies of replies I have received to my enquiries.

Signature.. Date........................

IV   FOR Copies required in connection with a judicial proceeding.
I hereby request you to make and supply to me..reproduction(s) of the publication(s) mentioned overleaf (all of) which I require for the purposes of a judicial proceeding or for the purposes of a report of a judicial proceeding. I undertake not to use it (them) for any other purpose.

Signature.. Date........................

V   FOR Works in which there is no U.K. copyright.
I hereby request you to make and supply to me..reproduction(s) of the publication(s) mentioned overleaf. The publication(s) in question does (do) not enjoy copyright protection in the United Kingdom because

....
....

Signature.. Date........................

The Library reserves the right to ask for further enquiries to be made or to refuse to make copies in any particular case. In particular, copies of Stationery Office publications should normally be obtained from H.M.S.O. or through a bookseller and only in exceptional circumstances will be supplied by the Library.
It is an infringement of copyright to make further copies of material supplied under this application.

FIG. 12. Reverse of request for photocopies (Fig. 11).

PHOTOCOPYING

Processes

Photocopying processes have improved considerably over the years and most modern appliances can be relied upon to give good copies, after the initial warming up, at the touch of a button. Some give contact copies of the same size as the original, but others produce their copies by projection, so that it is possible to obtain them either larger or smaller than the original. This enables a saving to be made by making the copies, say, two-thirds of the size of the original, and such copies are usually quite satisfactory. Most modern machines give direct positive copies, in which black appears as black, but some produce an intermediate negative from which one or more positives are printed either automatically or by a manual operation. Most modern machines also give dry copies, particularly those using the Xerox (trademark of the Xerox Corporation, USA, and of Rank-Xerox Ltd, UK) and electrostatic reprographic processes in which the image is transferred in the form of a coloured resin which is fused by heat on to the paper: in any machine in which the paper is heated for any purpose if it does not run smoothly and becomes stuck there is a risk of fire starting in a few seconds. Many modern machines will give up to a dozen prints of any frame by adjustment of a dial.

Quite a number of the reports held by an information centre are themselves likely to be represented only by photocopies, and the readability necessarily deteriorates with each 'generation' so that often it is not worth making a photocopy of the only document available. Normally the text and line diagrams copy well, but figures in which there are large areas of black reproduce very poorly in many photocopying processes, as do half-tone plates, so that if these are essential to the use of a report a photocopy will not give the user satisfaction even if the text is perfectly clear.

The permanence of photocopies varies greatly. Some processes involve treatment of the exposed paper by liquids which cannot in practice be completely removed and the images sometimes tend to fade in time, particularly with exposure to bright light.

Equipment

For information on photocopying equipment reference should be made to technical journals such as *Management Services in Government* (formerly the *O and M Bulletin*), *Business Equipment Digest*, which gives an annual review of new copying equipment, and *FID News Bulletin*, which occasionally includes a 'Document Reproduction Survey'. AGARD have published an AGARDograph by Hampshire which provides a guide to reprographic processes for the small user currently (1974) available, which covers photocopying, duplicating (spirit and stencil), offset-litho duplicating and printing, and micrographics.

Economics

It is, of course, clear that a point must come at which photocopying becomes uneconomical. The original document may be bulky, in which case the photocopy would be much more so and postal charges on it would be very high quite apart from the cost in materials, staff and machine time involved in making the photocopy, including collating the loose sheets. A decision should be made at an early stage and recorded on the master record of a report whether a request should normally be met by supplying a photocopy and this decision should not depend solely on the bulk, but also on the suitability of the illustrations to reproduce well.

In the paper by Hampshire, cited above, a table of comparative costs is included for various copying and duplicating processes, as at May 1974, in relation to the number of copies required.

MICROCOPYING AND MICROFORMS

Problems of storage space for large collections of paper copies have usually eventually been resolved by microcopying, i.e. transferring the reports on to film as microimages. The two forms most commonly used at the present time are roll microfilm, and microfiche which is a flat sheet of microfilm containing multiple microimages in a grid pattern. Micro-opaques, such as microcard, are also used but for information centres the transparencies are the more versatile. (See Baker, G. G. & Associates, 1974.)

The different forms

Microfilm has been used as a storage medium for many years. A roll of 35mm film will have a number of reports on each reel at a moderate optical reduction, so that a frame can be read if necessary without serious difficulty using a watchmaker's eye-glass or one of the fairly numerous hand viewers. There are plenty of projectors available that show a more or less full-sized image on a ground-glass screen or on an opaque screen, and some of them will also make a photocopy of any desired frame at the touch of a button. On the other hand a reel is likely to have about a thousand frames on it, comprising perhaps forty or fifty reports and it may take quite a time to find a desired report and still more to find a desired frame. The next stage is to use 16 mm film with roughly four times as many pages in the same size and weight, but it is far more difficult to read the film without a projector. Either form of roll film has the advantage that it is very unlikely for a roll to be mislaid.

Newer and more convenient methods of storing and using roll film are the cassette and cartridge, which are easier to store because the containers are nearly square and much easier to insert into a reader-printer (usually motorized) made for this type of storage; there are some commercial services which issue material on cassetted microfilm, and their number seems likely to increase. The main objection to their use is their limited capacity.

Sealy has shown that it is possible to run an information service based entirely on a microform store of reports. Optical coincidence cards are used for retrieval, and when a report is required the cassetted film is run through a reader-printer. The document store consists of the cassetted microfilm and microfiches received from other sources.

Microfiches are pieces of flat film containing multiple images in a grid pattern. In the past there has been a number of different sizes with differing numbers of frames, but the commonest form has been a 148×105 mm sheet with space for seventy-two image frames in six rows; the top row, however, is occupied by a title and other bibliographical information which can be read by the unaided eye, the first frame is conventionally left empty and the second is occupied by a reference number and a statement of the number of microfiches used for the report, and, recently, a resolution chart, while one frame is occupied by the word 'end' and the date of filming, so that space remains for fifty-seven frames at a reduction of 1/20. More recently an American (National Microfilm Association) standard (see the article by Avedon) has increased the reduction to 1/24 and this provides room for ninety-eight usable frames. The *British Standard* (*BS* 4187) has now been revised and issued in two parts (Part 1 60-frame format, Part 2 98-frame format). The 98-frame format has been generally adopted. There is also an ISO standard. The use of microfiches for scientific and technical reports is discussed in an AGARDograph by Williams & Broadhurst.

A relatively recent development is the ultrafiche such as the Photochromic Micro-Image (PCMI) system produced by the National Cash Register Co. Ltd (Tauber & Myers). In ultrafiches reduction can be 1/96 to 1/150, allowing 1,680 to 3,200 frames on a standard 148 × 105 mm fiche. Ultrafiches need specialized equipment for their production, not at present available to information centres, and are thus not suitable for reproduction and distribution on demand, but the system may be very useful for storing a large number of reports which are seldom going to be called for if the large savings in storage costs outweigh the high initial cost of having the ultrafiches produced. A retrieval system using ultrafiches will be described later in this chapter.

Aperture cards. Single frames of 35 mm film can be mounted in tab cards (the card format used for computer input). The film can contain a single image, e.g. an engineering drawing, or several small images, e.g. a short report. The body of the card can be punched with a retrieval code, and can also contain printed bibliographical information.

Micro-opaques such as microcard are losing popularity with the increasing use of microfiches. The microcard is in effect a microfiche on opaque card at about the same reduction in size. Since it has to be viewed by reflected light the projectors are more expensive and less satisfactory than those for microfiches, and it is almost impossible to reproduce a satisfactory full-size copy from a microcard. A number of US reports were, however, issued as microcards before microfiches became popular.

Microform retrieval systems

Microfilm systems. Information retrieval from microform has a long history. One of the earliest systems to be developed, which nevertheless embodied many of the features used in modern systems, was the Rapid Selector, first suggested by Vannevar Bush in 1938 (see paper by Shaw) and an experimental model of which was constructed at the Massachusetts Institute of Technology during the period 1938–1940. A reel of 35 mm film contained document frames accompanied by specific patterns of clear dots used as a selection code. In searching, the code pattern for each document frame was projected on to a bank of photocells. The photocells were masked by a cut-out that was the exact physical image of the selection code pattern, so that when a coded frame had the same hole pattern as the cut-out a match resulted which fired a Strobotron that projected the selected document frame on to a section of unexposed 16mm film allowing a replica to be made. The system was developed further by the National Bureau of Standards and Engineering Research Associates, and used operationally by the US Navy Department's Bureau of Ships as described in papers by Ball (1959, 1961). More details of the system will be found in the state-of-the-art report by Bagg & Stevens from the National Bureau of Standards.

Roll film is also used in the National Bureau of Standards system FOSDIC (Film Optical Scanning Device for Input to Computers). FOSDIC II developed for the US National Weather Records Center carries film records of punched cards of meteorological data. Output of the system is either a duplicate of the original punched card or magnetic tape. The system is also described in the review by Bagg & Stevens already mentioned.

Other systems employing roll film include FileSearch (FMA Inc.) used by the US Bureau of Ships Central Records Section and FLIP (Film Library Instantaneous Presentation) (Benson-Lehner Corporation).

More recently Kodak Ltd have developed the MIRACODE system in which the coded microfilm is contained in cassettes used with a Microstar reader-printer incorporating a push-button control unit into which the search requests are keyed. The system is described in Williams' *Miniaturized communication* and in the paper by Baffady. For a large collection the store would have to be broken down into a number of sub-sets, to avoid the necessity of searching all the cassettes for each enquiry. Baffady also describes the 3M Company's Microdisc system which is somewhat similar to Miracode but separates the filmed images from the retrieval codes. Microdisc combines a special-programme minicomputer, an input/output terminal with cathode ray tube display and a 3M Page Search dry silver reader-printer in an integrated configuration that allows random access to a 16mm microfilm cartridge file.

Index information is stored on magnetic disc. In response to searchers' requests the cathode-ray tube will display the precise cartridge and frame location of any microimage. Opaque document marks under each filmed image guide the Page Search retrieval unit to the appropriate frame.

Microfiches. Simple retrieval of standard fiches from a large and heavily used collection when a search has produced a list of accession numbers is provided by automated storage systems such as Roneo Vickers Conserv-a-trieve or Remington Rand Lektriever. In such systems push button selection of a particular drawer enables it to be delivered automatically to the operator's working level when seated in front of the machine.

Fiche-retrieval units are available in which push button selection from a keyboard selects a fiche and the frame on it required from a collection of fiches in a cartridge stored with the unit. The chosen frame is then projected on to a screen. The cartridges typically contain thirty fiches and can be changed quickly.

Information retrieval from microfiches or their equivalent can be effected by using coding similar to that used in the roll film systems. The early systems used film chips rather than the standard microfiches of the present day. In France Samain developed the Filmorex system and in the USA the Kodak Minicard system, reported by Tyler & others, was developed and at least four operational systems produced. In these systems each film chip contains code bits recorded in a selection area together with images of one or more document pages.

Microfiches can also be retrieved by a system in which the coding is not incorporated in the fiches but in binary-coded metal bars attached to their top edges. Such a system is the Image Systems Inc. CARD (Compact Automatic Retrieval Display) described in papers by Lyon and by Vernimb. (Details are obtainable in the UK from Image Systems Ltd, 548 Chiswick High Road, London, W4.) The microfiches are housed in a rotating carousel each containing 750 fiches and are retrieved by signals from a keyboard which operate a needle-sort system. The system includes a reader-printer. The unit can be computer-controlled through an interface module. The system described by Vernimb is that used in the European Nuclear Documentation Service (ENDS), and each microfiche frame contains four abstracts from the ENDS data-base. References retrieved from a computer search can thus be displayed on the screen of the reader-printer. Modified CARD units interfaced with a computer are used in the Massachusetts Institute of Technology's Project Intrex for full-text retrieval, as described in the paper by Overhage & Reintjes. Dimensions of the fiches are 150 × 100mm and reduction factor is eighteen to one, each fiche containing sixty frames.

Lyon also describes the Mohawk Industrial Laboratories System 4000, available in modules holding 4,000 tab size aperture cards which are encoded using a special punch. Retrieval is effected by entering the required code on a keyboard.

Duerden describes a computer-controllable ultrafiche terminal under development by GEC Marconi Electronics Ltd. The PCMI ultrafiches contain a 22-bit retrieval code at the edges of each frame. A page is selected by an external digital signal from a computer or keyboard.

Production of microfiches

If the centre has a microfilm camera, microfiches can be produced cheaply from the roll film using plastic jackets. The jackets are usually 148 × 105mm in size and consist of two very thin sheets of clear plastic cemented together at the top and bottom edges and at intervals of 16mm or 35mm across their width to form pockets into which strips of roll film can be inserted. Equipment is available to assist jacket loading. The main disadvantages of jacketed microfiches are that 'second generation' copies are less good than with unjacketed fiches because of the presence of the film, and the separation of the film strips caused by the pockets is slightly greater than standard. The latter only causes difficulties if it is desired to make full size paper copies using a production printer.

For large-scale fiche production a step-and-repeat camera is more suitable, in which the film is advanced a frame at a time up to the end of the line and then returned automatically to the beginning of the next line. Such cameras can use sheet film and incorporate a processor so that fully processed fiches are delivered, or separate processing can be employed. Other cameras work from 105mm roll stock which is cut into separate fiches in the camera and stored in a light-tight box ready for processing. A few (suitable for large numbers of masters) use 105mm roll film which is not cut and the output is a chain of masters which can be cut for individual duplication or copied on a roll-to-roll copier. Step-and-repeat cameras usually incorporate a separate 1:1 size-ratio camera for recording the eye-legible title at the head of each fiche. A minimum output of 300 frames per hour can be expected with step-and-repeat cameras.

Master fiches can be copied by exposing them in emulsion-to-emulsion contact with cut size diazo film under near-ultra-violet from a light box and developing the exposed film in an ammonia developer. Up to nine masters can be copied simultaneously by this process.

The main problem in microfiche production is to maintain quality and thus help to overcome the reluctance of users to accept fiches instead of paper copy. The best high-contrast film and development chemicals should be used but it is impossible to produce a good-quality fiche from a poor paper copy, and the points to remember in producing a report to ensure maximum legibility in the microfiche produced from it have already been enumerated in Chapter 2. For a detailed review of equipment for producing microfiches, reference should be made to G. G. Baker & Associates' *Guide* (1974).

When microfiches are made of new reports it is best to have a master copy and a number of 'second generation' copies made from it. The master copy on silver halide film is the archival copy, and should be handled only when it is necessary to make further 'second generation' copies. One of the latter should be used when enlarged paper copies are needed. The master copies should be stored separately to avoid the possibility of their being handled unnecessarily. This procedure means that the required storage capacity is considerably greater than if a single microfiche is made, but the method is desirable, particularly when considerable use is made of the collection, as is the case with the newer holdings in a large centre.

Requests for reports held as microfilm will in general be met by making paper copies of the appropriate frames. Requests for microfiches can be met either by supplying a duplicate fiche or by preparing a paper copy using a reader-printer or a production printer if this is available. Reader-printers are suitable for copying selected frames, or for short reports in their entirety, but are rather slow for lengthy reports. The possibility of recovering the cost of supplying paper copies by making a charge should be seriously considered. This should cut down the number of copies made which are subsequently returned as being of no interest.

There is a large number of microfiche readers and reader-printers now on the market. A useful guide is published by G. G. Baker & Associates (1973). In the USA, the American Library Association in its Library Technology Program (LTP) has prepared *Library Technology Reports* on microform equipment and in particular microfiche reading devices. In the UK, the National Reprographic Centre for documentation (NRCd) (Hatfield Polytechnic, Endymion Road Annexe, Hatfield, Herts.) has a similar programme, and issues objective test reports on microform equipment. NRCd and LTP have established an exchange programme whereby evaluation of microform equipment published by either of the organizations may be republished by the other. The paper by Sauter of the US Defense Documentation Center gives an excellent review of microfiche systems for the 'small user' (i.e. microfiche usage of between 200 and 1,000 per year), including recent advances in microfiche standards, reading equipment, and microfiche quality. The report by Williams & Broadhurst already cited also gives guidance on these points.

On-line information-retrieval systems can be made more immediately effective to terminal users distant from the main centre if a local collection of microfiches is maintained, duplicating the catalogue entries of the main centre. If security-classified information is involved, only unclassified search terms and accession numbers need to be transmitted on-line, and the local microfiche collection, which is kept under secure control, is consulted for the full details of the result of the search. Such a system is operated by the Defence Scientific Information Service of the Defence Research Board in Canada, and is described in the paper by Irvine.

Economics. Rising costs make it impossible to be dogmatic on the subject of the cost-benefit of replacing a collection of paper copies of reports by microfiches, and each centre considering such a step will have to make its own analysis. A guide to costings (as of 1971) will be found in *Methods in miniature*, an HMSO publication prepared by the Interdepartmental Group on Microcopying, and Parsons discusses the economics of microforms as a storage medium in libraries, with special reference to experience at the

British Library Lending Division. His paper includes detailed cost calculations (as at 1972) and it is understood that a similar study is planned for late 1975.

Microfiches and the user

There is considerable resistance among users to the use of microfiches. Economies in storage and distribution of reports in this form can be dissipated if the user requires a full-size paper copy to be made from each fiche supplied to him. However an indication that microfiche acceptability is increasing is given in the paper by Sheppard. Microfiche was used as the primary publication form for the preprints of papers presented at the Rotary-wing Aircraft Symposium held in Melbourne, Australia, in September 1973. A questionnaire seeking to ascertain user reaction to the microfiche preprints was circulated to 119 people who attended the conference and/or received copies of the preprints. Analysis of the ninety replies showed that fifty-seven found microfiches acceptable for the purpose.

The concept of individual desk-top microfiche readers as an essential tool for the working scientist should be vigorously encouraged, and libraries associated with the scientist's laboratory should have reader-printers available to reproduce the frames in the fiche required for detailed study. At the present time there are several portable readers marketed at a reasonable price.

References

AVEDON, D. M. The Federal Government takes three giant steps for micrographics. *Journal of Micrographics*, 5(4). March, 1972. 165–171.

BAFFADY, W. Microfilm equipment and retrieval systems for library picture collections. *Special Libraries*, 65(10/11). October–November, 1974. 440–444.

BAGG, T. C. and STEVENS, M. E. Information selection systems retrieving replica copies: a state-of-the-art report. Washington, National Bureau of Standards, 1961. pp. 173. *NBS Technical Note* 157.

BAKER, G. G. & ASSOCIATES. A guide to microfilm readers and reader-printers. 2nd ed. Guildford (England), 1973. ISBN 0 9502082 3X. pp. 128.

BAKER, G. G. & ASSOCIATES. A guide to the production of microforms. Guildford (England), 1974. ISBN 0 9502082 56. pp. 144.

BALL, H. R. Information retrieval in the Bureau of Ships. *Bureau of Ship Journal*. May, 1959. 5–8.

BALL, H. R. Bureau of Ships Rapid Selector. *Bureau of Ships Journal.* November, 1961. 6–7.

BARKER, R. E. Photocopying practices in the United Kingdom. London, Faber & Faber, 1970. pp. 104.

BRITISH STANDARDS INSTITUTION. Specification for microfiche. Part 1. 60-frame format. London, 1973. ISBN 0 580 07609 1. pp. 9. *BS* 4187 *Pt.* 1.

BRITISH STANDARDS INSTITUTION. Specification for microfiche. Part 2. 98-frame format. London, 1973. ISBN 0 580 07619 9. pp. 9. *BS* 4187 *Pt.* 2.

COPINGER, W. A. *and* SKONE JAMES. F. E. Copinger and Skone James on copyright . . . 11th ed., by E. P. Skone James. London, Sweet & Maxwell, 1971. pp. 968.

DUERDEN, F. A computer-controllable ultrafiche terminal. *AGARD Conference Proceedings* No. 136. *New developments in storage, retrieval and dissemination of aerospace information.* Neuilly-sur-Seine, AGARD, 1973. 11–1 – 11–7.

HAMPSHIRE, T. A guide to reprographic processes for the small user. Neuilly-sur-Seine, AGARD, 1975. *AGARDograph* No. 199.

INTERNATIONAL ORGANIZATION FOR STANDARDIZATION (ISO). Transparent A6 size microfiche of uniform division – image arrangements No. 1 and No. 2. Geneva, 1973. pp. 3. *ISO* 2707.

INTERDEPARTMENTAL GROUP ON MICROCOPYING (UK). Methods in miniature: an introduction to microcopying. London, HMSO, 1968. pp. 31.

IRVINE, J. J. A remote-terminal retrospective search facility using a hybrid of microform and computer storage. *Information Storage and Retrieval,* 9(1). November, 1973. 597–606.

LYON, C. C. Retrieval of microfiche – random access. *AGARD Conference Proceedings* No. 136. *New developments in storage, retrieval and dissemination of aerospace information.* Neuilly-sur-Seine, AGARD, 1973. 9–1 – 9–7.

NATIONAL BUREAU OF STANDARDS. FOSDIC – A film optical sensing device for input to computers. *National Bureau of Standards Technical News Bulletin,* 38(2). February, 1954. 24–27.

NATIONAL BUREAU OF STANDARDS. FOSDIC II – reads microfilmed punched cards. *National Bureau of Standards Technical News Bulletin,* 41(5). May, 1957. 72–74.

NATIONAL MICROFILM ASSOCIATION. Microfiche standard specification. Annapolis, Md., 1963. M–1–1963.

OVERHAGE, C. F. J. *and* REINTJES, J. F. Project Intrex, a general review. *Information Storage and Retrieval,* 10(5/6). May–June, 1974. 157–188.

PARLIAMENT. The Copyright Act 1956. Chapter 74, 4 & 5 Eliz. 2. London, HMSO, 1956.

PARSONS, R. B. The economics of microforms as a storage medium in libraries. *NLL Review,* 2(1). April, 1972. 45–55.

SAMAIN, J. FILMOREX – eine neue Technik elektronischer Dokumentation. *Nachrichten für Dokumentation,* 9(1). January, 1958. 35–40.

SAUTER, H. E. A microfiche system for small users. *AGARD Conference Proceedings* No. 136. *New developments in storage, retrieval and dissemination of aerospace information.* Neuilly-sur-Seine, AGARD, 1973. 10–1 – 10–10 and 10–A1.
SEALY, T. An effective use of microfilm in a technical information system. *Information Scientist*, 6(3). September, 1972. 111–115.
SHAW, R. R. The Rapid Selector. *J. Documentation*, 5(3). December, 1949. 164–171.
SHEPPARD, M. O. Microfiche preprints for conferences. *Aslib Proceedings*, 26(11). November, 1974. 435–446.
TAUBER, A. S. and MYERS, W. C. Photochromic micro-images, a key to practical microdocument storage and dissemination. *American Documentation*, 13(4). October, 1962. 403–409.
TYLER, A. W. and others. The application of the Kodak Minicard system to problems of documentation. *American Documentation*, 6(1). January, 1955. 18–30.
VERNIMB, C. O. Abstracts on microfiche for on-line retrieval. *AGARD Conference Proceedings* No. 136. *New developments in storage, retrieval and dissemination of aerospace information.* Neuilly-sur-Seine, AGARD, 1973. 12–1 – 12–13.
WILLIAMS, B. J. S. Miniaturized communications. London, Library Association, Hatfield, the National Reprographic Centre for documentation, 1970. ISBN 0 85365 112 4. pp. 190.
WILLIAMS, B. J. S. and BROADHURST, R. N. The use of microfiches for scientific and technical reports: considerations for the small user. Neuilly-sur-Seine, AGARD, 1974. *AGARDograph* No. 198.

SELECTED BIBLIOGRAPHY

CAVENDISH, J. M. A handbook of copyright in British publishing practice. London, Cassell, 1974. ISBN 0 304 29192 7. pp. 210.
... COPIERS '73. *Business equipment digest*, 13(7). July, 1973. 6–7, 9, 11, 13, 15, 17, 19.
DEUTSCH, A. Microfilm copyright problems. *Microfiche Foundation Newsletter*, no. 27. March, 1974. 3–10.
GORDON, H. F. 16 mm microfilm viewing equipment guide: directory. Alexandria, Va., Defense Documentation Centre, [1971?], *Report No.* DDC-TR-71-1. (Available NTIS as AD 718 000).
HENRY, N. I. Copyright: public policy and information technology. *Science*, 183(4123). 1 February, 1974. 384–391.
HOLLOWAY, A. H. A study of copyright. Neuilly-sur-Seine, AGARD, 1970. 32. *AGARD Advisory Report* No. 23.
LUTHER, F. The economics of microfilming. *Library Journal*, 96(19). November, 1961. 3743–3746.
NATIONAL MICROFILM ASSOCIATION. Proposed revision to industry standard: quality standards for Computer Output Microfilm. Silver Spring, Md., 1974.
NATIONAL REPROGRAPHIC CENTRE FOR DOCUMENTATION. Micro-

graphic cameras: a guide to types and equipment available in the UK. Hatfield, 1974. ISBN 0 85267 0524. pp. 84.

NELSON, C. E. Microfilm technology: engineering and related fields. New York, McGraw-Hill, 1965. pp. 397.

PLUMB, P. W., ed. The economics of microfilming and document reproduction: papers given at seminars 1966. London, Microfilm Association of Great Britain, 1966. pp. 55.

STAHL, N. Problems and opportunities with microfilm. *Journal of Micrographics*, 3(2). Winter, 1969–1970. 66–67.

UNIVERSAL COPYRIGHT CONVENTION (The). Paris, Unesco, 1952.

VEIT, F. Microforms, microform equipment and microform use in the educational environment. *Library Trends*, 19(4). April, 1971. 447–466.

VESSEY, H. F. The use of microfiche for scientific and technical reports. Neuilly-sur-Seine, AGARD, 1970. *AGARD Advisory Report* No. 27.

CHAPTER 9

Mechanization

Any present-day costing exercise will show the large element that staff costs contribute to the total. It is therefore vital in a large reports centre that staff should work at maximum productivity and that any piece of equipment that helps to cut down unnecessary work or eliminates routine work should be carefully considered. Mechanization does not only mean installing a computer: types of mechanized storage are described in Chapter 10, and there are also mechanized conveyer systems as installed at the British Library Lending Division which take much of the drudgery out of moving large piles of reports around a building. Automatic addressing machines assist in the routine work of a post room, and visits to exhibitions such as the annual Business Efficiency Exhibition in Britain will usually give an opportunity of seeing demonstrations of other new products which are designed to lighten clerical labour.

SIMPLE MECHANIZATION

Time-consuming operations in a reports centre using a manually produced card catalogue and announcement bulletin are the multiple typing and checking operations. If the centre is also responsible for report production, again multiple typing and checking may be necessary. Such operations can be considerably facilitated by using tape-typewriters. Multiple typing of reports or serials lists which need periodic updating can also be avoided by using eighty-column punched cards and a tabulator.

Tape-typewriters

These machines have already been mentioned briefly in Chapter 6 in connection with the preparation of announcement bulletins and computer-produced indexes to them. Tape-typewriters are essentially electric typewriters with associated paper tape (or edge-punched card) punches and readers. When the punch is switched on, each key depression of the typewriter results in a pattern of holes being punched across the tape, unique for the character typed. Text punched into the tape will be typed automatically when that tape is placed in the tape reader and the 'start read' key depressed. The machines have a number of control codes, such as non-print, print-restore, tape-skip, skip-restore, punch on, punch off, etc. Using these codes a programme tape can be punched which will control the machine when typing data in standard format, or a tape can be punched in which by the use of tape-skip and skip-restore codes selective reproduction of parts of the tape are possible.

The punched paper tape can be used for computer input, but if not required for this purpose, it can save a good deal of repetitive typing and checking. In producing draft reports which may be subject to amendments, the draft is typed and a tape produced. When typing the corrected draft the unchanged material is typed automatically at 120 words per minute (twice the speed of an average typist), simultaneously producing a new tape, and only the new material is typed manually. (The paper tape for the parts to be amended can be stepped character-by-character past the reading head with the punch switched off, using a 'single step' facility.) Only the new material has to be checked. When a completely correct tape has been produced this is used to type automatically the final version of the report on offset litho masters.

Wilson (1964) describes the use of a Friden Flexowriter with edge-punched cards instead of paper tape in the library at the Atomic Energy Research Establishment, Harwell, to produce catalogue cards and lists with a saving in clerical and typing effort estimated at 1,000 man-hours a year. Production of catalogue cards and accession lists at the Central Electricity Generating Board Library using tape-typewriters is described by Vickers. A twenty-five per cent saving in operating costs, a fifty-three per cent saving in typing time, and a seventy-six per cent saving in clerical time, were obtained compared with the original procedure.

DATA PREPARATION

It is not necessary to have a computer in the centre to benefit from computer processing. Provided that the bibliographical data for reports are prepared in the centre in machine-readable form such as punched paper tape, the tapes can be processed by a computer bureau using programmes provided by the centre, and, if the centre has no staff trained in computer programming, the programmes can be written under contract. Printed indexes to announcement bulletins, KWIC or KWOC indexes, and SDI are all tasks which can be carried out by a bureau on a regular basis. Each increment of data processed by the bureau can be cumulated, so that a magnetic tape data-base is gradually built up. This data-base will form the retrospective search file. Batch searches can be carried out using a bureau, but interactive, on-line searches, such as described in Chapter 5, will require an in-house computer or a terminal in the centre linked to a computer to which the centre has guaranteed access, and where the operators will load the centre's data-base when required.

Tape-typewriters have already been described. The advantages of using this method of data preparation is that hard copy is simultaneously provided which can be used e.g. for offset litho masters for announcement bulletins. Other methods of data preparation include magnetic tape-typewriters, OCR (optical character recognition) typing, or direct entry into a computer using a visual display unit. A review of data preparation methods is given in the paper by Bernhardt.

For computer processing, the bibliographical data must be structured into fields which the computer can recognize. This is a matter for arrangement between the users and the programmers. One way is to have a unique functional character to terminate each field. There must also be other unique characters to indicate the beginning and end of each bibliographic unit, and all these characters must be inserted during the data preparation.

Quality control of the machine-readable data is vital. Nothing shows up small inconsistencies so cruelly as computer printout of index entries where an extra space or misplaced comma will separate entries which should follow sequentially. Punched paper tape processed by a bureau can only be checked in the centre by electronically 'reading' it through the tape-typewriter and typing out the contents, the product then being checked by human scanning. Each block of bibliographical data on the tape should be separated by a length of blank tape. Errors can then be corrected by hand punching a 'kill code' before the item containing the error and repunching the item on a separate correction tape. (The 'kill code' must be agreed with the programmers and must be a code not used for any other purpose.) This procedure is time-consuming and correction programmes should be written when an in-house computer is available so that entries can be displayed on a visual display unit and corrections entered from the keyboard. Fern & Bagnall describe 'Editrec', an on-line editing programme for bibliographic records for the Newcastle-upon-Tyne University IBM 360/67 Newcastle File Handling System in which corrections are made by this method. Another source of errors is faulty transcription of descriptors from the centre's thesaurus which could mean that the item is lost for retrospective search. This can be overcome by having a master magnetic tape of the thesaurus used in the centre, and a programme should be written to compare the descriptor field of each new item against the master thesaurus tape. Mismatches are displayed or printed out for checking.

Some operational data preparation systems

Paper tape. Barnett (1972, 1973) describes the system developed at the Aircraft Research Association Ltd, for producing KWOC, title, report number and author indexes for their report accessions. The system uses punched-paper-tape input to the Association's ICL 4130 computer, and programmes were written in-house in Algol. The KWOC index is based on descriptors allocated by the library staff.

The abstract journal *Bulletin Signalétique*, issued by the Documentation Centre of the Centre National de la Recherche Scientifique (CNRS) is prepared initially on punched paper tape as part of the PASCAL system (Programme Appliqué à la Sélection et à la Compilation Automatiques de la Littérature). The keyboard operators are given standard worksheets for each item in which each element is identified, and which include abstracts and keywords. The tapes are computer processed daily and sent through photocomposition which prints out the first draft on diazo paper. Proof reading of this draft results in the operators editing correction tapes which are then merged with the main tapes. The corrected data for each item are stored on magnetic tape until publication date, and author and subject indexes are computer produced for each issue. The system is described by d'Olier & Dusoulier.

The system used at the Ministry of Technology's Technology Reports Centre from 1968 to 1971 is described in papers by Vessey and by Schuler. After each report had been recorded, using a standard process sheet, abstracted, and TEST descriptors allocated, the bibliographical data were typed on a carbon-backed flimsy/card combination using Vonomatic tape-typewriters controlled by a tape programme. The card was used as the master record card for the report, subsequent distribution and loan transactions being entered on it. The flimsy was used for assembling into COSATI field and group order for an issue of the twice-monthly announcement bulletin *R & D Abstracts*. When preparing an issue of *R & D Abstracts* each report paper tape was electronically 'read' through one of the tape-typewriters, automatically typing an offset litho master and simultaneously punching a continuous tape for the computer. At this stage the typist inserted any necessary corrections. Otherwise the only manual typing operations consisted in typing the COSATI field and group headings (which did not appear on the computer tape), and inserting the serial number of each item. The computer tapes were processed by the Central Computer Agency's computer at Norwich to produce the printed indexes for the corresponding issue of *R & D Abstracts*, and an experimental SDI service was also provided, using the ICL FIND 2 programme package.

OCR (Optical character recognition) is used in the SHARP (Ships Analysis and Retrieval Project) system of the US Department of the Navy Ship Systems and Scientific Documentation Division described in the paper by Smith. Bibliographical data for the report input (3,500 titles per year) are typed on standard OCR forms in the library and scanned by an OCR reader in the computer centre, resulting in a magnetic tape which is processed by the computer. OCR was found to be a great improvement over keypunching; errors were virtually eliminated and processing time significantly reduced.

Direct entry into the computer from an on-line terminal using a visual display unit is used in the TITUS system (Traitement de l'Information Textile Universelle et Sélective) developed by the Institut Textile de France and described in an article by Bousselet. Error detection programmes verify the data and the type of error and its location are displayed on the screen.

Direct entry is also used for the creation of a library catalogue in the in-house mechanized information system developed at the Strip Mills Division of the British Steel Corporation and described in the paper by Patten. The system includes editorial features to assist the operators, the next accession number and a blank format being displayed on the visual display unit screen after each record has been transmitted to the computer.

LIBRARY 'HOUSEKEEPING'

The uses of a computer for information retrieval and SDI have been described in Chapters 5 and 7. To get the best utilization out of an in-house computer, however, it should also be used to assist in clerical or 'housekeeping' operations. There are many systems already in operation, both batch and on-line. McAllister surveys a number of such on-line systems in the USA, including acquisitions, cataloguing, circulation, loans and management information.

Loans

Computer-operated loans systems have been developed in a number of libraries and developments are summarized in a paper by Wilson (1973). Systems developed in libraries holding extensive report collections include those at the Atomic Energy Research Establishment, Harwell, and the Atomic Weapons Research Establishments at Aldermaston and Foulness. Wilson & Greenhalgh describe the system developed for the AERE library – COBLOS (Computer-based Loans System). This is an off-line system operational since December 1970. Two teletypewriters in the library produce eight track punched paper tape which is input to Harwell's IBM 360/165 computer. The principal output consists of printed loans lists, reissue and recall notices, diagnostics, error messages, and statistical information. A teletypewriter, on-line to the IBM 360/165 computer at AWRE, Aldermaston, is used by the AWRE Foulness library for its loans system, UPDATE, described by Eunson. The system used in the main AWRE library, and described by Searle & Corbett, is a punched card system in which transaction cards are punched daily using an IBM 029 card punch, and these form the computer input to update and process the library loans files on disc once each fortnight.

Another computerized method of organizing a loans service is by means of the 'library pen' developed by Plessey Telecommunications Data Systems (Sopers Lane, Poole, Dorset BH17 7ER). In this system a light-sensitive 'pen' reads bar-coded labels on books or reports and borrowers' cards. The information is recorded on magnetic tape for subsequent transmission to any computer to which the centre has access. The stored information can be processed to produce overdue lists or management data. The original system allowed for ten terminals, but by inclusion of a miniprocessor the system has been enhanced to allow for up to sixty-four terminals ('Enhancements . . .').

The cost of computerized loans systems in comparison with manual systems is discussed by Ross & Brooks. They calculated the cost per loan for manual and computerized loans systems (for the University of Essex library) for 1970/71 with predictions for 1973/74 and 1976/77. They conclude that an off-line system is as economical as a manual system, and with disc drives becoming cheaper, costs of on-line systems should reduce almost to the level of off-line systems. They emphasize the rate of increase of staff salaries as the over-riding factor in costing library circulation.

MINICOMPUTERS

The capital cost of large computers has, up to the last few years, made their purchase difficult to justify for use purely for information work except in the largest centres. Much of the work already cited on the development of information retrieval, SDI, and cataloguing and ordering systems has been carried out in the libraries of research establishments or universities where large computers are installed for scientific research purposes, and time on them can be allocated for library purposes. However, during the last few years small or 'mini' computers have been developed on a considerable scale, with core stores of up to 32 K words and ability for this to be raised. The Electrical Research Association has published a guide to minicomputers, and their use in information centres is growing. McIvor describes a minicomputer-based information system—the Defence Scientific Information Service of the Canadian Defence Research Board. The system uses two Varian 620 machines, one for data input and the other for maintaining the master files and producing catalogue cards, COM (Computer Output Microform) cartridges, KWOC indexes, indexed *Document Digests* and SDI notices, It was found that production was more economical than an earlier system using a large computer.

PREPARING FOR AN IN-HOUSE COMPUTER

When it is proposed to automate a system it is necessary first to make a thorough study of the existing system. It is usually advisable to have staff trained in systems analysis to carry out this task, but they should first spend some time in acquiring knowledge of the existing systems and of the objectives of the reports centre, and work closely with the staff of the centre. Simpson, in describing the steps to be taken 'before the machines come' gives a useful outline of systems analysis for the manager who has to do the job himself. He lists the essential steps as: (a) define what the system is to do; (b) lay out the procedure in flow chart form; (c) make a preliminary system design; (d) determine the system requirements to meet the original definition of what the system is to do; (e) design the subsystems; (f) evaluate the new design; (g) plan the design and manufacture of systems equipment; (h) assess the improvements which would be gained by adopting the system; (i) revise the model; (j) test the model; (k) develop system specifications; (l) install, debug, modify and extend the system; (m) organize systems service to ensure maintenance to keep the system working. This approach will show where the existing system can be improved: perhaps some jobs can be simplified, others may serve no useful purpose, and a systems analysis is a very useful exercise even if the installation of a computer has to be postponed. It is also useful to study the experiences of other centres who have operated computer installations for some time; thus Bauer describes lessons learned from the automation of the Technical Information Department of Lockheed Georgia Company in 1962. He emphasizes the necessity for the systems analysis and the development of new concepts for the benefit of the user, not automation with rules of the conventional library in mind.

Mechanization

PRACTICAL PROBLEMS OF INSTALLING A COMPUTER

When a computer is to be installed, preparations must be made well in advance. There may be building alterations to be put in hand, installation of an air conditioning system etc. and this will take some time. When the computer is installed, it will not immediately be productive. There will be a period of testing and programme writing, and to test the programmes the data preparation staff will have to supply test data which must incorporate all the likely problems which will occur in the final computerized system. When the new system is ready to be introduced the manual system must be run in parallel with it until the new system has been thoroughly proved. This period must not be curtailed, even if it means some weeks of overtime working, or it may be found that important records are lost which will be difficult to reconstitute, and the service will suffer.

The examples of successful computer systems described in this chapter and those on information retrieval and SDI show that a computer can be a most powerful tool for the information scientist. Provided the systems analysis is properly carried out, the computer programmes adequately tested, and the computer staff work closely with the information staff, a computer system can produce results which are far beyond the capacity of manual systems, and the service given by an information centre can be greatly extended without increase in staff.

MECHANIZATION

Section by Mr Marvin E. Wilson

There was a time, and probably that time is still with us for many people, when it was imagined that mechanization was the answer to most of the difficulties of large information centres. It is not a rare phenomenon that most mechanization efforts in information centres have led to difficulties and/or disappointments nor is it rare that these could have been foreseen.

Definitions

Perhaps the definition of the word 'mechanization' has contributed to many of the problems. The interchanging of the words 'mechanization', 'automation', and 'computerization' occurs constantly. 'Computerization' is normally understood to mean a process accomplished on a computer. 'Automation' is defined as a process in which some portion of a function is accomplished by some automatic means without needing manual labour. 'Mechanization' is defined as using a mechanical means to aid in a work function. It is understandable then that a manager who approves a 'mechanization' project, and thereby expects a sophisticated computer system, is disappointed when the project is only the filming of some documents for improved storage techniques. The manager, since thinking 'computerization', expected the improved storage techniques to be some advanced computer technology. At the other end of the scale would be the manager who approves a project expecting some modest 'mechanization' advancement and ends up with a computer application which creates difficulties because of the costs involved. These would obviously be extreme cases, which fortunately do not happen often. Misunderstanding of what is expected from 'mechanization' does happen often and can usually be foreseen, if people will make the necessary effort to be sure their goals are clearly understood by all.

For clarity then this section on 'Mechanization' will treat the word as including any application of mechanical and/or electronic equipment to aid in the management and operation of an information centre. If the reader chooses to think of it as 'automation' or

Mechanization

'computerization' in the context it is used, then he should do so. Also, for clarity, this section is not presented as being all inclusive as regards techniques and/or types of equipment. Nor is it presented as endorsing any specific techniques or types of equipment. It is based on the writer's knowledge and experiences in the mechanization of functions in support of information centres. Some useful references for anyone seeking additional information are given at the end of the chapter.

Planning mechanization

Mechanization, in some form, can be applied to all work functions of an information centre. Applied correctly the mechanization effort will result in improved service. It is important that mechanization efforts be planned and implemented very carefully. Frequently an increase in the overall costs will be experienced by such an effort, so the benefits of the added service to the users must be examined as an important step in the decision process. Efforts that are expected to produce cost savings are seemingly easy to approve but they must be carefully examined to be sure the savings will be achieved. The most difficult effort to examine is one which is undertaken to increase the capability or capacity of the information centre. This type of effort normally involves expenditure of funds without an apparent immediate gain. Without these efforts, however, an information centre is likely to fall behind in utilization of new technology, will ultimately be outdated in techniques and will reach a saturation point in work capacity.

The work of management then is easy to define. Managers must encourage mechanized efforts that will facilitate improved service from the information centre considering such factors as new technologies, availability of funds, availability of human resources, availability of facilities, and certainly at the present time the availability of material resources. The present world energy shortage has highlighted the limits of our material resources. Perhaps it is an appropriate time for each manager of an information centre to think about how information would be transferred if an alternative method to paper was needed. Probably the most important step in planning a mechanized effort is to plan how the effort will be evaluated in its development and implementation stages. Technical developers of new mechanization efforts will not be concerned with anything as mundane as whether the effort can and will achieve expected goals. It is the job of management to be sure that monitoring and evaluation will be an important and enforced part of every mechanization plan. More aspects of this part of management's job will be dealt with in subsequent paragraphs.

Equipment

Up to now little mechanical and/or electronic equipment has been designed and developed for exclusive use in information centres. Certainly information centres have benefited from equipment that has been developed for other specific functions. It is hard to imagine the existence of today's information centre had we not had chains of equipment development such as the high-speed electrically driven printing presses which replaced those worked by turning a handle, which replaced jelly duplicators, which replaced hand copying. Advances in filming and computer techniques have been just as dramatic with measurable benefits for information centres but the fact remains that the developments were not made exclusively for information centres.

A valid question then is: 'How have information centres managed to design and implement such highly sophisticated mechanization schemes if specific equipment was not designed for the task?' The answer lies in the innovative minds and skills of the operators of the information centres. They have taken equipment and technologies developed for other purposes and adapted them to the specialized needs of the information centres. Nowhere is this adaptation better displayed than in the remarkable computer-software applications that have been developed by operators of information centres to service the needs of the centres. The integration of specialized computer processes or products with the other resources of information centres has enabled the centres to reach a level of sophistication achieved only in a very few occupational areas.

Stages of mechanization

In all occupations it is human nature to point to the most visible portion of one's accomplishments as being the height of achievement. For information centres, if we are considering mechanization efforts, this would be the on-line information retrieval systems. While the accomplishments in on-line retrieval systems have been truly outstanding there are other applications of mechanization in information centres that must be cited. It is not possible to put an order of priority on the importance of different applications of mechanization since they would vary from centre to centre, but it is definite that the on-line systems that are given such high visibility would not be possible without many other mechanization efforts.

While most people would not generally think of card cabinets as pieces of mechanical equipment, they in fact fall into the broad interpretation of mechanization of an information centre. Certainly they are a mechanical aid in filing the thousands of index cards that are necessary to facilitate manual searching of files. The introduction of KARDEX files was certainly an advance in filing techniques, but because it involved a cost to convert to them it required the same application of decision process as is involved today in converting from a manual search to an on-line system. Management had to decide if the improved service justified the cost.

Microcopying and microforms

One of the earlier mechanization efforts that is still with us today is the production of microcopies of paper reports. It is done in the interest of historical value, conserving space, exchanging reports, or any number of other reasons. Initially it was accomplished by filming on a continuous roll of 16mm film. This was a fairly simple operation and a wide variety of cameras with different capabilities were and still are available. Roll film did not lend itself to shorter articles or books so other forms of microcopies were developed, the most popular being microfiche.

Microfiche. This is a sheet of film containing varying numbers of pages or images. The advantage of microfiche over roll film for shorter articles is the time needed to locate the page one wishes to look at.

Microfiche can be prepared with two camera techniques. One is to film initially on roll film and then cut the film into strips and insert the strips into jackets to make a microfiche. The second is to film the article with a camera which incorporates a step-and-repeat motion so that the film is advanced a frame at a time up to the end of a line and then returned automatically to the beginning of the next line. The step-and-repeat camera is naturally much more expensive than a camera for 16mm film made or adapted for the purpose, but there are other problems that need to be considered. Although the photography is mechanized there is still the necessity of turning over the pages of the paper report for which there is no satisfactory machine; it is not difficult to arrange that the person who does this also presses a button to make an exposure when the next page is ready to be photographed, but the complications do not end here – for while a very junior staff member is quite capable of turning pages, he is likely not to be unduly careful about seeing that each page is in the correct position to produce ultimately a microfiche whose frames are evenly spaced in straight lines. In fact it is often found that microfiche frames are in pairs of verso and recto although they are photographed separately. Management must make the decision what method to use based on workload costs, etc.

Easier use of microforms. Several manufacturers of reading equipment for microfilm have put considerable effort into coding schemes and loading techniques to make the use of film more attractive. It is now possible to key on a regular keyboard identifying information for a specific record and have the equipment select and display the frame that contains the desired record. Different loading techniques have lessened the required time to less than ten seconds. Advances have been made in film bases to reduce the thickness of film to the point that four times as many feet of film can be put on a roll as was possible five years ago.

Microfiche-handling equipment has been developed that permits almost any level of manual or automatic selection of a specific microfiche. Some of the manual methods are notching techniques and are quite efficient on a cost-comparison basis. Microfiche can also be coded so that a desired frame from a desired sheet of film can be displayed through the use of a keyboard. Microfiche is also easily enlarged (Plate 4).

Computer Output Microform (COM) is the latest technology for using film. This technology provides for a computer to generate a

Mechanization

page/frame of printing on a cathode-ray-tube, and the page being automatically filmed by a synchronized camera system. The page/frame generation and filming is very fast, less than one second for most equipment. (Plate 5 refers.) Using this technique it is now possible to produce either microfilm or microfiche at considerably lower cost per page/frame. There are savings in both computer time and the lower cost of film than of paper. The problems of page positioning experienced in using cameras are not found in this technique. COM offers a much greater selection of reduction ratios than was possible when using cameras. It is fairly standard to place about 350 pages on a sheet of 6 × 4in (150mm × 100mm) microfiche using COM against about one hundred pages using a camera. One manufacturer has equipment that uses a packing technique for roll film that permits twenty times the number of frames to be placed on a roll of film using COM compared with using a camera.

The advent of COM applications has greatly broadened the types of data it is feasible to put on film. It is not difficult now to produce a film subject index for a huge collection of source material. This was not possible before COM because it could not be kept up to date. Many entrepreneurs have developed integrated COM-produced microfilm or microfiche and computer interfaces that cause the computer to drive the reading equipment. Such an application might be to store a summary of a report on COM-produced microfilm, conduct an on-line search on the computer, then have the computer drive the film-reading equipment to display the desired frame or frames. Such a system could greatly reduce computer storage requirements and thus costs. New applications are constantly being developed for COM equipment. Because of the interest, equipment manufacturers are investing in a wide range of general-purpose software that is available at a minimum cost.

Advances in COM in recent years are in many ways as exciting and challenging as the rapid development of on-line computer capabilities in the late 1960s. It has given managers of information centres a new set of options to consider when making operating decisions. It is not difficult to compare the costs of using COM files as a supplement to or a part of a computer system. When a COM file will meet the operating requirements considerable savings will normally be recognized. The challenge for the manager is in selecting the correct media to meet the requirement.

Computer-controlled composition

Related to COM but somewhat different is the computer controlled composition equipment that is now available to produce fully composed print masters in either positive or negative form. The major difference between COM and publication quality composition equipment is the sophistication in the composition equipment. While COM equipment generally is limited to one size and style of type, composition equipment generally offers ten or more type styles in both plain or bold face and in a size range of 4–6 point up to 20–25 point. The computer software used with the composition equipment is much more complex and offers more options. Most provide word checking for recognized hyphenation points so that book-set even-line spacing can be achieved, preselected or encoded headings, automatic page numbering, etc. The cost in using composition equipment with the normal pre-process software routine is considerably more than the costs for COM. While an industry standard is not available the writer believes the ratio is about 150 to 1. One should not be too concerned with this ratio, however, as COM per page/frame cost is measured in very low pennies.

Data in machine-readable form

One common result of using either COM or composition equipment is that the data will be in some machine-readable form. There are many options available to prepare data in a machine-readable form. All involve some type of keyboarding. The method to be used will be dependent on many factors such as availability of equipment within the organization that is primarily for other functions, the type of equipment that will be used to process the data, and others. The four most used methods are typewriter and optical-scan equipment, key-punch machines, key-to-disc mini-computer systems, and direct computer input. Each method offers advantages under certain conditions and requirements. A very careful analysis is needed to select the best method for a given centre. Selection of the wrong method could result in both higher costs and insufficient capacity to do the work.

One of the values of having records in machine-readable form is that they can then be used for many purposes other than the one requiring the initial creation. Since keyboarding of records, by any means, is fairly expensive it is necessary to have the records serve as many uses as possible. Therefore careful planning should be given to record form and content once the decision is made to convert them to machine-readable form. Two pitfalls to avoid are: keyboarding the same data more than once and failing to keyboard all data that will ever be needed by any future plan. Data in the record can be ignored by programming or other techniques but data that is not in the record cannot be put in economically.

On-line information retrieval

The most glamorous task performed in information centres, as noted earlier in this chapter, is on-line retrieval. As collections have grown, it has become almost an impossible task to be able to maintain manual index-files that would permit doing comprehensive searches of the file. It is in this area that computers have excelled. The heart of the on-line system is the data-base or -bases that may be accessed. The value of any search made of the data-base will be dependent on the accuracy and completeness of the access points provided when the data-base was assembled. As noted in the discussion on the multiple use of machine-readable records, the same basic record used to produce a composed publication might also be used to form the data-base. This emphasizes the need to completely define all uses of the record before it is keyboarded.

One of the critical data elements contained in a data-base is the subject terms associated with the report. Most current data-bases have the subject terms assigned by a senior analyst qualified in the technical area of the report. This has been the practice for the past several years. A new trend is to have a computer determine the subject terms that will be used in indexing the report by matching the words in the title and abstract to an authorized list of terms for the technical area and using any words that match as subject terms. The use of the computer is still too new to make a meaningful decision but all indications are that the technique, given a fair chance, will work. The quality of the list of authorized terms is of vital importance. Of course, the abstracts must be well written also.

Terminals and software. There are numerous options available to information centres in performing on-line searches. Many different commercial vendors offer software packages to search different data-bases. Most of them are very good and will do the job. Most of them are interactive conversational mode, meaning that the searcher can interact with the computer in primarily English words. There is a complete range of terminal equipment available. The range is both in costs and capabilities. The job of the manager is to select the combination of software and terminal equipment that will best meet the requirement. Many managers make a mistake in selecting low-speed terminals because they cost less but end up paying more because of additional computer time required. No one set of software and terminal equipment is right for all centres but the range available should make it possible for a centre to make a desired selection based on performance and costs.

Methods of access to a computer. The previous paragraphs on COM, composition equipment, and on-line retrieval imply that an information centre must have access to a computer to use the techniques. Certainly this is true. The major decision facing managers of information centres is what method should be used for this computer access. The cost of computer systems today makes it doubtful if many information centres could afford systems of their own. While initial costs of acquiring equipment are high, the costs to operate the system over two or three years are likely to be even higher. Many managers, in their desire to have their own computer, do not give full consideration to the costs for occupied space, electricity, water, heating, cooling, machine maintenance, software maintenance, programming staff, operating staff, special supplies such as tapes, and many other factors. The decision made by the manager on computer access could well put the centre on a firm basis or could put it out of business.

There are four choices open to the manager for computer support. The first is for the centre to acquire and operate its own computer (see Plate 6). The second is to utilize available time on a computer operated by the organization of which the information centre is a part. The third is to buy the services needed from a service bureau. The fourth is to use a combination of the first three. Any of the methods will work. Each centre must carefully consider all possibilities that will provide the service needed and then select the best offering. The criteria to be used for the selection will vary from centre to centre so each will need to develop its own. Perhaps the most important factor is to be sure the individual making the decision is qualified to do so.

On-line searching is one function that may prove to be more economical to do with a service-bureau arrangement. It is a common practice for an information centre to have a local computer terminal linked on-line to one or more of the large computerized information retrieval networks, so that the request information is transmitted at once to the computer, which may be hundreds of miles away. Most of these networks deal with openly published information, notably INSPEC for electronic papers, UKCIS for chemical and the oldest and best known of them, MEDLARS, for medical publications. Some, however, such as RECON from NASA and GRA from NTIS, have files not only for published papers but also for unpublished reports. These files contain the reports announced in NASA *Scientific and Technical Aerospace Reports (STAR)* and *Government Reports Announcements (GRA)*. The computer maintains indexes of these reports, and they are updated at twice-monthly intervals. The files may be used to operate a selective current-awareness service as well as the information retrieval service.

Decision-making

Given that there are many new mechanization approaches for information centres to consider, there is always the question of when any project becomes profitable when compared with whatever preceded it. It certainly does not follow that if some development is profitable in one centre it will necessarily be so in another. Almost invariably mechanization means an increase in capital expenditure and in upkeep. It is not simply a matter of balancing these costs on an annual basis against the salaries of the staff whose services might be dispensed with or deployed elsewhere. A more realistic but much more difficult assessment might be made by comparing the unit costs of the operation before and after mechanization, but even so there are usually imponderables which need to be taken into account, for example the value of the time saved by the quicker appearance of the output or a new output not previously provided.

In this section, as elsewhere, emphasis has been placed on cost-benefit analysis to reach the decision as to whether any piece of mechanization is going to pay for itself. No numerical data have been presented. Each manager must develop his own criteria and methods of analysis, for what applies for one centre will not be valid at another. An analysis which is sound for one centre at one time will be useless for another or at another time. In many cases it will be quite obvious that some innovation is worthwhile, but it should always be considered whether a change is desirable in itself and in its consequences. Carried to extremes this could delay if not prevent any advance, but change for the sake of change seldom confers much benefit except perhaps to the makers of the equipment.

References

BARNETT, C. C. Report cataloguing in the Aircraft Research Association library. *Program*, 6(1). January, 1972. 60–73.

BARNETT, C. C. A computer-produced keyword indexing system for technical reports in the library of the Aircraft Research Association Limited. *AGARD Conference Proceedings* No. 136. *New developments in storage, retrieval and dissemination of aerospace information.* Neuilly-sur-Seine, AGARD, 1973. 1-1 – 1-7.

BERNHARDT, R. Problems of data recording and data interchange. *AGARD Conference Proceedings* No. 117. *Government assistance for technical information in industry and simple mechanization for small information centres.* Neuilly-sur-Seine, AGARD, 1973. 5-1 – 5-6.

BAUER, C. K. Automation and its lessons. *Special Libraries*, 63(2). February, 1972. 47–52.

BOUSSELET, P. Le système 'Titus'. *Nachrichten-Nouvelles-Notizie*, 49(4). 1973. 157–163.

D'OLIER, J. H. and DUSOULIER, N. *Bulletin Signalétique* mechanization: the PASCAL system. *Program*, 5(4). October, 1971. 228–238.

ELECTRICAL RESEARCH ASSOCIATION. The ERA guide to minicomputers. London, Ovum Ltd, 1972. ISBN 0 9501842 5 x. pp. 303.

ENHANCEMENTS TO THE PLESSEY 'LIBRARY PEN'. *Program*, 8(1). January, 1974. 52–53.

EUNSON, B. G. UPDATE – an on-line loans control system in use in a small research library. *Program*, 8(2). April, 1974. 88–101.

EYRE, J. J. Structure and handling of MARC files for the AMCOS (Aldermaston Mechanized Cataloguing and Ordering System) update program. *Program*, 4(1). January, 1970. 30–41.

FERN, R. and BAGNALL, J. An on-line editing program for bibliographic records. *Program*, 6(2). April, 1972. 117–119.

MCALLISTER, C. On-line library housekeeping systems: a survey. *Special Libraries*, 62(11). November, 1971. 457–468.

MCIVOR, R. A. A mini-computer based information system. *AGARD Conference Proceedings* No. 136. *New developments in storage, retrieval and dissemination of aerospace information.* Neuilly-sur-Seine, AGARD, 1973. 2-1 – 2-7.

PATTEN, M. N. Experiences with an in-house mechanized information system. *Aslib Proceedings*, 26(5). May, 1974. 189–209.

ROSS, J. *and* BROOKS, J. Costing manual and computerized library circulation systems. *Program*, 6(3). July, 1972. 217–227.

SCHULER, S. C. Mintech [Ministry of Technology] Reports Centre services and mechanization programme. *Information Scientist*, 4(2). June, 1970. 47–64.

SEARLE, R. H. *and* CORBETT, L. The computerized, punched card loans control system at AWRE, Aldermaston. *Program*, 6(2). April, 1972. 163–166.

SIMPSON, D. J. Before the machines come. *Aslib Proceedings*, 20(1). January, 1968. 21–33.

SMITH, R. C. SHARP: experiences in library automation. *Special Libraries*, 65(2). February, 1974. 61–65.

VESSEY, H. F. Plans for the computer control of large collections. INSTITUTE OF INFORMATION SCIENTISTS CONFERENCE. *3rd, Sheffield, 1968. Proceedings.* London, 1969. 47–63.

VICKERS, P. H. Tape typewriters: practical aspects of their use in information work. *Information Scientist*, 1(1). July, 1967. 17–34.

WILSON, C. W. J. Use of the Friden Flexowriter in the library of the Atomic Energy Research Establishment, Harwell. *Journal of Documentation*, 20(1). March, 1964. 16–24.

WILSON, C. W. J. Developments with computer-based loans system in the United Kingdom. *Program*, 7(4). October, 1973. 165–171.

WILSON, C. W. J. *and* GREENHALGH, K. R. AERE Library computer-based loans system – COBLOS. *Program*, 5(2). May, 1971. 89–118.

SELECTED BIBLIOGRAPHY

AYRES, F. H. Some basic laws of library automation. *Program*, 4(2). April, 1970. 68–69.

BAKER, G. G. & ASSOCIATES. A guide to COM in the UK. 3rd ed. Guildford, 1974. ISBN 0 9502082 21. pp. 60.

BIERMAN, K. J. Library automation. *Annual review of Information Science and Technology*, Vol. 9. Washington, American Society for Information Science, 1974. ISBN 0 87715 209 8. 123–172.

DUCHESNE, R. M. The use of computers in British libraries and information services: an analysis. *Program*, 8(4). October, 1974. 183–190.

FORD, G. Library automation: guidelines to costing. London, OSTI, 1973. *OSTI Report* No. 5153. (Available BLLD.)

HAYES, R. M. *and* BECHER, J. Handbook of data processing for libraries. Sponsored by the Council on Library Requirements. New York, Wiley, 1971. ISBN 0 471 364843. pp. 585.

HEATH, J. T. *and* TOWNSEND, C. INPUT: a generalized IBM 360

MARC file handling system. London, *British National Bibliography*, 1971. ISBN 0 900220 27 9. pp. 99. *MARC Documentation Service Publication* No. 4.

IRVINE, R. MARC for cataloguers: an explanation of its use. Southampton, the University, 1972. ISBN 0 85432 090 3. pp. 40. *Automation Project Report* No. 4.

KIMBER, R. T. Automation in libraries. Oxford, Pergamon Press, 1968. ISBN 0 08 12987 0. pp. 140.

LANCASTER, F. W., ed. Proceedings of the 1972 clinic on library applications of data processing: applications of on-line computers to library problems. London, Clive Bingley, 1972. ISBN 0 85157 158 1.

MURPHY, J. COM: computer output microfilm, select bibliography. Hatfield, Herts (England), Hertis, 1974. pp. 34.

ROBINSON, F. The uses of OCR and COM in information work. *Program*, 8(3). July, 1974. 137–148.

SPENCER, J. R. An appraisal of computer output microform for library catalogues: the final report on the findings and work of an investigation from December 1971 to July 1973, directed by B. J. S. Williams. Hatfield, Herts. (England), National Reprographic Centre for documentation, 1974. pp. 173. *OSTI Report* 5196.

SWIHART, S. J. and HEFLEY, B. F. Computer systems in the library: a handbook for managers and designers. Los Angeles, Melville Publishing Co., 1973. ISBN 0 471 83995 7. pp. 338.

TINKER, L., comp. An annotated bibliography of library automation 1968–1972. London, Aslib, 1973. ISBN 0 85142 050 8. pp. 85.

TORKINGTON, R. B. MARC and its application to library automation. *Advances in librarianship*, 4. 1974. 2–23.

WARHEIT, I. A. The automation of libraries. *Special Libraries*, 63(1). January, 1972. 1–7.

WILSON, C. W. J., ed. Directory of operational computer applications in United Kingdom libraries and information units. London, Aslib, 1973. ISBN 0 85142 054 0. pp. 160.

CHAPTER 10

Security, Storage and Weeding

There are two aspects to security in information centres – that of the material which is handled and that of the people who handle it, and these have to be considered separately although they are closely related. It is almost useless to give physical protection to valuable documents if the people who deal with them are unreliable, as has unfortunately often been demonstrated, but the emphasis here is on the methods to be employed to make it more difficult for evilly-disposed people to get access to what has to be guarded.

The weight of emphasis also has to be upon military security, the safeguarding of information related, perhaps indirectly, to the work of the armed forces, and although most information officers will be more aware of commercial security if only because of the publicity now being given to industrial spying, they must also be aware of the requirements of military security. The value of unique copies of reports has also to be considered, especially by those responsible for their custody, and expensive equipment must also be safeguarded.

SECURITY OF MATERIAL

Although security considerations must start with the primary documents in an information centre, it should not be forgotten that the secondary or derived documents such as abstract bulletins and catalogue cards are also important and that memories of the contents of documents have value and are not susceptible to the same precautions as pieces of paper.

The documents may have value not only from the military point of view but also from the purely commercial aspect; these values may be to the organization which holds them or to the one which produced them or even to third parties, and although the originating agencies may allow access to their reports to approved outside recipients, it will usually be with conditions stipulated which are unlikely to be less stringent than those applied by the originating organization.

It is vital that all documents which have security value shall be clearly marked to indicate this fact and also the degree and kind of value. Though the view has been put forward that these markings give an intruder a strong clue as to what is worth taking, the important effect is to remind the user of the precautions he is committed to taking to preserve security. The more dangerous evilly-disposed person does not need much guidance as to what he is looking for.

Although for the present purpose attention is concentrated upon reports security, value attaches to many other things, such as plans, photographs and equipment, and also to parts of any of them, though all the parts are unlikely to have equal value.

Physical security protection

The broad principles here are that documents requiring protection must be stored in secure accommodation, that their movements must be recorded and that they should be supplied only to people who have been authorized by the originators to see them and who have established a need to use them.

The documents may, of course, come from other countries, in which case the regulations of the originating countries have to be followed. These may show some variations: naturally the markings on the documents are in the language of the originating country, but there are generally recognized equivalents, and there is a broad agreement on the way they have to be handled, though here also there are some variations. It should be noted, for example, that the British 'Restricted' grading is not used in the USA.

Documents requiring special protection have (as already stated) to be stored in secure accommodation and this is commonly interpreted as meaning that the containers or rooms in which they are kept should be capable of resisting unauthorized entry for a reasonable period and that the building should be patrolled at about the same interval. When a protected document is removed from its container it is, of course, subject to special handling procedures by which the user is required to abide.

The fact that some of the documents in the holdings of an information centre need to be handled in a different way from the great majority of these holdings raises a series of problems. One way of dealing with them is to segregate the special documents from the others and store and handle them in a different way. The other method is to give the entire holdings the same secure treatment and only to separate the special documents when they leave the centre or are supplied to an authorized enquirer for use within the centre.

This second approach means that the secure accommodation has to be much more ample than would otherwise be necessary, but it may be easier to make the whole premises secure than only part of them and the method has merits which may outweigh the disadvantages. All the personnel in the centre have access to the special material in the course of their work and have, of course, been authorized by the relevant authorities to handle it. Handling and storage are simplified if all the holdings are in one continuous series without internal differentiation. There are so many variations of gradings and other security markings that complete segregation could easily raise more problems than it solves, and a very important point is that documents carrying a protective classification often do not retain their grading permanently.

Security gradings

The normal British security gradings, in rising order of security, are 'Restricted', 'Confidential' and 'Secret'; and access to documents so marked has to be authorized by their originating authority or a delegated authority. In addition to the security gradings, reports may carry other protective markings or warnings which may indicate that they contain valuable commercial or proprietary information. If the meaning or consequence of any markings on a report is not known it is essential that advice be sought from the custodian or originator of the document. Commercial organizations sometimes mark their reports 'Confidential' or 'Secret' when they contain information private to the organization. These markings do not mean that the reports are subject to military security although at first sight they may be difficult to distinguish from those that are. Such reports should be given secure treatment until it is ascertained from the originators that the markings can be amended, e.g. to 'Confidential to members', or 'In confidence' or other statement indicating the actual meaning of the original form of wording.

Any secondary document which contains classified information is of course subject to the same grading as the parent document. A quotation from a classified document should be graded on its own content and it is clearly possible for a quotation from a 'Secret' document to be unclassified, though it is unlikely that such a quotation would be useful. On the other hand an abstract of a classified report would normally have the same security grading as its parent, although the practice by document originators of marking the security gradings of report titles and abstracts independently of that of the whole report is increasing. Thus a 'Secret' report might have an 'Unclassified' title and a 'Confidential' abstract. Bibliographical references to a classified document will be classified if they are explicit, particularly if they disclose that the document is classified. Hence in a published paper classified documents are only referred to in terms such as 'Jones, 1955. Unpublished report'.

During a war all documents having any relation to a project requiring protection are marked with the grading of that project, whether they have any security value of their own or not, on the grounds that if any enemy obtained a sufficient quantity of documents relating to a project, even the most innocent related document might enable him to solve some quite important outstanding detail. However with the passage of time this security value vanishes. An important new weapon will have a very high security value in its early stages of development, but when it is issued to the armed services for general use some security aspects cannot be maintained and a number of the related documents may be declassified, i.e. removed from the 'protected' list.

The processes of declassification, however, present their own problems. At the end of the Second World War, for example, there was an enormous quantity of classified documents which no longer had any security value, but the declassification regulations required that each document should be examined and regraded. It was clear that the skilled manpower needed for this was not available and consequently the documents retained their old gradings or received draconian treatment in the mass declassification of large collections of documents without individual inspection of their contents. The usual method on presumably

Security, Storage and Weeding

over-classified old reports is that they are examined as they are called up from storage for use. Although it may be apparent that the grading of a classified document is too high or totally unnecessary, it must retain that grading until it has been reviewed by the appropriate authority, which is normally the organization which first produced it. When a classified document is downgraded the known recipients are informed, but with the passage of time documents issued to individuals may have been passed to the information centre for secure storage. The information centre cannot therefore be certain that it has received all downgrading notifications. Enquiry should always be made to the originator of a report if it appears that the document may have been downgraded or that it may need consideration for such action.

When a computer is available in the information centre to assist in 'housekeeping' operations, the control of classified documents can be facilitated. The article by Berlin describes a computer-based system for security control of classified documents according to the US Department of Defense Industrial Security manual specifications, the system including automatic downgrading (This *Manual* is not generally available.)

ACCESS TO PROTECTED INFORMATION

Classified military documents may only be seen by people who have been authorized by the Ministry of Defence in the UK or the corresponding department in the user's own country, and then only when they can demonstrate that access to the documents is necessary in connection with defence work upon which they are engaged. It follows therefore that a national information centre which deals with classified documents will be staffed only by people specially authorized to handle them. The centre is likely to be supplying reports and information about them to other smaller authorized centres far more often than to individuals, but it is not uncommon for individuals representing other organizations to visit the centre to find what material is held which may help work being done on defence projects. (The process for authorizing staff to obtain access to classified information is outside the scope of this monograph as it takes place outside the information centre. The security officer of any organization undertaking defence projects will know the necessary procedures.)

When individuals wish to visit a centre in search of information which may be classified they are advised to submit their request in writing to the head of the centre giving reasons for wishing to examine the 'classified' documents. It is obvious that an individual who arrives unannounced at a centre will have no chance of seeing any classified material whether he is a private individual or the representative of a defence contractor. In general, too, the individual will be unable to take away any classified documents with him, even if his visit has been arranged beforehand: any classified documents for which he may establish a need will be sent to a competent person in his organization to whom the responsibility for their safekeeping may properly be delegated. This person will normally be the security officer or chief librarian of his organization, and it is the usual practice in any national information centre to send any classified documents to the authorized person in the requesting organization whether the request comes from him or from some other source in his organization.

Some of the documents in a large information centre will be the only known copies in the country or even in the world, so that they might be impossible to replace. Such reports clearly have a very great value even if they are not subject to military protection, and would only be released with precautions comparable with those for protected reports. The obvious method of dealing with them is to make a photocopy, but this may present difficulties because of bulk or poor quality of the original. In such cases the requester should be asked to consult the document in the information centre.

STORAGE

One of the most acute problems in information centres is certainly that of storage space. Even if the centre starts with ample accommodation, it is surprising how quickly this becomes filled up and 'bursting at the seams'. The usual immediate relief is by the use of remote storage accommodation, and even if 'remote' means no more than a hundred yards away, the problem of access becomes much more severe. If the remote storage is not controlled by the information centre then new problems arise, for the holdings may be transferred from one site to another without the consent of the centre, or there may be a series of more or less forcible requests for the storage space to be reduced or for the holdings to be reduced to make room for the new additions.

The second resort is to weed out non-essential stock and reduce the holdings of older essential stock by stages to single copies as soon as the records show that this can be done without serious interference with efficient operation of the centre. This weeding process is dealt with in a separate section.

The third resort is to make a micro-copy of each report, to accelerate the weeding programme and to advance it to the stage at which no paper copy is held at the centre and the micro-copy serves all demands. The last paper copy of any document becomes archive material and should be preserved as such, preferably in an appropriate collection. Microcopying, dealt with in more detail in Chapters 9 and 10, can, if the facilities are available, come into operation at an early stage, even on first receipt of the report.

Storage accommodation usually satisfies reasonable requirements if it is protected from damp and maintained at a fairly steady temperature, not excessively hot or dry. It should be remembered that these needs are equally applicable to both the main and remote storage areas. Some reports are printed on indifferent paper and some are photocopies which deteriorate, so that occasional inspection of the storage area and of a random sample of the reports is highly desirable. Old microfilm may be on nitrate stock (not now used) which deteriorates markedly on storage in other than ideal conditions. It is wise to transfer any reports which may be the only available copies and which seem likely to become defective on prolonged storage to a more permanent form photographically at an early stage, before any general policy of using microforms catches up with them. Storage has to accommodate all the forms in which stock is held, paper copies of different sizes, cans of film, microfiche or microcards, and these require at least three different forms of storage, which will be growing at different rates, though the paper copies present the severest growth problem.

Storage of paper copies

Storage space is most economically used if the accessions can be filed serially with no gaps left for report series whose expansion rates cannot be easily predicted. This is a strong argument in favour of the system in which the intake is identified by a single, unique, accession number and stored in this number order. Such a system does away with the need for shelf-marks or other location cues, though at the cost of popular old reports being in remote storage. When the records show that a copy of a requested report is in stock, there is one single place to look for it. The shelves, moreover, will only need to be disturbed when a report is called for or when the weeding or cleaning are being done.

For medium-size collections suspended pocket filing is convenient and reduces mis-filing. For large collections the stock will almost certainly be on open shelves in fixed racks (Plate 7), but there are several forms of sliding or rolling racks which multiply the storage capacity of a given area by a factor of two or more. These systems have the further advantage that most of the holdings are no longer in effect on open racks so that dust is much reduced and security improved, as in some of the systems at least it is only the solid end of the rack which is presented to view and this end can be locked. The accession numbers of the contents can be displayed but the disadvantage is that when a report is needed the whole of the heavy rack has to be moved; this does not require as much effort as might be thought, as the racks are on wheels which run on tracks and in some systems the moving is done by an electric motor. These systems are of course considerably more expensive than the usual open racks, and the more refinements that are incorporated the higher the cost. Such systems involve a great increase in the floor loading and are therefore mostly installed in basements. The floor loading should always be borne in mind when storage is being organized, or it may be found that a scheme is impracticable since the loading limitations in a building would be exceeded.

It may well be that old reports are not in a single series of accession numbers, although this system is used for newer acquisitions. If this is so it is seldom worthwhile to renumber the old stock, and more than one series will have to be maintained. It often happens in such cases that each is dealt with by a different section of the staff and different storage is used. The risk of error is then small provided that there is a simple and certain method of distinguishing the various series, known and used not only by the centre's staff but also by the customers. If small rooms are used for storage, different series will be kept in different rooms substantially independent of each other, but if a single large area is used for storage of different report series, the older closed series can occupy a fixed area which will not be disturbed except when the weeding programme comes into operation.

Storage of microforms

Cans of film are probably the most awkward form of holdings to store. There is the advantage that the cans protect the contents, but they are of an inconvenient shape, and the awkwardness is multiplied if they are of different sizes. Large cans of 35 mm film are best kept on open racking with two battens about six inches apart on which the cans rest on their edges with labels which can be read easily; the method is hardly practicable if there are different sizes of cans and then it is usually most convenient to store the different sizes separately. The records must then be adequate to direct a searcher to the type and size of container as well as the accession number of the report required. This complication is a strong argument for standardizing on a single size and gauge of film. Non-standard accessions can be transferred to the standard size, but if this is to be considered it would probably be more advantageous in the long run to convert the film to microfiche.

Microfiches of reports are now almost invariably produced in a standard 146×105 mm format, with bibliographical information readable by the unaided eye at the top, and kept in paper envelopes. One microfiche will hold an average-length report and they can be kept in standard index drawers which are preferably kept in lockable cabinets. Although paper copies of reports are usually kept on racks extending from the floor to as high as one can reach, and sometimes higher, cabinets of microfiches should be on stands so that the lowest drawer is about two feet from the floor and the highest not too high to be used without being extracted from the cabinet. Most microcards are 125×75 mm and if necessary the two forms can be interfiled in the same drawers. When there is a master microfiche used for the production of copies it should not be filed with the copies used for issue.

Saving of storage space is much greater with microfiches than with roll film and a standard filing cabinet drawer will hold 600 to 800 fiches. Since the prime need is the ability to find the microfiche for a given report with the minimum of delay, the obvious method of filing is by accession number, and this is essential in an automated system. For small collections it is equally possible to file the fiches in some other order, say by corporate author and under that by accession number, and thus to eliminate one card catalogue. Many requests will not quote the accession number, and hence it will be necessary to refer to a catalogue when dealing with a request. Two difficulties arise in such a system: it is no longer possible to see at once if one fiche is missing from a set, and it becomes necessary periodically to reorganize the contents of filing drawers as the collection grows. When fiches are filed in accession number order, growth is coped with simply by adding further filing drawers.

If very large quantities of microfiches are held, consideration should be given to the installation of an automated filing system such as the Remington Kard-veyer or Roneo-Vickers Spacemiser. In such systems, which work from any standard AC power outlet, the filing drawers are placed on shelves in a rotating conveyer system within a lockable cabinet. The shelf required is brought to the working level by pressing the appropriate button. Units are available in different sizes holding up to several hundred thousand cards or microfiches. Considerable saving in floor space results, and ease of access is greatly facilitated.

Storage of other retrieval tools

Printed index volumes are referred to daily by many staff. For such multiple access it is useful to store them on rotating shelves or carousels. The automated filing systems described earlier in this chapter for microfiche storage are equally useful for drawers of catalogue cards. When card catalogues are discontinued and replaced by printed indexes, consideration should be given to microfilming the index cards, and storing the microfilms in cassettes near a reader printer. Provided the cassettes are properly labelled and filed in the correct order, reference to the correct part of the index is simple and relatively quick, and considerable floor space is saved.

Security aspects of storage

When reports subject to protective classification markings are held, a decision has to be reached as to whether they should be separated from other holdings for storage in secure accommodation or whether all the holdings should be kept together, in which case the precautions necessary for the highest protective classification must be applied to them all. Each method has its own advantages and disadvantages, but when a number of the unclassified or unmarked documents have their own value, for example from scarcity, the advantage would be with keeping all the holdings together.

Security requires that no document needing protection should be left accessible and unattended at any time and that when any considerable number of them are held together they must be protected against any form of unauthorized access and must be accounted for at all times.

Checking of holdings is thus chiefly controlled from the records, and although it is simplified if the reports requiring protection are segregated, the difference is not great. On the other hand if all such reports are kept together in one place additional precautions are needed to protect that place since it would otherwise make the work of an intruder easier. Further information on the subject is contained in the section on Security.

WEEDING

Weeding may be done in two ways; at the input stage or on the shelved stock, or, of course, both. The principles are the same in both cases, i.e. how many copies of a report must be held, or must even one copy be held?

Weeding at the input stage

A large information centre is likely to have a large intake of reports which come in automatically, and not all of them will be relevant to its interests. An early decision has then to be made as to what is to be done with these irrelevant reports. Some of them will be available elsewhere in some quantity and such reports can be disposed of without being recorded unless there is some reason to suppose that the centre will be asked for them. It would then be at least as easy to supply a copy as to advise the enquirer to apply elsewhere, and would be of more benefit to good customer relations.

Some irrelevant reports may appear to be the only available ones in the country and these should be recorded in sufficient detail to enable subsequent identification of the reports without the entire processing procedure being brought into play. There will be no need for an abstract or for any detailed subject analysis, but a potentially unique document cannot be destroyed without further thought and a decision on what to do with it has to be made before unnecessary time and money are spent on it. Normally the choice is between including the report in the collection with the knowledge that it is unlikely to be called for and the preferable alternative of sending it for retention to another centre with whose interests it can be identified. Needless to say if this alternative is adopted the receiving centre should be warned that the copy may well be unique and the new location noted on the record cards.

Reports in some quantity may be received by a centre which seem to have no relation to the probable demand for them although their relevance is plain. If the centre is the distributing agency for some classes of reports the number sent may be that required for the standard distribution or a considerably greater number without much consideration of the demand for the particular report, and either way the fate of the apparently excessive supply has to be considered. Perhaps a number of copies may be needed for consideration by some committee, and it may be that the sender is unable to account for the number sent. Unless there is some good reason for another course the best procedure is to keep all the copies supplied for a reasonable period of, say, six months, and then to weed them down to what experience suggests is a suitable number, perhaps half a dozen. In view of the world paper shortage, however, the problem of surplus copies at the input stage is likely to diminish considerably in the future.

Weeding existing stock

There must be a weeding programme in which the stocks held are reviewed at intervals until only a single copy of a report is held, but this has to be done with discretion. Since it is apparently a clerical operation which can be organized from the stock record cards, there is some tendency for it to become purely mechanical, but a number of circumstances have to be taken into account. Fortunately these circumstances are to some extent foreseeable and can be marked on the record card so that some reports are exempted from the standard weeding procedure.

Security, Storage and Weeding

For reports originating within the same organization as the centre it has to be considered whether some other unit holds stocks and if so how many copies are held. The difficulty of reprinting if this is called for must also be taken into account. On the other hand the likely demand has to be estimated, and experience usually allows this to be done with some accuracy, though bad estimates are sometimes made. If a stock is held against some possible contingency one can usually predict a period after which the need may have lapsed.

For reports originating outside the centre's parent organization there is a similar balance between potential supply and potential demand, but for most of these reports only a single copy will have been received, and there are no weeding problems except for its disposal.

The stage at which only a single copy of a report is held brings about some new problems. Are requests for it to be met by loans of that single copy or by photocopying it, and if a photocopy is lent and returned, should it be retained when it is established that interest in the report is not dead? Should the paper copy be retained or should a microcopy replace it and the paper copy be disposed of? There is likely to be a standing policy at the centre on this point, but there may be circumstances which require a departure from it, for example the paper copy may be in poor condition or be too faint for photocopying to be successful.

The problem of unique copies has always to be borne in mind. Most large centres will have copies of old reports which are considered to be unique in the country if not in the world, and some at least of these unique copies will be peripheral to the interests of the centre. Even if it is known that such a report has been superseded by a later one there are probably sections of it which have not been repeated and have a remaining value. Information officers like librarians have an aversion to the destruction of unique documents. It may be that some other information centre is known to be willing to accept and preserve such reports and to have a greater interest in the subject matter than the holding centre. In such cases the reports may be passed on, with a warning that they are thought to be unique. More often no such centre will be known and then the best solution is to have a microfiche made and to offer the paper copy to the British Library, or to the Public Record Office in the case of British government reports. The Public

Record Office will normally only accept originals, but the British Library accepts reproduced copies.

Although the use of a set programme for weeding is economical of effort and the level of the staff needed to carry it out, it involves risks when a report is subject to demands which were not foreseen when it was first entered on the weeding programme. A standing order should be made to ensure that when this happens the weeding programme is suspended for that report while the case is looked into. This could happen, for example, if a report is called for more than once during the third year that it is held in the centre. In such cases the stock record card for the report must be annotated.

References

BERLIN, S. An advanced classified document control system. *Special Libraries*, 58(3). March, 1967. 160–165.

SELECTED BIBLIOGRAPHY

DOWNIE, C. S. Barriers to the flow of technical information: limitation statements – legal basis. Arlington, Va., Office of Aerospace Research, 1969. *Report* No. OAR–69–0014. (Available NTIS as AD 692 400.)

GERRARD, S. A. *and* LYLE, D. F. Handling industrial (scientific and technical) confidential report material. *Aslib Proceedings*, 18(8). August, 1966. 206–217.

JERMY, K. E. Control of commercially confidential information in reports. *Aslib Proceedings*, 18(8). August, 1966. 221–225.

WALKINS, P. S. Filing and storage of reports. *Aslib Proceedings*, 5(4). November, 1953. 335–340.

CHAPTER II

Organization and Management

THE INFORMATION CENTRE – SUB-UNITS AND CENTRALIZATION

An information centre may be organized as a single centralized unit, or it may consist of a main information centre with sub-units in different buildings or remote establishments, and it may be part of a larger division, perhaps called 'information' which includes publicity and public relations. Again the centre may be almost entirely self-contained but it is more likely to make use of various common services and some at least of its staff may be under the control of management outside the centre. There are both advantages and disadvantages in centralization.

In the United States, sub-units and centralization might encompass centralized, decentralized, and network information centres, which may be distinguished from the decentralized operation. The National Library of Medicine operates an extensive network whereby individual libraries and information centres can participate in a time-shared retrieval system. It also offers tapes so that individual libraries and information centres can operate their own decentralized system. The NLM operation is centralized as to input, preparation of indexes, and data maintenance. See the description of ERIC in Chapter 3 for an example of a clearinghouse activity that is decentralized. Many gradations of these terms exist in real-life information services.

The pros and cons of centralization

It is clearly possible to have much greater specialization in a large unit than in a small one or in a centralized system than in one which involves a loose linkage of independent units. Many jobs can be done once for the whole system instead of being repeated for each unit. The head of a centralized system has greater responsibilities, greater opportunities and greater rewards than are possible in a collection of separate units, and there are more opportunities for junior staff to obtain promotion within the centre. Centralized purchasing can lead to economies and centralized ordering can ensure that the reference material provides a better coverage than would be possible with small independent units and includes unusual or expensive items which would otherwise not be available, while avoiding unnecessary duplication of items which are seldom used. Centralization can provide opportunities for enterprises which would not otherwise occur, including increased mechanization, and minor research projects.

On the other hand, some information scientists have no liking for such specialization, which can involve a lack of variety in their work and an increasing absence of contact with the general field of information work. The one-man information unit has a fascination all its own for many information workers. The centralization of tasks tends to eliminate the personal touch, and contact with users can be reduced. Though the head of a centralized system has his opportunities, it is at the cost of being more of a manager than an information scientist. The heads of small autonomous units have the satisfaction of achieving responsibility in a lower grade and at an earlier age, and a number of people prefer to look for promotion accompanied by a change of scene rather than wait to step into dead men's shoes.

Centralized purchasing often results in supplies being not quite what was wanted, and the chain of ordering may lead to delays. A large centre is more likely to be subject to staff cuts in periods of recession, so that the scope for developing new tasks may be more apparent than real.

Balancing the pros and cons could be continued indefinitely and it is not possible to ensure that all the benefits shall be guaranteed and all the disadvantages avoided. It is probably true that the right man at the head of a centralized system could gain most of the advantages and avoid most of the shortcomings, and it is certain that such a man is more likely to be found in a large organization than in any of the small units.

Centralization involves as a rule the use of equipment which would not otherwise be available, and this emphasizes the fact that there is centralization not only of authority but also of work and services. Specialized equipment will be used by the whole system, and work done on this equipment will be forwarded by all the units to wherever the equipment is sited, normally at the centre, but not necessarily there, though control would be exercised from the centre. There may be good reasons for placing equipment at outlying units (such as availability of suitable staff, lower cost of floor space, etc.), but complete divorce between an information centre and its major equipment is to be deprecated. However, in a large centre with outlying sub-units the siting of an important piece of equipment at one of the sub-units will be useful in increasing the self-respect of the staff of the sub-unit and giving them the opportunity of developing specialized expertise. The problem of communication is of great importance. It is useless to place important equipment at an outlying unit if communications cannot be relied on. The typical example of specialized equipment is a computer used for information retrieval. This is satisfactory if there is reliable and rapid access to it, by the provision of remote terminals, with a guarantee of on-line availability between stated hours. If this is the case there is no need for the computer to be in the information system at all, and it may be outside the whole organization.

The need for sub-units

Many large information centres exist primarily to provide technical information to workers in their own organization. The geographical disposition of the organization will then determine the way in which the information service is organized. With an organization occupying various buildings in one area it may be necessary to set up sub-units of the centre in each building which may either be a small reference library or a smaller version of the centre. The parent organization may have a number of research establishments remote from the main information centre, and each establishment will need its own information unit. These are the main types of sub-unit which are most commonly met with, and the information units at remote establishments tend to be the more autonomous.

Types of sub-unit

The first type of sub-unit will of necessity be rather small and its holdings will be confined to general reference material and specialized material relevant to the work which goes on in the building. It may be operated part-time by one of the technical staff located in the building, and its operations may be limited to those of a small library. This will, however, very much depend on the officer in charge. The sub-unit may have a limited authority to obtain material directly from suppliers of its choice or more probably from a prescribed list. It may, however, have to rely entirely on what is sent from the main centre. Few of these small sub-units will have the effort or perhaps the skill necessary to prepare indexes, though catalogue cards supplied from outside may be filed. Their value as information centres depends largely on whether technical staff is available to interpret the information gleaned from the indexes and documents, but there must always be facilities for feeding back the more difficult enquiries to the main centre. If the organization has a computerized information system there may well be an on-line terminal in the sub-unit which enables enquiries to be put into the system and replies received without the main centre being called into action.

The main centre will in general have the responsibility for providing these sub-units with the materials, facilities and expertise that they need. In some cases the sub-units will specialize in a particular discipline but will still need the backing of a general information service: the more restricted the range of coverage the better any topic within that range will be documented. The sub-unit will need indexes and must be supplied either with printed issues or with cards which can be filed: printed indexes may be the more popular at the unit since they do not require much local work, and if catalogue cards are sent they must be sufficient in coverage to satisfy the more urgent needs without being so numerous as to impose an unmanageable task in sorting, weeding and filing. The head of the main centre will have to ensure that the officer in charge of the sub-unit thoroughly understands the system used, and agree with him on how far he can deal with enquiries himself and what should be passed back to the main centre. The main centre should be prepared to give enquiries sent by the sub-unit some priority, as time has already been spent on them and the reputation of the main centre as well as that of the sub-unit is affected by the speed and quality of the service.

A second type of sub-unit is that set up by the main centre as a branch in order to provide users with a conveniently situated service essentially similar to that provided by the main centre. With this type there is usually no question of subject specialization, though this may sometimes be needed: in general what is wanted is a smaller version of the main information centre. In its favour is the fact that the staff is provided by the main centre as well as the methods and the bulk of the material. A proper balance has to be maintained between the staff available and the work, but it is important that the sub-unit should neither be nor appear to be a mere post-office and that all the interesting work should not be passed on to the main centre as a matter of course. It will seldom be practicable to duplicate massive indexes, but full indexes of new accessions should be maintained as far as is needed to cover local interests and a good supply of information tools, particularly abstracts of the centre's own holdings should be provided. Microfiches provide a very convenient way of holding a good stock of primary reports in a small space and the sub-unit should be provided with portable microfiche readers and a reader-printer.

It always gives satisfaction to users to have a place nearby which they can easily visit for their information needs and in particular to find a familiar and knowledgeable person there. Although the most economical use of staff involves their being concentrated in one place with emphasis on specialization, the goodwill arising from personal contact is worth the loss involved in having some members less efficiently used in detached sub-units with generalized work.

The third type of sub-unit is that situated in a research establishment of the same organization as the main centre, and here there is a wide variation in arrangements. Some may be staffed, supplied and controlled by the main centre, while others may be quite independent, using their own systems and acknowledging no more than a degree of voluntary co-operation with the main unit, and there are many intermediate types.

Where the main centre provides the staff, the sub-unit is not noticeably different from a branch of the main centre except that usually a high degree of subject specialization is involved and the staff has a loyalty towards the establishment as well as towards the main centre. The head of the establishment may well wish to have the information unit entirely under his control and will always have some degree of control, while the staff will be anxious to give satisfaction to users among whom they are themselves working. The sub-unit must be able to work independently to a large extent and it must be provided with all the necessary resources; it will usually purchase much of its material without more interference from the main centre than is necessary to see that its budget is not exceeded and in fact the clerical and ancillary staff will normally be supplied by the establishment, as will the furniture and fittings.

At the other end of the scale the information centre at a major establishment will commonly be substantially autonomous. It may have facilities lacking at the main centre and use systems appropriate to local needs rather than to more general requirements and it may have resources not appropriate to the main centre. There will be an important difference between the main centre and sub-units in that the latter almost always deal face-to-face with their users while the main centre works mostly by correspondence.

The attitude of the main centre towards such an autonomous unit is one of co-operation and of supplying services which are necessary but not otherwise available. The main centre gives a lead to sub-units, large and small alike, though they may not be alike in following the lead. The head of the main centre does well to arrange periodical meetings between the senior staff of all establishment information units, so that they become familiar not only with the main centre but also with each other's situations, facilities and problems and all can offer suggestions for solutions and improvements in any area. The emphasis on co-operation is good for its own sake and also for its effect in minimizing the strains which arise between leader and led and between controller and controlled, as well as those which concern the problems of semi-autonomy.

STAFF

The staff of a large information centre will consist of different classes and grades. There will be technical, supervisory, clerical and ancillary staff such as typists, machine operators, messengers and paperkeepers.

It is natural for some rivalry to develop between some of the classes of the staff: A may think he could do B's work better than B does it and is only prevented from doing so by his grading: C may resent D's seniority, which seems to him to depend only on some paper qualification: E thinks that he is overworked while F does very little all day. It is an important task of management to avoid these rivalries as far as possible and to smooth them away when they do arise. Important principles are that there should be no obvious injustice, that work should be fairly distributed, that everyone should be able to see some prospects of advancement and that all should appreciate the importance of co-operation to advance the work and reputation of the centre.

The head of every information centre is convinced that he has not the staff necessary to fulfil his obligations and that this shortage is in all grades and types. He nearly always has a mental list of developments and improvements which are being held up by the necessities of day-to-day working, and he will know of a number of services which he should be giving but for which he lacks the necessary staff. He will contrive to bring about savings in some directions by more efficient working or by quietly dropping unrewarding jobs in order to devote his resources to more appealing ends, and he will be divided between the urge to publicize his successes and risk possible consequent staff cuts, and lying low and avoiding any reputation as a go-getter while doing what he thinks needs to be done.

Technical staff

The technical staff will be largely used for abstracting and subject analysis of the new accessions and dealing with subject enquiries. They will also provide assistance to clerical staff when in difficulties with the enquiries falling to their share, and they are responsible for producing such things as special bibliographies and state-of-the-art reports as opportunity and need arise. The technical staff will be expected to give thought to ways of improving the systems used: if subject analysis is based on a thesaurus, this will need review in the light of experience just as a classification system needs constant expansion in the fields in which most advances are being made. Subject enquiries which call for digested information rather than the supply of documents will be the responsibility of the technical staff, and these may range from a single factual question to a request for a literature survey.

Technical staff should be encouraged to write reports on new services or methods which they have helped to develop. These are always of interest to other workers in information science. They should also be encouraged to undertake special investigations such as surveys of user needs, and the potential market for new services.

The technical staff will be chosen to provide, as far as possible, expertise on the whole range of subjects covered by the information centre, though this will not always be possible, and it will then be necessary for one or more of the staff to make themselves conversant with the missing subjects. A majority of the technical staff will be graduates specializing in the subjects with, if possible, a post-graduate qualification in information science, but there will usually be room for some whose experience is practical rather than academic. Although recruiting will to some extent be dictated by the need to fill gaps as quickly as possible, it will aim at filling subject gaps as well as vacant chairs and also at maintaining a good range of ages among the staff. Although a number of comings and goings are to be expected, a considerable number of the technical staff will expect to make a career in the centre and it would be an embarrassment if a number of them came up to retirement age in very rapid succession. The fact that the technical staff has a blend of career officers and 'birds of passage' is probably an advantage rather than otherwise as it improves the career prospects of the stayers and also gives a chance of changing or widening the field of interest. In an organization with experimental establishments there may be an opportunity of arranging that the staff from the establishments may do a tour of duty in the information centre, to the benefit of both sides, though it must be admitted that these opportunities are not often taken up, mainly because the experimental staff have a suspicion that their absence from their normal posts may have a bad effect on their promotion prospects there. There may also be a chance of the information staff doing a tour of duty on experimental work in the establishments, which is highly desirable though it will result in empty chairs in the information centre during the tour of duty.

One specialization which will often be found in the technical staff is the ability to translate technical papers from foreign languages. Sometimes this is done by specialists who may come to do little else, and if the centre offers a translation service this is essential. Such specialist translators should also be expected to abstract and preferably to index as well the foreign language

Organization and Management

material they are dealing with. (If they do not index, others can do so from their abstracts.) At the same time, other staff who have some ability with languages should be encouraged to develop that ability and be given occasional jobs in which it needs to be used.

Technical staff with sufficient experience are likely to be invited to serve on committees in the information science field, and although such co-operation may not directly benefit the information centre it does so indirectly, both in increasing its reputation for useful collaboration and in bringing in a further sort of expertise and advance knowledge of coming developments, apart from the value of the experience to the individual. Collaboration in the United Kingdom is also increased if the centre becomes a member of Aslib, and the staff are encouraged to attend the meetings organized by Aslib and its specialist groups. Suitably qualified professional staff should be encouraged to apply for membership of the Institute of Information Scientists. By such means they keep themselves abreast of new developments and meet others working in the information field for discussion of common problems. Attendance at conferences and symposia on topics of interest to the centre should also be encouraged. All these activities bring about absences from the working chairs, but this is compensated for not only in the ways already mentioned but also by giving the staff some change from their everyday work and by suggesting to them that they are not regarded as mere wage-slaves or clock-watchers.

Supervisory staff

The numbers of supervisory staff will be proportional to those of the clerical or ancillary staff whom they supervise, and some of them will be posted so that advantage may be taken of some special expertise they possess such as computing experience. In such cases they are more or less equivalent to technical staff and often work among them. In large organizations the posting of supervisory staff is commonly controlled from outside the information centre, so that a particularly bright member is likely to be posted on quite quickly for the benefit of his career prospects. This is to be expected and it is important that any new procedures he may have introduced are fully documented and understood before he is posted away.

There is often an idea that supervisory staff sit around doing little but supervising and that they would not dream of getting their hands dirty. This is not usually the case and in fact good supervisors should be able to do all the jobs they supervise, and be ready to do so in an emergency. As with other grades it is a matter of prime importance that they should be interested in what they are doing and not thinking only of what their next assignment will be, and that they should be anxious to improve methods and efficiency.

Clerical staff

The clerical staff will, at least in the beginning, not be obviously different from clerical staff in other parts of the organization, but their work is decidedly different from that which clerical staff in general are used to; the better ones develop an interest in information work and a degree of expertise which can be surprising and is by no means limited to their own particular jobs. It is advantageous to encourage them and to help them to see how they fit into the scheme of things and how their work affects not only the information centre but the organization in general.

The clerical staff will be responsible not only for nearly all the cataloguing which forms such an important part of the work of an information centre. They will also deal with the simpler requests and enquiries which can be satisfied by the supply of documents held by the centre about which sufficient information is supplied and also the preliminary and final stages of the more complex enquiries about which they have to seek advice from their supervisors or which they have to pass on to the technical staff. This involves co-operation with the technical staff in deciding at what stage to pass on an enquiry and doing so in a way that avoids the risk of the technical staff having to do unnecessary clerical work.

The clerical staff will have access to all the card catalogues and printed indexes, but will not often use the subject index which will be maintained by the technical staff and kept in their area. The remaining card catalogues, on the other hand, will be maintained by the clerical staff and located in their area though the technical staff will also use them as occasion arises and give advice on their arrangement. It is commonly found that filing catalogue cards is a highly unpopular duty, although a few people find it interesting and congenial. It is therefore wise to arrange that this chore is taken in rotation and even if there is someone who likes filing catalogue cards he should not be given a monopoly, so that when he is not available for any reason the job can still be carried on efficiently.

Ancillary staff

Ancillary staff include typists, though it is advantageous that some at least of the clerical staff are able to type and encouraged to do the simpler typing arising from their own work. If there are enough specialist typists they will work in a pool under their own supervisor, a system which has its own advantages though it involves a degree of organization unnecessary when there are only a few typists, working among the people who generate their work.

When very large stocks of paper reports are held it is usually an advantage, and when remote storage is used it is almost always necessary, to use paperkeepers to put reports away in their proper place and to extract them again when needed. The paperkeepers will use a system and will know in what area a report with a given accession number is to be found; sometimes another person will need to extract a paper and then it is important that he should understand and follow the system used (for example in leaving a token in the place of a document taken) and know where to look for what he wants; it is better that the putting away should be left entirely to the paperkeepers. This recognition of a minor specialization does not interfere with the necessity for the senior staff keeping an eye on the arrangements and proposing any alterations which seem desirable. As in all similar cases the operating staff should be given every opportunity of making comments and suggestions: they may know of some important objection which is not obvious, and their suggestions may be improvements on what is proposed. The suggestions of the operating staff will not always be taken up: there will sometimes be an overriding necessity to make some change, but when a proposal is turned down the reason for doing so should be given.

Cleaning operations call for some attention. Reports stored on open shelves get dusty and when they are being cleaned it is vital that they should be replaced where they belong, though when any reshelving is being done it can with advantage be combined with dusting. When security-classified reports are held it is necessary that there should be active supervision of the cleaners to ensure the integrity of the collection, and as cleaning is usually done out of normal working hours, special arrangements have to be made for this.

The ancillary staff will commonly be recruited and controlled from outside the information centre, and it is then necessary to secure the co-operation of those responsible to ensure that unsuitable staff are not placed in the centre or at least are reposted quickly, that substitutes are provided when staff are absent through leave or sickness and that suitable staff are left in the centre long enough to give useful service after learning the ropes, and are not posted only for short periods for the sake of their career prospects. Nearly all types of ancillary staff will have their own specializations, minor as these may be, and they should be respected and treated accordingly; a good machine operator or a good cleaner is a valuable member of a team and will appreciate signs that he or she is being recognized as such.

Access to supervisors

All staff should have ready access to higher management and not only to their immediate seniors. Access to the most senior staff should normally be arranged through the immediate senior, but the head of the centre and his immediate deputies should make a point of seeing all their staff at frequent but irregular intervals and usually while the staff are actually at their work. When a staff member seeks an interview with higher management the interview should take place in private and the immediate senior should not be present at the start of the interview, though he may be called in later either to offer his comment or to be made aware of what is going on.

Training

All new staff will need on-the-job training even if they have already had experience of similar work, since most information centres use some systems and techniques of their own, and at least a proportion of the new staff will have had no previous experience of such work. Much of this instruction will be given by the immediate senior, or even by fellow staff members in the course of the work being done, but it will sometimes be useful to have definite training sessions, particularly when some important change is being made in a system. On-the-job training is also facilitated if the procedures of the centre are formalized and reproduced as printed instructions. Some more complicated procedures should be written up as manuals, and the compiling of such manuals is in itself a useful exercise for some of the experienced staff. All staff, and technical staff in particular, should be encouraged to make efforts to improve themselves in various ways, thus enhancing their promotion prospects and also increasing their value to the information centre and to the community in general. Apart from the old-established courses in information science, which are now day-release or even sandwich courses rather than evening classes, there are now numbers of short courses, arranged e.g. by Aslib in the United Kingdom, especially for information and library workers. Staff showing management potential should be sent on one or more of the management courses which are now available.

Useful reviews of information staff training will be found in the articles by Mack (1972) and Liebesny, and the subject was treated in more detail by Mack in 1973.

Assessment of staff

It is usual for annual reports to be made on staff; these will concern how they do their work, their personal characteristics, their suitability for their work and for promotion, and general evaluations and observations. These reports are usually confidential, though there are often arrangements for the person reported upon to be informed of any particularly adverse marking. It is, of course, vital that all reporting should be objective and it is important that reasonably uniform standards should be used, though some reporting officers will inevitably get a reputation for high or low marking and allowances are made for this when their assessments are being considered. It is also important that the views of both the immediate superior and the head of the centre should appear either as separate assessments or in successive sections, and it is very useful to have two independent assessments on each person reported on. The completion of annual reports is a good opportunity for the senior reporting officer to give the staff member reported on an interview at which topics discussed would include his progress, his view of his future, and whether he would benefit from further training or a change of duties.

In all dealings it is most important that the principle of co-operation should be emphasized; all classes of staff and all members of them should be working together for the objects of the information centre, and the success or failure of a centre depends to no small extent on the degree to which this principle is accepted and followed and on staff members appreciating the relevance and value of their work, together with its relation to the work of others.

ASSESSMENT OF METHODS

The head of the centre must keep its operations continuously under review, and for this purpose it is important that monthly work returns be submitted by all the sections of the centre. These should be charted so that figures for similar months in previous years can be compared.

When a case has to be made for the purchase of new and expensive equipment, or for an increase in the numbers of staff, it will usually be necessary to produce figures showing the costs of the operations under consideration and it is a useful exercise to cost the centre's operations at regular periods. The paper by Taylor describes a costing exercise on a library service which was to be repeated annually. It includes cost of individual library products, including accession list, abstracts, and major and minor enquiries. This paper was written in 1961, and it would be interesting and salutary to see the results of a similar survey at the present time. Klintøe describes the cost-analysis procedures in the Danish Technical Information Service in which data are gathered using weekly time sheets. Representative cost breakdowns are given for each type of service. In 1972 the Aslib Engineering Group devoted its annual conference to discussing the costing of library and information services. The proceedings included a paper by Overton on costing a government library/information service, an account by Vickery of Aslib's research into costing information services, and a paper by Cook on financing a library/information service by operating a cost recovery system. D. S. Price, deputy director of the ERIC Processing and Reference Facility, describes a system he terms 'building block costing'. This is based on three premises: first, the most useful display of costs is in terms of unit costs, but, since no single unit can measure an entire information system, a process of subdivision, unit costing of the subdivisions, and reassembly, must be applied. Second, unit costs are meaningful only in a framework of all costs, and third, cost collection must be continuous, with costs relatable to resultant production.

One of the difficulties of costing studies has been that it has not been possible to apply data collected in one organization to the different circumstances obtaining in another. Because of this the Aslib Research Department has undertaken a research project to collect cost data with widespread application. Some of this work is described in the paper by Wilkin & others which presents a method for data collection and analysis to obtain standard times for information systems procedures. Data collection is by a self-recording (diary) method, completed at the time of the operation. More recently, Vickers of the Aslib Research Department has reported on a survey made of eighteen mechanized information systems in Europe and the USA using a structured cost-analysis scheme. The sample included data-base producers and self-contained systems that both create, and provide services from, a data-base. Unit costs were derived for most operations. It appeared that costs were affected more significantly by factors such as system management, salary variations, and productivity of staff, than by technical factors such as depth of indexing, data preparation methods, or computer programming.

Some of the newer management techniques can be applied in the environment of an information service, but caution is necessary in that techniques proved effective in measuring or increasing output from a factory production line cannot be transferred without change to a production situation where a variable amount of intellectual effort is required. In this field some classic work was carried out in the USA during the period 1966–68 by John I. Thomson and Company, New York, under the ATLIS Program (Army Technical Library Improvement Studies), and reported on by Wessel (November, 1968). He provides examples of the use of cost-effectiveness analysis to a search service, and of the applicability of classical utility criteria for measuring the value of commodities (services and products) and for making determinations of equilibrium conditions which maximize utility within given budget constraints. Complete details of the study are given in a series of openly available reports by Wessel & others (1967, 1968, 1969). In the final report (Wessel & Moore, 1969) four techniques are proposed. These are (1) SCORE Analysis (Service COmponents Reliability and Efficiency Analysis) – a technique to measure the effectiveness of a service and the associated change in effectiveness due to a change in operations or costs; (2) SCOUT Analysis (Service COmponents Utility Analysis) – a technique to determine the optimum balance between operations which yields maximum effectiveness within budget constraints; (3) CORE Analysis (COrrelation, Regression and Effectiveness Analysis) – a technique to derive unit cost standards for given operations which produces a given quality of output, and (4) GAME Analysis (Group Attainment and MEthods Analysis) – a technique to eliminate unnecessary work or excessive delays, to arrange work in the best order; to standardize usage of proper work methods, and to develop time standards to accomplish essential events.

Lancaster & Climenson give some criteria for economic efficiency of a document-retrieval system including coverage, usability (the value of the documents retrieved in terms of age, reliability and comprehensibility), recall, precision, response time, presentation and amount of user effort required. A later article by Lancaster on cost-effectiveness of information retrieval and dissemination systems lists three viewpoints from which an information system can be evaluated: how well the system is satisfying its objectives, i.e. system effectiveness; how efficiently (in terms of costs) it is satisfying its objectives, i.e. cost effectiveness; and whether the system justifies its existence, i.e. cost-benefit. The paper by Gilchrist gives a useful summary of these and other studies on cost effectiveness. Mason (March, 1973) considers that although it is usually impossible to put a quantified value on information supplied by an information service, a method for demonstrating cost effectiveness is the next best thing, and that the necessary techniques are available in programmed budgeting.

A useful review of modern management methods is given in a later paper by Mason (November, 1973). He has tried out a number of them in an information service and he describes those he has found most useful and some of the pitfalls encountered. The interrelation of modern techniques to give a practical system is described by Magson, who links management by objectives, work measurement, activity sampling, and programmed budgeting into a cost-benefit analysis of some typical activities of an information centre. The results are based on the difference between two sets of cost-analyses, representing a 'present' and an 'alternative' situation respectively.

The techniques of operational research developed in the Second World War as an aid to military decision-making should also find application in the management of an information centre. In 1971 Aslib, with OSTI support, commissioned a review by the Institute for Operational Research on the scope for operational research in the library and information field. The review was published as an OSTI report, and the results of discussions between the Institute and Aslib are surveyed in a paper by Elton & Vickery. They conclude that there is a strong case for the application of operational research methods to be applied to a system if there are difficult decisions to take regarding alternative courses of action; if these alternatives differ significantly in cost and/or effectiveness; and if there is relatively unconstrained freedom to choose between them.

It must constantly be borne in mind that the main aim of an information centre in science and technology is to provide an information service to working scientists and technologists, either to facilitate new research and development, or to prevent the wasteful reduplication of work. It is in this latter respect that cost-benefit of information services could be demonstrated and it is not very well documented. Martyn estimates that one-quarter to one-third of research is duplicated. Heads of information centres would perform a most useful service in demonstrating to the community that information services are an economic asset if they would record and publicize where possible all cases where information provided by their centres has prevented expensive research being repeated unnecessarily.

References

COOK, J. Financing a library/information service by operating a cost-recovery system. *Aslib Proceedings*, 24(6). June, 1972. 342–349.

ELTON, M. *and* VICKERY, B. The scope for operational research in the library and information field. *Aslib Proceedings*, 25(8). August, 1973. 305–319.

GILCHRIST, A. Cost-effectiveness. *Aslib Proceedings*, 23(9). September, 1971. 455–464.

INSTITUTE FOR OPERATIONAL RESEARCH. The scope for OR in the library and information services field. London, OSTI, 1972, *OSTI Report* 5136. (Available BLLD.)

KLINTØE, K. Cost analysis of a technical information unit. *Aslib Proceedings*, 23(7). July, 1971. 362–371.

LANCASTER, P. W. The cost-effectiveness analysis of information retrieval and dissemination systems. *Journal of the American Society for Information Science*, 22(1). January/February, 1971. 12–27.

LANCASTER, P. W. *and* CLIMENSON, W. D. Evaluating the economic efficiency of a document retrieval system. *Journal of Documentation*, 24(1). March, 1968. 16–40.

LIEBESNY, F. Education and technical training for technical information. *AGARD Conference Proceedings* No. 136. *New developments in storage, retrieval and dissemination of aerospace information.* Neuilly-sur-Seine, AGARD, 1973. 6–1 – 6–3.

MACK, E. Information staff training. *Information Scientist*, 6(2). June, 1972. 51–59.

MACK, E. In-training in information and special library units. London, Aslib, 1973. ISBN 0 85142 062 1. pp. 53.

MAGSON, M. S. Measurement of cost-benefit in information centres. *Aslib Proceedings*, 25(5). May, 1973. 164–185.

MARTYN, J. Unintentional duplication of research. *New Scientist*, 21(377). 1964. 338.

MASON, D. Management techniques applied to the operation of information services. *Aslib Proceedings*, 25(11). November, 1973. 445–458.

MASON, D. Programmed budgeting and cost-effectiveness. *Aslib Proceedings*, 25(3). March, 1973. 100–110.

OVERTON, C. D. Value for money in Government library/information services. *Aslib Proceedings*, 24(6). June, 1972. 325–336.

PRICE, D. S. Rational cost information. *Special Libraries*, 65(2). February, 1974. 49–57.

TAYLOR, L. Cost research on a library service. *Aslib Proceedings*, 13(9). September, 1961. 238–248.

VICKERS, P. H. A cost survey of mechanized information systems. *Journal of Documentation*, 29(3). September, 1973. 258–280.

VICKERY, B. C. Research by Aslib into costing of information services. *Aslib Proceedings*, 24(6). June, 1972. 336–341.

WESSEL, C. J. Criteria for evaluating the technical library effectiveness. *Aslib Proceedings*, 20(11). November, 1968. 455–481.

WESSEL, C. J. *and* COHRSSEN, B. A. Criteria for evaluating the effectiveness of library operations and services. Phase I: Literature search and state-of-the-art. *ATLIS Report* No. 10. February, 1967. (Available NTIS as AD 649 468.)

WESSEL, C. J. *and others*. Criteria for evaluating the effectiveness of library operations and services. Phase II: Data gathering and evaluation. Final report. *ATLIS Report* No. 19. August, 1968. (Available NTIS as AD 676 188.)

WESSEL, C. J. *and* MOORE, K. L. Criteria for evaluating the effectiveness of library operations and services. Phase III: Recommended criteria and methods for their utilization. Final report. *ATLIS Report* No. 21. January, 1969. (Available NTIS as AD 682 758.)

WILKIN, A. P. *and others*. Standard times for information systems: a method for data collection and analysis. *Journal of Documentation,* 28(2). June, 1972. 131-150.

SELECTED BIBLIOGRAPHY

BROPHY, P. *and* BUCKLAND, M. K. Simulation in education for library and information service administration. *Information Scientist,* 6(3). September, 1972. 93-100.

DUTTON, B. G. Staff management and staff participation. *Aslib Proceedings,* 25(3). March, 1973. 111-125.

FLOWERDEW, A. D. J. *and* WHITEHEAD, C. M. E. Cost-effectiveness and cost/benefit analysis in information science. London, London School of Economics and Political Science, 1974. pp. 72. *OSTI Report* No. 5208. (Available BLLD.)

FUSSLER, H. H. *and others.* Management education: implications for libraries and library schools. Chicago, University of Chicago Press, 1974. ISBN 0 226 27560 4. pp. 115.

HANSON, C. W. Selection of staff. *INSTITUTE OF INFORMATION SCIENTISTS. CONFERENCE. 3rd, Sheffield, 1968. Proceedings...* London, 1969. 54-61.

KENNINGTON, D. Managing effectively: some tips for special librarians. *Aslib Proceedings,* 23(6). June, 1971. 287-291.

MCCLELLAND, W. G. Management in a service environment. *Aslib Proceedings,* 25(3). March, 1973. 93-99.

PROSSER, C. Cost analysis without tears: some hints for librarians. *New Library World,* 75(890). August, 1974. 163-165.

ROBINSON, F. Getting into management. *Information Scientist,* 8(3). September, 1974. 107-115.

THOMAS, P. A. *and* WARD, V. A. Librarians as managers, an exploratory study: where the time goes. London, Aslib, 1973. ISBN 0 85142 051 6. pp. 43. *Aslib Occasional Publication,* 12.

Conclusion

The reader will not fail to have seen that much of the information work with unpublished reports in large information centres does not differ in kind from work with other materials in other information departments, however much it may differ in detail. Some aspects of the work are indeed different in kind, but it is quite impossible to separate those which are exclusively concerned with the stated subject of the monograph from those which are equally relevant to other kinds of information and library work; this is true of almost all specialized subjects and also of specialized points of view: a monograph which kept strictly within the bounds of its subject could not be used without constant reference to other works.

Most of the chapters contain sections which have been written from different points of view from others: to some extent this has resulted from the fact that the monograph will be read by a very wide range of people, but principally from a recognition of the need to see both sides of any argument. It has been said before that there is no black or white, but only different shades of grey, and there can be no cause in which every consideration favours the same side, no matter how convinced its protagonists may be. Every information centre has to take note of the interests of its users, its staff and its source of funds, and in every enterprise there has to be some compromise: it may be clear what the ideal would be, but in the long march towards this ideal, consideration has always to be given to what is practicable at the time, and sometimes it is difficult enough to accomplish that.

Other Relevant Literature

ASHWORTH, W., *ed*. Handbook of special librarianship and information work. 3rd ed. London, Aslib, 1967. pp. 624.
AUGER, C. P., *ed*. Use of reports literature. London, Butterworth, 1975. pp. 276.
BATTEN, W. E., *ed*. Handbook of special librarianship and information work. 4th ed. London, Aslib, 1975. ISBN 0 85142 073 7 (hardback); ISBN 0 85142 074 5 (paperback). pp. 438.
CUADRA, C., *ed*. Annual review of information science and technology. Vol. 9. Washington, American Society for Information Science, 1974. ISBN 0 87715 209 8.
HANSON, C. W. Introduction to science-information work. London, Aslib, 1971. ISBN 0 85142 033 8. pp. 199.
HERNER, S. *and* VELLUCCI, M. J., *eds*. Selected federal computer-based information systems. Washington, Information Resources Press, 1971. ISBN 0 87815 007 2. pp. 215.
KENT, A. *and* LANCOUR, H. Encyclopedia of library and information science. Vols. 1-14 (A-Lib). New York, Marcel Dekker, 1968-1975.
KRUZAS, A. T., *ed*. Encyclopedia of information systems and services. 2nd international ed. Ann Arbor, Edwards Bros. Inc., 1974. pp. 1271.
LYNCH, M. F. Computer-based information services in science and technology – principles and techniques. Stevenage, Peter Peregrinus Ltd., 1974. ISBN 0901223 55 7. pp. 96.
LOOSJES, T. P. On documentation of scientific literature. London, Butterworth, 1973. ISBN 0 0408 704292. pp. 196.
NATIONAL SCIENCE FOUNDATION. Non-conventional scientific and technical information systems in current use. No. 4. Washington, National Science Foundation, 1966. *NSF 66-24*.
PFOUTZ, D. R. Guide to report literature. Library Journal, 84(11). November, 1959. 3363-3366.
VICKERY, B. C. Information systems. London, Butterworth, 1973. ISBN 0 408 70456 x. pp. 360.
WEIL, B. H., *ed*. The technical report. New York, Reinhold, 1954. pp. 497.

APPENDIX I

Acronyms and Abbreviations

(Titles etc., are preceded by the name of the country, for governmental organizations)

(These are not all referred to in the text)

ADSATIS	(Australia) Australian Defence Science and Technology Information System
AERE	(UK) Atomic Energy Research Establishment (Harwell)
AGARD	(NATO) Advisory Group for Aerospace Research and Development (Neuilly-sur-Seine)
AGRIS	Agricultural Information System (International Information System for the Agricultural Sciences and Technology, Rome)
AIAA	American Institute for Aeronautics and Astronautics (New York)
AIDS	Automated Information Dissemination System, (SDI service at Standard Telecommunication Laboratories Ltd, Harlow, UK)
AMCOS	Aldermaston Mechanized Cataloguing and Ordering System (Atomic Weapons Research Establishment, Aldermaston, UK)
ASSASSIN	Agricultural System for Storage and Subsequent Selection of Information (Imperial Chemical Industries Ltd., Agricultural Division, Billingham, Teesside, UK)
ASTIA	(US) Armed Services Technical Information Agency (Cameron Station, Va.) now the Defense Documentation Center
AUDACIOUS	Automatic Direct Access to Information with On-line UDC System (American Institute of Physics project)
AWRE	(UK) Atomic Weapons Research Establishment (Aldermaston)

BECAN	Biomedical Engineering Current Awareness Notification (UK Medical Research Council, Project FAIR)
BIOS	(UK) British Intelligence Objectives Subcommittee
BLLD	(UK) British Library Lending Division (Boston Spa, Wetherby, West Yorks., England)
BNB	*British National Bibliography* (now part of British Library)
BT	Broader term
CAB	Commonwealth Agricultural Bureaux (Farnham Royal, Slough, UK)
CAC	Chemical Abstracts Condensates
CADO	(US) Central Air Documents Office, later merged into ASTIA
CAIN	Catalog-Indexing System
CARD	Compact Automatic Retrieval Display (Image Systems Inc., USA)
CAS	Chemical Abstracts Service (Columbus, Ohio, USA)
CBAC	Chemical-Biological Activities (part of Chemical Abstracts Service)
CFSTI	(US) Clearinghouse for Federal Scientific and Technical Information (now NTIS)
CIOS	Combined Intelligence Objectives Subcommittee
CNDST	(France) Centre National de Documentation Scientifique et Technique (Paris)
CNRS	(France) Centre National de la Recherche Scientifique (Paris)
COBLOS	Computer Based Loans System (Atomic Energy Research Establishment)
COM	Computer Output Microform
COMPENDEX	*Engineering Index* on-line service
CORE	Correlation, Regression and Effectiveness (analysis)
COSATI	(US) Committee on Scientific and Technical Information (Washington)
CSIRO	(Australia) Commonwealth Scientific and Industrial Research Organization (Canberra)
CT	Chemical Titles (part of Chemical Abstracts Service)
DDC	(US) Defense Documentation Center (Cameron Station, Va.
DEVIL	Direct Evaluation of Indexing Languages (Institution of Electrical Engineers, INSPEC, UK)
DRIC	(UK) Defence Research Information Centre (St Mary Cray, Kent)
DSIS	(Canada) Defence Science Information Service (Ottawa)
DTI	(UK) Department of Trade and Industry (London)

Appendix 1

DTO	(Denmark) Dansk Teknisk Oplysningstjeneste (Copenhagen)
EARS	Epilepsy Abstracts Retrieval System (US National Institute of Neurological Diseases and Strokes)
EIRMA	European Industrial Research Management Association (Paris)
EJC	Engineers Joint Council (New York)
ENDS	European Nuclear Documentation Service
ERDA	(US) Energy Research and Development Administration
ERIC	Educational Resources Information Center
ESA	European Space Agency, formerly European Space Research Organization
ESDU	Engineering Sciences Data Unit (London)
ESRO	European Space Research Organization (now European Space Agency)
ETC	European Translations Centre (Delft)
EUSIDIC	European Association of Scientific Information Dissemination Centres (The Hague)
FAIR	Fast Access Information Retrieval (UK Medical Research Council)
FID	International Federation for Documentation (The Hague)
FLIP	Film Library Instantaneous Presentation
FOSDIC	(US) Film Optical Scanning Device for Input to Computers (US National Bureau of Standards)
GAO	General Accounting Office (Washington)
GAME	Group Attainment and Methods (analysis)
GPO	(US) Government Printing Office (Washington)
GRA	(US) *Government Reports Announcements*
HMSO	(UK) Her Majesty's Stationery Office (London)
HTFS	Heat Transfer and Fluid Flow Information Service (Atomic Energy Research Establishment, Harwell, UK)
IAC	Information Analysis Centre
IAEA	International Atomic Energy Agency (Vienna)
IBBRIS	*International Biodeterioration Bulletin Reference Index Supplement*
IFT	Institute of Food Technology
IDW	Institut für Dokumentationswesen (Frankfurt a/Main)
INFIRS	Inverted File Information Retrieval System (UKCIS)
INIS	International Nuclear Information System
INSDOC	Indian National Scientific Documentation Centre (New Delhi)

INSPEC	International Services in Physics, Electrotechnology, Computers and Control (Institution of Electrical Engineers, London)
INTREX	Information Transfer Experiments (Massachusetts Institute of Technology, USA)
IRBEL	*Indexed References to Biomedical Engineering Literature* (UK Medical Research Council, Project FAIR)
IRMS	Information Retrieval and Management System
IRRD	International Road Research Documentation Scheme
ISIS	Integrated Scientific Information System (International Labour Office, Geneva)
ISO	International Organization for Standardization (commonly known as International Standards Organization, Geneva)
JURIS	(US) Department of Justice on-line service
KWAC	Keyword and context
KWIC	Keyword in context
KWOC	Keyword out of context
MARC	Machine readable cataloguing
MEDLARS	Medical Literature Analysis and Retrieval System (National Library of Medicine, Bethesda, Md., USA)
MEDLINE	MEDLARS on-line service
MINICS	Minimum Input Cataloguing System (Loughborough University of Technology, UK)
NACA	(US) National Advisory Committee for Aeronautics (now NASA)
NASA	(US) National Aeronautics and Space Administration, (Washington DC)
NATO	North Atlantic Treaty Organization (Brussels)
NBS	(US) National Bureau of Standards (Washington)
NIH	(US) National Institutes of Health (Bethesda, Md.)
NLLST	(UK) National Lending Library for Science and Technology (now BLLD)
NLM	(US) National Library of Medicine (Bethesda, Md.)
NRCd	National Reprographic Centre for documentation (Hatfield, Herts.)
NRLSI	(UK) National Reference Library for Science and Invention (now Science Reference Library, London)
NRC	(Canada) National Research Council (Ottawa)
NRC	(US) National Research Council (Washington)
NSA	*Nuclear Science Abstracts*
NSF	(US) National Science Foundation (Washington)
NT	Narrower term

NTIS	(US) National Technical Information Service (Springfield, Va.)
OECD	Organization for Economic Co-operation and Development (Paris)
ONERA	(France) Office National des Études et Recherches Aéronautiques (Chatillon-sous-Baigneux, Seine, France)
OSRD	(US) Office of Scientific Research and Development (wound up in 1947)
OSTI	(UK) Office of Scientific and Technical Information (Department of Education and Science, London) (now British Library Research and Development Department)
OTS	(US) Office of Technical Services, transferred to National Bureau of Standards
OVID	On-line VDU Interrogation of Data bases (British Steel Corporation, Strip Mills Division)
PASCAL	Programme Appliqué à la Sélection et à la Compilation Automatiques de la Littérature
PC	Paper copy
PCMI	Photochromic Micro-Image
PRECIS	Preserved Context Index System (British Library)
PUDOC	(Netherlands) Centrum voor Landbouwpublikation en Landbouwdocumentatie
QUIS	Queen's University (Belfast) Information Systems
QUOBIRD	Queen's University (Belfast) On-line Bibliographical Information Retrieval and Dissemination
QUODAMP	Queen's University (Belfast) Data base on Atomic and Molecular Potentials
RA	Research Association
R and D	Research and Development
RECON	Remote Console (an on-line computer system developed by Lockheed Laboratories, Palo Alto, Calif., USA)
RIOT	Retrieval of Information by On-line Terminal (UKAEA, Culham Laboratory)
RT	Related term
SCORE	Service Components Reliability and Efficiency (analysis)
SCOUT	Service Components Utility (analysis)
SDI	Selective Dissemination of Information
SDS	(ESRO) Space Documentation Service
SHARP	Ships Analysis and Retrieval Program (US Depart-

	ment of the Navy Ship Systems and Scientific Documentation Division)
SLIC	Selective Listing in Combination
SLIP	Symmetric List Processor
SOCRATES	System for Organizing Current Reports to Aid Technologists and Scientists (Defence Research Board, Ottawa, Canada)
SOD	(US) Superintendent of Documents (at US Government Printing Office)
SRIM	Standing Order Microfiche Service (NTIS)
SSIE	Smithsonian Science Information Exchange (Washington DC, USA)
STAR	*Scientific and Technical Aerospace Reports*
TEST	*Thesaurus of engineering and scientific terms*
TITUS	Traitement de l'Information Textile Universelle et Sélective (Institut Textile de France)
TRC	(UK) Technology Reports Centre (St Mary Cray, Kent)
TRRL	(UK) Transport and Road Research Laboratory (Crowthorne, Berks.)
UDC	Universal Decimal Classification (maintained by FID)
UKAEA	(UK) United Kingdom Atomic Energy Authority (London)
UKCIS	United Kingdom Chemical Information Service (Nottingham University)
USAEC	(US) United States Atomic Energy Commission (Oak Ridge, Tenn.)

APPENDIX 2

Names and Addresses of National Information Centres

(Main sources: Bauer, C. K. International information systems for physical scientists. AGARD *Lecture Series*, 69, pp. 6-1–6A3-60.
Williams, C. H. Guide to European sources of technical information. 3rd ed. Guernsey, Francis Hodgson, 1970.
FID News Bulletins)
The UK and US centres are described with addresses in Chapter 3

ALGERIA
Centre Cultural Scientifique et Technique Français d'Alger, Section de Diffusion Scientifique et Technique, 7 Rue Kassani Issad, Algiers

ARGENTINE
Secretaria del Consejo Nacional de Desarrollo, (Secretariat of the National Council of Development) Biblioteca Buenos Aires, Buenos Aires

AUSTRALIA
CSIRO Central Library and Information Service, 314 Albert Street, East Melbourne, VIC 3002

AUSTRIA
Gesellschaft für Dokumentation und Bibliographie, Josefsplatz 1, 1014 Vienna

BELGIUM
Centre National de Documentation Scientifique et Technique (CNDST), Boulevard de l'Empereur 4, B-1000 Brussels

BOLIVIA
Centro Nacional de Documentacion Cientifica y Tecnologica-Universidad Mayor de San Andres, Plaza del Obelisco, La Paz

BRAZIL
Instituto Brasileiro de Bibliografia e Documentaçao, Avenue General Justo 171, Rio de Janeiro

Appendix 2

CANADA
Information Canada, (for Canadian Government publications), Canadian Government Printing Bureau, 45 Sacred Heart Boulevard, Hull, Quebec, K1A 0S7

Technical Information Services, National Research Council of Canada, 100 Sussex Drive, Ottawa, Ontario

CHILE
Centro Nacional de Información y Documentación, Canada No. 308—Casilla 297–V, Santiago

CHINA
National Library of Peking, Peking

COLOMBIA
Fondo Colombiano de Investigaciones Cientificas y Proyectos Especiales 'Francisco Jose de Caldas' (COLCIENCIAS), Division de Documentación, Avenida 30 No. 52–A–77, Bogota

CUBA
Instituto de Documentación e Información Cientifica y Tecnica de la Academia de Ciencias de Cuba, Calle 15, no. 551, e/Cyd. Vedado, La Havana

DENMARK
Dansk Teknisk Oplysningstjeneste, (Danish Technical Information Service), Ørnevej 30, DK–2400 Copenhagen

Danmarks Tekniske Bibliotek, (National Technological Library of Denmark), Anker Engelunds Vej 1, DK–2800 Lyngby

ECUADOR
Servicios de Información Tecnica, CENDES, P.O. Box 5833, Guayaquil

EGYPT
National Information and Documentation Centre, Al-Tahreer Street, Dokki, Cairo

FINLAND
Technical Research Centre of Finland, Lonnrotinkatu, 37, Helsinki 18

FRANCE
Centre de Documentation du Centre National de La Recherche Scientifique (CNRS), 75971 Paris CEDEX 20

GERMANY, FEDERAL REPUBLIC OF, Technische Informationsbibliothek, Wolfengarten 1B, D–3000 Hanover 1

GHANA
Central Reference and Research Library, Council for Scientific and Industrial Research, P.O. Box M32, Accra

GREECE
Greek Productivity Centre, 28 Kapodistriou Street, Athens

ICELAND
Idnadarmalastofnun Islands, (Industrial Institute of Iceland), Skipholt 37, Rejkavik

INDIA
Indian National Scientific Documentation Centre (INSDOC), Hillside Road, New Delhi 12

IRAN
Iranian Documentation Centre, Institute for Research and Planning in Science and Education, Tehran

IRELAND, REPUBLIC OF, Institute for Industrial Research and Standards, Technical Information Division, Glasnevin House, Ballymun Road, Dublin 9

ISRAEL
National Centre of Scientific and Technological Information, P.O. Box 20125, Tel-Aviv

ITALY
Laboratorio di Studi sulla ricerca e sulla documentazione, (Research and Documention Laboratory), Piazzale della Scienze 7, 00100 Rome

JAPAN
Japan Information Centre for Science and Technology, 2-5-2 Nagata-Cho, Chiyoda-ku, Tokyo

KOREA
Korea Scientific and Technological Information Centre (KORSTIC), 206-9 Cheongryangi-dong, Donbdaimum-ku, Seoul

MOROCCO
Centre National de Documentation, 5 Zankat Mostaghenem, B.P.826, Rabat-Mechouar

NETHERLANDS
Nederlands Instituut voor Documentatie en Registratuur (NIDER), 6 Willem Witsenplein, 's Gravenhage

NEW ZEALAND
Department of Scientific and Industrial Research Library, Wellington

NORWAY
Norsk Senter for Informasjon, (Norwegian Centre for Information), Forskningsveien 1, Oslo 3

POLAND
Centralny Instytut Informacji Naukowo-Technicznej i Ekonomicznej, (Institute for Scientific, Technical and Economic Information), Al. Niepodleglosci 188, 00-931 Warsaw

PORTUGAL
Instituto Nacional de Investigaçao Industrial, Centro de Documentaçao e Informaçao (National Institute for Industrial Research, Documentation and Information Centre), Rua Garcia de Orta 68-1, Lisbon 2

ROMANIA
Institutul National de Informaresi Documentare Stiintifica si Tehnica (INID) (National Institute for Scientific and Technical Information and Documentation), 27-9 Cosmonautilor Street, Bucharest

SPAIN
Centro de Información y Documentación, Joaquín Costa, 22, Madrid, 6

SWEDEN
Kungliga Tekniska Hogskolan (Royal Institute of Technology), Library-Documentation Department, S-100 44 Stockholm

SWITZERLAND
Eidgenössische Technische Hochschule (Bibliothek), Information and Documentation Centre, Leonhardstrasse 33, CH-8006 Zürich

TAIWAN (Formosa)
Scientific Documentation Centre, 128-1 Yen Chiu Road, Section 2, Nankang, Taipei

THAILAND
Thai National Documentation Centre, 196 Phahonyothin Road, Bang Khan, Bangkok 9

TURKEY
Scientific and Technical Documentation Centre of Turkey (TURDOK), Bayindir Sokak 33, Yenisehir-Ankara

YUGOSLAVIA
Referral Centre, University of Zagreb, 3 Trg marsala Tita, 41000 Zagreb

PART II

Work in Company-based Information Units

B. Yates

*Director, Australian National Science and Technology Library
Formerly Group Technical Communications Manager,
Pilkington Brothers Limited*

The author wishes to thank the Directors of Pilkington Brothers Limited and Dr D. S. Oliver, Director of Group Research and Development, for permission to publish this monograph. The author and editor wish to thank Mr W. T. Knox and Mr D. F. Lyle for helpful comments.

Introduction

WHAT REPORTS ARE FOR

Reports are now common working documents in many company-based information units. Their use and availability have increased dramatically since the Second World War, especially within information units dealing with scientific and technical subjects.

There are particular advantages usually associated with reports which make them valuable to an information unit: (1) reports are often the first indication or first record of work done; (2) reports are produced and published far more quickly than is usual for journal articles; (3) much report material never appears in any other published form; (4) if a report does form the basis of a subsequent journal article this article is rarely as comprehensive as the original report.

Reports exist, and are being published, which cover almost every conceivable topic in which an information unit could be interested. It must therefore be quite an unusual unit which has no interest in report literature or has no reports in its holdings.

DEFINITION OF REPORTS

There is no international (ISO) standard defining reports. *British Standard* 4811:1972 defines a report as 'A document which formally states the results of, or progress made with, research and/or development investigations, which, where appropriate, draws conclusions and makes recommendations, and which is initially submitted to the person or body for whom the work was done'.

The reference to research and/or development in this definition may perhaps lead the reader to assume that it is only usefully defining scientific research and development reports. A closer examination, however, will show that the definition is also suitable for reports written by commercial or government organizations covering marketing, economic, social or any other investigations.

The term 'unpublished' which is used in the title requires clarification. It is a term which is frequently used in information circles; however, it has not achieved a precise definition though most people attempting a definition would do so within a small range of meanings. For the purpose of this monograph unpublished reports are taken to be those which, when first distributed, are not available as of right to anyone who wishes to have a copy. Within the definition of a report given previously, the key phrase in this context is 'initially submitted to the person or body for whom the work was done'. This indicates that the work need not automatically be made available outside the organization for which the work was done. Virtually all reports are unpublished in the sense that publishers and the book trade have nothing to do with them, except for government and similar reports intended for anyone interested in the subjects covered.

The vast majority of reports prepared by or on behalf of industrial and commercial concerns are never published outside the organization itself. There are several possible reasons for this: (a) to protect concepts at an early stage of development; (b) to protect development work proceeding or concluded; (c) to protect detail of a developed technical idea before or after patenting; (d) to protect the commercial advantage to be gained from a new project, process or other development of a company's business or strategy; (e) to give the first benefit of results to collaborating organizations; (f) to safeguard information which has been given in confidence.

Whatever their origin, reports are vital tools which the information unit must use if it is to fulfil its task of helping to keep its parent body in the forefront of its chosen area of commercial or industrial activity.

STAFFING

Of course staff are needed to handle unpublished reports and an information unit needs to have good quality staff, for good staff are the essence of a successful unit. Good staff can make the poorest system work reasonably well whilst poor staff can ruin the best system. Good staff will be those with the right sort of personality, with a real interest in information work, a real motivation to do it well, and with the right sort of academic, scientific, technical, commercial or other background.

A good information unit by its very professionalism, by the way the staff handle themselves as well as the way they handle enquiries, establishes in managers a confidence in the service. It is this confidence which encourages managers to allow the information unit to have all the company's internal reports, including the most secret ones. This confidence is based on the feeling that all the staff of the unit have the company's interests at heart and are completely aware of the confidentiality of the reports entrusted to their care. This confidence can easily be shattered if the information unit becomes known as a source of gossip, particularly harmful gossip about people and happenings in the company.

AIMS OF THE MONOGRAPH

The purpose of this monograph is to suggest how the company-based information unit should organize itself to cope with report literature.

In a monograph of this nature it is not possible to set out in detail all the possible methods for dealing with every part of the operation but the intention is always to suggest alternatives whereever possible. However, it is of course more than likely that the author's particularly favoured method is presented more strongly than the others. To try to counter this some references are given at the end of the chapters and at the end of the monograph which will enable the reader to obtain more information or to get a different approach to a topic.

We have tried to consider areas in which reports originate inside and outside the organization, and then how the information unit can locate and obtain such reports. How such reports are produced is sketched out, without involving too much printing expertise, and then some indication is given of the meaning and origins of report serial numbers. The report in retrospect is useless if the information in it cannot be retrieved, so indexing is included, and then information dissemination and filing of reports. Finally the most important question of security control is dealt with.

CHAPTER I

The Origins of Reports and How to Find Them

The value of unpublished reports to any industrial or commercial concern can be very great indeed, for the simple reason that the information contained in such a report does not often appear in a periodical or in any other easily accessible form. When it does, often only a digest of the report or selected sections of it are printed, not the report in full. Thus in serving the organization to which it is responsible any information unit must constantly seek unpublished reports which are useful. Depending on the type of work being done by the parent company of the information unit, useful reports can originate from several sources particular to that company. However, they can nearly always be placed in one of two categories:—internal, that is—produced internally to the company, including subsidiaries; and external, or produced externally.

INTERNAL REPORTS

'In-house' is another way of saying 'internal'. In this instance, we are considering those reports which originate within the information unit's company. They may be written and reproduced or just reproduced by the company, the writing having been done elsewhere. The determining point is that someone in the company will have authorized the text and also authorized its issue.

Reports are produced at various locations within a company, and these may be extremely widely scattered in the case of a multinational company. Nevertheless such reports should logically be considered as 'in-house' reports. This type of company brings problems to the information unit wishing to obtain reports and these problems will be discussed in a later section.

Internal documents which come under the broad heading of reports can have several names; they can be called notes, memoranda, progress reports, project notes or reports, to instance merely a few names. They originate from almost any department within the company; production, research and development, marketing, sales, advertising, finance and planning. They can contain information on current work, analysis of future trends, outlines of future plans. They represent aspects of the company's knowledge in certain areas, and can be a clear guide to the company's strengths and weaknesses. As well as being formal reports of work done they can also be reports of discussions, visits or appraisals.

Two special forms of unpublished reports require highlighting. One is the minutes of committee meetings and the other is laboratory notebooks.

Minutes of committee meetings

In meetings, points of view are raised, plans made and decisions taken and this information will not be available from any other source. Reports usually cite references to other reports or to patents or articles in periodicals but rarely to minutes of meetings. Although largely regarded to be of current awareness value, in that they continually review a company's knowledge in certain areas, minutes are worth more consideration than the term 'current' implies. An example will suffice to illustrate this point. Let us imagine that a report analysing a certain commercial situation is presented to committee. During the discussion of the report more information is produced which reinforces, adds to, or changes the report in some way. Following the discussion some decision about action will probably be taken. All the information generated at the meeting is available in one place only, in the minutes of the meeting, but anyone requiring information in the subject area of the report requires both the report and the record of discussion in order to get a complete picture. It is often the case that the link between the report and the committee to which it was submitted is overlooked.

Minutes are thus extremely valuable unpublished reports. They are often not indexed in any 'in-house' system and the information in them which can be very important, is lost. Methods of providing a means of retrieving this information will be discussed later.

Laboratory notebooks

Laboratory notebooks are issued to scientists and technicians in industrial and government laboratories. They are used to record the day-to-day work done by the individual and therefore predate the report proper.

Laboratories often issue guidelines indicating how information is to be recorded in the laboratory notebook to ensure that all information is recorded in an understandable form. Since the information in such notebooks could be used during patent litigation many laboratories require each entry in the notebook to be dated, signed by the individual who has done the work and countersigned by his supervisor.

It may also happen that the work recorded in the notebook is never written up in the form of a report, and therefore it could remain as the only documentary source of that piece of work. Laboratory notebooks are therefore a particular, but equally important, type of unpublished report. Whereas it is not usual for a notebook to provide conclusions to an investigation, it does however provide more detail on the method used in the investigation and the results obtained. Hence, it is a most useful document for checking the results of the investigation and the way in which the investigation was progressed. This is particularly useful in retrospect to check that the right conclusions have been drawn in the reports issued.

Source of internal reports

Internal reports, then, are records of work done in or on behalf of a company or commercial organization, and in the main, this work will have been done for commercial or technical reasons. For these reasons the report is not likely to be made available to anyone outside the company except in special circumstances which will be considered later. Some reports contain so much vital information to a company that their distribution will be restricted within the company. (Treatment of this type of report is to be found in the section on security control – p. 280.) For internal reports there is only one possible source, the company itself, whereas for other reports there are often several sources: libraries, clearing houses, reports centres, etc.

The information in such a report will not be available elsewhere, and if the information is not available when discussions are taking place in the company on particular topics, this could lead to seriously incorrect and damaging decisions being taken. For any company its own reports are the most important reports of all and therefore every information unit must ensure that it has a copy of every internal report. To further emphasize the importance of these reports, it should be remembered that the reports can represent the investment of the company in research and/or development, licence fees, etc.

EXTERNAL REPORTS

External reports can have many origins and many sources, some of which will be considered here. Each particular information unit in each company will place a different value on the different types of reports, depending on its organization's activities. The origins of external reports therefore cannot be categorized in any order of importance. It is, however, a most useful exercise for each information unit to analyse those areas and organizations which may be producing relevant useful reports and for it to consider possible ways of knowing of these reports and of obtaining copies as necessary.

Reports of other companies

Several companies, or two companies, may agree to exchange information regarding certain technical or commercial activities. Usually the agreement is in the form of a legal document, usually signed by an authorized representative of each participating company, which lays down the areas in which the collaboration is to be effective. Such collaboration often leads to the exchange of reports which are naturally confidential to the parties to the agreement. Since each company has specifically chosen and agreed a technical or commercial area, it tries to ensure that it receives information from the other participants, at least equal to that which it provides, and certainly that it receives all information to which it is entitled. An information unit then should treat these reports as secondary only to its own.

Some reports which companies produce are made widely available without much restriction. Possible reasons for this are:

(a) the report contains no information which can in any way be used to the detriment of the company (in other words the company's competitors cannot gain any advantage from the knowledge, but the report could be useful to others); (b) the technical activities described in the report have already been patented; (c) the company is seeking to disclose information which it is not going to patent but for which it wishes to establish a claim of 'prior art', that is so that it can claim to have been the first company to have had the idea and made it work, thus preventing any other company from patenting the idea; (d) the company may feel that open release could benefit it in terms of good public relations.

Consultancy reports

It is not unusual for companies to commission reports to be produced by external agencies on a consultancy basis. A market assessment may be done by an agency for a fee or a private technical laboratory may be paid to do certain research or testing work. The results of the work will be written up in the form of a report, which will be confidential to the company or companies paying the fee.

There are several agencies (Predicasts in the United States and the Economist Intelligence Unit in the United Kingdom are just two examples) which produce reports, usually of a market research nature, in anticipation of a demand. These reports are then sold to anyone who is prepared to pay the necessary fee. These are on the border line of our definition of unpublished reports. They are not usually available from any library source, though details of their existence are usually freely available. Certainly they are reports, they are available and they can be most useful.

Stanford Research Institute Long Range Planning Service Reports are also of this kind. The topics of the reports are selected and treated so as to maintain a balance in five major categories: markets, industry, technical, business environment, and management and planning. The June 1972 *Newsletter* of the Long Range Planning Service reminds members that reports are confidential to members and they must sign an agreement not to circulate reports outside their own organization.

Another example is the reports produced by the various working groups of the European Industrial Research Management

Association (EIRMA). These reports deal with topics of interest to those concerned with the direction of research and development activities and are available to members only. Even the topics covered by the reports are not generally known to non-members.

Government reports

Agencies of the United States Government produce thousands of reports in a year and many of these reports are made available to non-government enquirers. Reports for the United Kingdom and other governments do not equal these in number but reports are produced and some of them are available on request. Some reports are sold through the printing office or 'stationery office' of the particular country. The *Monthly Catalog of US Government Publications* and the United Kingdom *Daily List*, with its monthly and annual cumulations contain details of these. The monthly listings are by originating department and there are subject indexes, though experience leads one to be rather careful of these. The indexing is done in little detail.

The reports listed here are only a small proportion of the total produced. One can think of the vast number of reports produced concerning military research, nuclear power research, as well as those concerned with commercial and financial matters which never reach beyond a very strictly controlled group of organizations. These organizations will in general be those companies who are doing work on contract for a government agency and will thus need the information in order to do their work properly, or those companies undertaking a joint exercise with government who are therefore entitled to the information produced as a result of the work. In either case access to the reports will be strictly controlled within the company. This measure will be laid down either by the government, by the company or both.

The range and scope of government reports and government-sponsored reports is surprising to those who have not had cause to look in this direction. The reports cover technical, commercial, economic and social subjects. As some indication the following titles have been taken from recent listings:

(a) Office of the Assistant Secretary for Policy, Plans and International Affairs (DOT), Washington D.C.
PB 236 701/9GA

Economic Aspects of Refinery and Deep-Water Port Location in the United States: volume 1, Report.
May 1974. pp. 344.
(b) Federal Highway Administration, Materials Division, Washington D.C.
PB 236 481/8GA
Concrete Patching Materials.
April 1974. pp. 41.
(c) United Kingdom Atomic Energy Authority, Culcheth, Lancashire, England.
SRD-R. 30
Second Survey of Defects in Pressure Vessels Built to High Standards of Construction and its Relevance to Nuclear Primary Circuits.
1974. pp. 35

Trade association and research association reports

Regardless of whether these associations are commercially or technically based, they often produce reports for the benefit of their members only. It may be that after a few years, when the report becomes dated, it will be released for wider distribution, but in the first instance it is certainly unpublished.

University reports

One cannot say that all the work done by universities for industry and commerce is unpublished. The university may well reserve the right to publish some information regarding the work either immediately, or after a patent has been granted, or after the company has had the benefit of the work for a certain time.

Theses

A university thesis can be considered as a special kind of report and can be, and is, useful to commerce and industry as the following examples taken from recent listings will indicate.

(a) A. T. Stewart
Some deformation studies in two phase alloys.
University of Oxford, 1972.

(b) S. Jeckovich
An economic study of the US glass industry 1899–1947. University of Pittsburgh, 1961.

The existence of theses can be found from certain specialized sources, discussed in Part I of this book (pp. 36–8, 72), and they are available from specialized services or from the university accepting the thesis. In the latter case it is not unusual for the university to provide a copy only on loan, to put restrictions on the use of the thesis, to forbid its being copied and to lay down stringent rules governing where the thesis may be read.

Conference papers

At first sight it may be considered that conference papers have nothing to do with reports. It is not suggested that they should be considered as reports just because they are a report to a conference, but rather that since some of the material is valuable, they should be considered as a specialized source of information. Many papers given to conferences are never published in full either because no proceedings are published, or the organizers feel that discussion at the conference would be inhibited if the paper and discussions were to be published and have deliberately announced that nothing will be published. Another reason could be because the author of the paper does not submit it to any journal or periodical for acceptance. Surveys by Hanson & Janes, and by Liebesny have shown that only about half the published papers from a sample selection of conferences were noted in English-language abstracting journals.

Thus information which could be valuable is being continually lost. Fortunately there are sources which guide the enquirer to at least some conference papers and these are indicated in Part I (pp. 109, 128).

FORM OF REPORTS

Reports from various sources come in different sizes, layouts and typefaces. They come in 'hard copy' i.e. full size copy, microfiche, microfilm and magnetic tape, and information units must be prepared to store these and provide a means for readers to use them.

Storage is considered elsewhere and there are no real problems in the use of hard copy. Microfiche, however, is an entirely different matter. There are many microfiche readers and reader/printers available and it is not the purpose of this monograph to suggest the best one to buy. The best advice will come from discussions with other information units or from advisory organizations such as the National Reprographic Centre for documentation, Hatfield, Herts., England. This serves its members only; membership costs £12 a year in the UK and £14 a year overseas for the basic service.

A useful listing of microfiche-viewing equipment available in America was made by Gordon and published in 1971.

The main problem with reports on microfiche is still that of the reluctance of the user to use this form. As more and more reports are becoming available only, or only cheaply, in microfiche form, the situation will probably soon arise that the user has available to him only reports on microfiche.

Reports on magnetic tape present no problems in that there are many acceptable types of machines for playing the tape. Users however are again somewhat reluctant to use this type of report in that they cannot skim through it but must listen to all, or most of, the tape at least once.

HOW TO LOCATE REPORTS

Internal

A measure of the standing of an information unit in any company is the number and variety of the company internal reports it holds. Does it hold a copy of every report produced? Does it receive the minutes of every committee which meets in the company?

The lack of an internal document is very serious. It cuts out important information which no amount of published information can replace. The value of such irreplaceable information has earlier been highlighted. It is thus incumbent on any information unit to ensure that it receives all such reports. The simplest way is for senior management in the organization to direct that reports will be written in a certain style at certain dates in the life of an investigation and to stipulate who should receive copies. Another effective way is for the information unit to have a management link with the 'in-house' printers and in this way to know of all reports being produced, to obtain copies and to check the distribution of them. If an organization has a project-planning system then the system should be generating signals at various stages of the project, and if the information unit arranges to receive these signals then it can easily check what reports have been or will be written about the project and can obtain copies.

Committee minutes should similarly have their distribution specified by senior management, but if this does not happen then the information unit must be in a position to know what committees exist in the company and, knowing this, to approach the chairmen or secretaries in order to receive copies regularly. The case to receive committee minutes may need to be made forcibly to a chairman but sound arguments can be made from the ideas outlined earlier.

Committees are empowered to, and often do, call for special reports which may be considered to be outside the project planning system. It is quite possible that these could slip through the net of the information unit unless it receives the committee minutes; it is often only in this medium that reference is made to the report.

Laboratory notebooks and the information they contain, as has been said previously, are most important documents in any organization and an information unit should have complete access to them. One efficient way of doing this is for the information unit to be responsible for the issuing of such notebooks. Thus, when a notebook becomes full, its user would bring it back to the information unit to obtain another. The information unit can then check what information in the notebook forms part of a report. Reports should refer to laboratory notebooks so that additional information can be obtained, if required, by anyone reading the report. Of the rest perhaps some is routine test work which does not need indexing and perhaps some is novel work which requires indexing. This can be done and an index entry made referring to the laboratory notebook.

If the information unit does not issue the notebook, it should always be in a position which enables it to check a completed notebook before a new one is issued. It is open to argument whether an information unit should hold the completed notebooks or whether they should be retained by the section whose work is recorded therein. On balance they are probably more useful if located in the issuing section, particularly if the section needs to make use of the information fairly frequently.

External

Reports produced externally to the company, but yet to which it is entitled for instance because of a licensing agreement, reach the company in various ways, not usually directly through the information unit. If a joint project is being undertaken with government it is usual for the company to appoint a leader of its team and for this leader to be the initial recipient of reports relating to the project from government sources. This leader will undoubtedly show the reports to some or all members of the team but he may not, and most certainly initially will not, think of showing them to the information unit; least of all will he consider depositing them in the information unit. Thus to be aware of all this valuable information coming in from this type of external source, the information unit must know all the leaders of collaborative projects and all leaders of sponsored work.

Reports from collaborative or sponsored work or received as a result of licences are particular types of external reports. There are many more without the restrictions necessarily surrounding these and since no organization is completely self-sufficient on the internal resources it has available, it must capitalize on the work and information available from these external sources. It needs to do this to avoid duplicating expensive technical or commercial work, to monitor activities in areas peripheral to its main business, and to obtain advance warning of social, economic or commercial developments which may affect its future.

The major abstract journals tend to ignore those reports which lie outside well defined and easily identified series. Reasons for this include: (a) existing services are only just able to keep up with conventionally published literature, and as report literature is so difficult to obtain it would be impossible to control efficiently; (b) even if report literature were covered by abstract journals, it would be extremely difficult for the reader to obtain many reports listed; (c) reports have a relatively short 'life' and in many cases are not worth listing; (d) unedited technical reports in which the material is not adequately presented should not be considered as part of the open literature.

Though these reasons may have been pertinent at the time (1959) they were made by M. and S. Herner, the comments regarding the availability of reports are no longer valid and the comment about the short life of reports would seem to have been arguable even at the time it was written. Examples of publications containing report listings are given in Part 1 (pp. 120-8).

Pandex is a tape service having a data-base containing US Government reports as well as scientific and technical books and scientific, technical and medical journals. Eighteen per cent of the input to the data-base is taken from government reports. It is produced by CCM Information Corporation, 800 Third Avenue, New York City, New York 10022, USA.

References

GORDON, R. F. Microfiche viewing equipment guide. Alexandria, Va., Defense Documentation Center, 1971. *Report* AD 734 400.

HANSON, C. W. *and* JANES, M. Coverage by abstracting journals of conference papers. *Journal of Documentation*, 17(3). March, 1961. 143-149.

HERNER, M. *and* HERNER, S. The current status of the government research report in the United States of America. *Unesco Bulletin for Libraries*, 13(8-9). August-September, 1959. 187-196.

LIEBESNY, F. Lost information: unpublished conference papers. *INTERNATIONAL CONFERENCE ON SCIENTIFIC INFORMATION, WASHINGTON, 1958. Proceedings*. Washington, National Academy of Sciences – National Research Council, 1959. 475-479.

SELECTED BIBLIOGRAPHY

ASLIB. Information department. Report literature in the UK. *Aslib Proceedings*, 25(8). August, 1973. 330-334.

CARROLL, V. D., *ed*. Survey of scientific and technical tape services. New York, American Institute of Physics, 1970. pp. 64.

FINER, R. A guide to selected computer based information services. London, Aslib, 1972. pp. 113.

CHAPTER 2

Editing, Reproducing and Numbering Reports

TYPES OF REPORT

In any fairly large commercial organization there will be several types of unpublished reports produced on a routine basis. These will range from technical memoranda to records of technical visits, technical notes and technical reports. The precise purpose of each of these documents will vary with each organization although in general terms technical memoranda will be the least important from our point of view. Since they are rapid and often informal communications which do not require editing, they can be considered to fall outside the scope of this chapter. Records of technical visits and technical notes are more formal documents, generally used as vehicles for transmitting brief technical information rapidly. These documents do not normally involve the intervention of a technical editor but they will be subject to some form of vetting or approval system laid down by the particular establishment; they will also carry some identification number for retrieval purposes and they are likely to be handled or stored by the information unit within the company.

The technical report is a formal document which records the results of a research and/or development investigation and where appropriate draws conclusions and makes recommendations (*BS* 4811). It is this document which will normally require some editorial treatment and it will usually be issued as part of a series and will carry an identification number. It will probably be bound into a semi-stiff cover and will have a wider circulation than the other types of document, generally including senior research management, patents, licensing and planning departments as well as the central information unit.

It will normally be the editor's responsibility to define the type of document which will fall in each particular category and also, in the case of technical reports, to allot the actual document number.

THE EDITORIAL FUNCTION

Some organizations will have one person, normally called the Technical Editor, whose principal function is to edit and control the reproduction of the company's internal technical reports. In other organizations this responsibility may be a part-time duty of the Information Officer, Librarian, Communications Officer or some similar person. Brookes' book is a useful guide.

In those organizations which do not feel the need for such an editor, its technical notes and reports will be processed through some form of established vetting procedure which will take account of technical validity. It may be considered appropriate to sacrifice final editorial polish and some degree of standardization in the interests of rapid communication. In these cases the onus lies more heavily on the author's immediate manager to ensure that the report is technically accurate and also that its presentation meets the company's specifications. The manager will also inevitably become involved in some form of editorial correction and to a lesser extent will perform the duties of a technical editor.

If the company has an editorial department, this will normally consist of a full-time editor and possibly a subeditor or clerk plus two or more technical typists and technical illustrators, and the department may well also include a reprographic section in which the reports are finally printed, collated and bound.

Forms for recording progress

To maintain an efficient editorial department the Technical Editor will need to set up a procedural system for report presentation. He is likely to use some form of internal progress sheet such as the one shown in Figure 1. This will indicate when the report was first received, how many illustrations and photographs there are and the various dates for editing, typing and producing illustrative material. The most important part of the sheet is the deadline which will be fixed by the Technical Editor. The last date on the sheet should be earlier than or the same as the deadline date.

Report no._____	Deadline [_____]
Title_____	
Author(s)_____	
Department_____	
Manuscript received_____	
Draft to editor_____	Edited and discussed_____ with author
No. of illustrations_____	No. of photographs_____
For camera copy typing_____	To author for checking_____
	Approved_____
Illustrations ordered_____	To author for checking_____
	Approved_____
Photographs ordered_____	Received_____
Covers ordered_____	OK for printing_____
Received from printer_____	
Checked and distributed_____	

FIG. 1. Internal Progress Sheet for an Editorial Department.

If reports are to be processed efficiently and effectively, each stage on the progress sheet will be allotted a certain time. On average the total time for individual reports, including printing, is four to five weeks.

It is often found useful to display the progress of each report on some kind of wall chart so that at a glance the editor can tell to what stage each report has progressed and, if there are any hold-ups, where they are occurring. The chart may be broken down into sections indicating the various stages through which the report will pass such as editing, typing, illustration preparation, etc. Different colours of ink can be used to indicate dates when the job is begun and to be completed and a section included for the person responsible for the work to initial the completion date. If the department is to maintain its credibility, particularly in the eyes of the authors with whom it deals, it must stick rigidly to its production schedules.

It is also common to use some sort of vetting or approval form (Figure 2) which acts as a routing sheet for the draft report before it reaches the editorial department for final processing. In addition to the report number, the title, author, and his department, the form will detail by title the various managers whose signature of approval is required. It will also probably contain a section to indicate the security grading of the document and the name of the person who has allotted the grading. A final section will be reserved for the signature of a senior manager or director if the report is to be sent outside the company. When the report has been through the technical and security vetting system, it will then be passed to the editorial department for copy editing and sub-editing in preparation for printing.

Editing unpublished reports

The fundamental role of the editor is to review the paper from a detached and objective standpoint; in fact the editor must try to become the intended reader and ask of the text the sort of questions the reader is likely to ask. He will not primarily be concerned with technical accuracy since this will already have been checked by the author's colleagues and managers. However, any fault in logical exposition may highlight some technical ambiguity or gap.

With this in mind, the editor will, during the first reading, go

Title			
Document No.			
Author(s)	Author(s) location and department		
	Security grading* 1 2 3 4	Security grading allocated by:	Complete this block if the document is security-graded and attach this vetting form to the manuscript. I certify that no other draft copies, including stencils of the document, are in existence. Signature: Date:
Author's signature		Date:	
Section head approval		Date:	
Departmental manager approval		Date:	
Report distributed		Date:	
Vetting form returned to information unit with required no. of copies of report			Date:
Director approval if report is to go outside the company		Signature: Date:	

*Delete whichever is not appropriate

FIG. 2. Approval Form for Reports.

through the text completely so that he gets an overall 'feel' for the subject matter of the report. This will enable him to judge the cohesion and logical exposition of ideas and to check whether the paper achieves its stated aims. He will be critical of the structure of the text and the balance of content. As a result of the first reading he may re-read certain parts of the report again, possibly as a prelude to some structural rearrangement to improve the juxtaposition and development of ideas. He will also at this stage examine the relevance and organization of any tables and illustrations which might be included and consider whether points could be made more succinctly through some form of illustration. The amount of reshaping required will vary enormously from author to author. On occasions the editor may also discover that certain critical steps in the development of the text have been omitted, generally because the author is too close to his work. He will mark these and raise them together with any proposed reshaping during a subsequent editorial session with the author.

The first reading by the editor will be one of assimilation and structural appraisal, so that he will initially pay little attention to the finer detail of language. This he will normally cover in a second reading, during which he will deal with grammatical inaccuracies, spelling errors, inconsistencies in style and appropriate levels of language, including abstractions and verbosity as well as jargon, colloquialisms and slang. He will also check tables and illustrations for obvious numerical inaccuracy, poor layout or inconsistencies in captions.

Having made a broad general examination and a close detailed examination of the report, the editor usually follows this up with an editorial session with the author. During this session he will need to exercise diplomacy, tact and subtlety if he is to gain first the respect of the author and then his agreement to any changes that the editor proposes should be made. This is perhaps the most difficult stage of all and one which must be handled with great delicacy and sensitivity by the editor, so that when it is finished, both author and editor will feel that they have achieved something positive and constructive.

When any agreed alterations have been made the editor will re-read once again the final text to check on continuity and accuracy of any corrections made and then he will finally subedit the report so that it is suitable to be prepared for printing. This subediting will involve 'mechanical' details such as weight and balance of headings, indentations and general layout and will include, for some printing processes, instructions on text width and type style and size.

REPRODUCING REPORTS

There are basically three ways in which reports can be reproduced. They may be run off on an office stencil machine or they may be printed using either the hot-metal or offset-lithography processes. Since we are dealing specifically with unpublished reports only, it is unlikely that many will be reproduced by the letterpress hot-metal process; this is generally reserved for commercial printing of what we might consider as openly published material. Since most unpublished reports are reproduced within the organization from which they originate, they are more likely to be reproduced by either some form of stencil or some form of in-house offset-litho duplicating system.

Reproduction from stencils

Wax stencils of, for example, the Gestetner type, are used most frequently in small establishments. They are the simplest method of reproducing documents and machines for reproducing documents from stencils are normally standard equipment in the small office. This method is suitable for the reproduction of up to five hundred copies of a document which may then be bound into preprinted covers.

Advantages. Stencilling is a fairly rapid and simple method of reproducing a document to an acceptable level of presentation. It does not require a great deal of operator skill and capital outlay is very low.

Disadvantages. There is a tendency for stencils to tear, especially if not handled carefully in the typewriter. Also the method uses fairly thick absorbent paper which results in a less attractive standard of presentation and does not give a professional finish. A common difficulty with this method is that many closed letters such as o, a, d, p, etc., tend to fill in with ink if the stencil is not properly cut. Once a cut stencil has been run on a machine it is virtually impossible to re-use it and consequently if further copies of a report are required at some future date – say ten years on – then either new stencils have to be cut or the original stencilled copy has to be photocopied with a resultant loss in quality and often of legibility.

Offset lithography

By far the most widely used method of reproducing unpublished reports is offset lithography. It is now common for many organizations, including even fairly small ones, to have their own printing department which reproduces all the internally-produced documentation, ranging from simple standard forms to reports and even special booklets. There is a large variety of printing machines on the market, ranging from fairly small manually controlled office machines through medium-output machines with manual, semi-automatic and fully automatic control to the larger machines, capable of taking A3 sheets and above, and also able to provide full colour reproduction. The size and versatility of the machine chosen will depend to a large extent on the amount of work passing through the print shop and the complexity of demand. Some of the larger companies have complete printing departments that would rival the facilities offered by a commercial printer. It is more usual however to have a small duplicating/print section with one or two machines plus collating and binding facilities. A process camera for plate preparation is also required although some of the smaller units reproduce from electrostatic paper masters, which can give quite acceptable quality. Camera-ready copy, that is the final draft ready for printing, is frequently typed in the editorial department on specially prepared paper, which may be coated on one side to give a sharper contrast. This paper may be marked in a yellow non-reproducible ink, to show the acceptable areas within which to type and the positioning of page numbers. To improve standardization and finished quality still further electric typewriters are preferred for report preparation.

Advantages. Offset litho offers a high degree of standardization and reproducibility. It gives professional-quality reproduction at a comparatively low cost per copy and work can be reproduced rapidly by the small internal unit. In addition, since printing is done by the organization producing the report, control is retained close to the point of origination within the company and no external correspondence is necessary. Metal plates can be retained so that reproduction at any future date becomes a simple matter of recovering the plates from storage and putting them back on to the print machine. If paper masters are used for printing, the camera copy may be retained in storage for any future further reproduction.

Disadvantages. An in-house offset litho unit will involve a company initially in a high capital expenditure and space requirements will also be fairly large. Furthermore a certain degree of printing skill will be needed.

Paper quality and sizes

All reports should be produced on a fairly good quality of paper suitable for the chosen reproduction process (cartridge paper of 112 g/m^2 weight is acceptable for offset litho work, printed two sides). The paper size should conform to the principal (A) series of the ISO recommended trimmed sizes. These sizes are detailed in *British Standard BS* 4000:1968. In general A4 page size (297mm × 210mm) should be used although on occasions it may be permitted to use A3 size (420mm × 297mm) folded over for large tables or graphs.

NUMBERING REPORTS

Series codes

Report series codes and numbers serve as a means of identification of a report. Reports can be ordered by this code and number: they can also be filed by it and the code and number should be quoted as part of a bibliographic reference. This presupposes that each report-series code and number is unique and that no other document will bear the same code and number. This happy state of affairs does not always exist in reality, for there is no central body allotting report codes, but it is surprising that from the vast number of reports already in existence and being continuously produced, there is not more duplication of series codes.

Most series codes when properly understood identify the originating body fairly precisely. This may not be immediately obvious to the newcomer handling reports for the first time, but most organizations have gone to much trouble to devise an easy, workable and recognizable method of allocating serial numbers to their reports. Series codes in several cases start with an alphabetical designation which identifies the originating body, e.g.,

SLAC	Stanford University Linear Accelerator Center
AERE	Atomic Energy Research Establishment
NAMRU	Naval Medical Research Unit
ORNL	Oak Ridge National Laboratory

Serial report numbers and other codes

This initial designation can then be followed by either a number, being the next number in a sequential series indicating the total number of reports issued, or by a further alphabetical code indicating the particular department responsible for the authorship of the document. In the latter case a number, from the sequential series, as noted previously, will follow. There may also be interspersed somewhere in the series code an indication of the year of issue, e.g. 73 indicating 1973, 74 indicating 1974. Finally there may be some indication of the type of report presented, PR – progress report, R – report, TN – technical note, TM – technical memorandum.

Examples

Some examples will illustrate these points:

(a) IC – AERO – 72 – 10
    IC   = Imperial College London
    AERO = Aeronautics Department
    72   = year of issue 1972
    10   = number of the report in the sequence.

IC – AERO – 72 – 10 is the report serial code and number for a report from the Aeronautics Department, Imperial College,

London, issued in March, 1972, and entitled 'Two more wind tunnels driven by aerofoil type centrifugal blowers'.

(b) HSRI – 71 – 103
        HSRI = Highway Safety Research Institute, Michigan University
        71 = Year of issue 1971
        103 = number of the report in the sequence.

HSRI – 71 – 103 is the report serial code and number for a report from the Highway Safety Research Institute, Michigan University, issued in June, 1971, and entitled 'Deployable head restraints'.

(c) SU – SEL – 71 – 038
        SU = Stanford University
        SEL = Electronics Laboratory
        71 = year of issue 1971
        038 = number of the report in the sequence.

SU – SEL – 71 – 038 is the report serial code and number for a report from the Electronics Laboratory, Stanford University, issued in June, 1971, and entitled 'Fault equivalence in sequential machines'.

The examples given are fairly straightforward but the reader should not be misled into thinking that all reports which he receives, or all reports which he is trying to trace, will have such easily identifiable series codes.

An information unit often has to try to trace work done by a particular laboratory. If the series codes that the laboratory uses are known, then a depository library can provide any reports it holds which bear these codes. If the codes are not known then to try to find them can be a long task. The serial and corporate author indexes of listings such as *Government Research Announcements (GRA)* and *R & D Abstracts* can be checked to try to get a lead to the serial code. There is a list of codes, prepared by Godfrey & Redman which could also be helpful.

Creating an internal series code and numbering system

If an information unit is given the task of devising a coding and numbering system for reports produced within the company, the method by which this is done could vary depending on the size and nature of the company. However, general guidelines can be suggested which if followed will at least lead to a rational system being employed.

The first and perhaps most necessary question to ask is – is a series code system required at all? In a small company it may well be satisfactory if each document merely bears a number, in a sequential series; there may be no need to indicate the department responsible for the report, or its location. In this case the information unit could allocate the report number and thus be in a position to ensure that it obtains copies of all internal reports. In a medium or large company there could well be a stronger case for adopting a series code. If this is so then one has to consider what needs to be indicated in the series code. Associated with the code should be a number. Whether there is a date associated with this or not, is not usually very important, but a firm decision must be taken whether to include such a date code or not. There will of course be a date in the body of the report indicating when it was written. To improve filing it will be found better to have the date code before the number code, e.g. 72/147 not 147/72.

The main problems come in deciding the alphabetical designations to be used. Should each works or department be designated and if so, how? In a medium/large company on one site it will be found useful just to designate each issuing department but in a large company having many works or laboratories, each works or laboratory should be designated and each issuing department within these works also designated. Wherever possible the alphabetical designations should be meaningful in their own right. Thus if a works is in Washington it is far better to use WA than AB to indicate this. Needless to say, each designation should be unique so that it immediately identifies one, and only one, location.

Having worked out a scheme which is acceptable to management, the information unit should publicize the scheme. In a large organization adopting such a system, the information unit cannot issue every report with its appropriate series code and number but it should certainly be in a position to see that whoever is responsible for doing this is well trained in the methods to be used. It should also ensure that it receives a copy of the report. A series code and numbering scheme which has been properly thought out during the initial stages will be capable of dealing with any changes in a company situation where new departments or works are created.

References

BRITISH STANDARDS INSTITUTION. Specification for sizes of papers and boards. London, 1968. pp. 20. *BS* 4000.

BRITISH STANDARDS INSTITUTION. The presentation of research and development reports. London, 1972. pp. 18. *BS* 4811.

BROOKES, B. C., *ed.* Editorial practice in libraries. London, Aslib, 1961. pp. 204.

FEDERAL SUPPLY SERVICE (USA). Diazotype paper sheet sizes. Washington, 1968. pp. 2. *Federal Standard* No. 131.

GODFREY, L. E. *and* REDMAN, K. F., *ed.* Dictionary of report series codes. 2nd ed. New York, Special Libraries Association, 1973. ISBN 0 87111 209 4. pp. 645.

INTERNATIONAL ORGANIZATION FOR STANDARDIZATION (ISO). Methods of expression of dimensions of processed writing paper and certain classes of printed matter. Geneva, 1963. pp. 4. *ISO R* 353.

——. Paper and board: folders and files. Geneva, 1967. p. 1. *ISO R* 623.

——. Paper: articles of stationery that includes detachable sheets, overall trimmed sizes, Geneva, 1967. pp. 2. *ISO R* 618.

——. Paper, untrimmed sizes, designation and tolerances. Geneva, 1966. p. 1. *ISO R* 479.

——. Paper, untrimmed stock sizes for the ISO A series, ISO primary range. Geneva, 1966. pp. 2. *ISO R* 478.

——. Paper, untrimmed stock sizes for the ISO A series, ISO supplementary range. Geneva. 1966. p. 1. *ISO R* 593.

——. Trimmed sizes of writing paper and certain classes of printed matter. Geneva, 1961. pp. 6. *ISO R* 216.

CHAPTER 3

Cataloguing, Classification, Indexing and Dissemination

CATALOGUING

It is becoming the rule rather than the exception for the industrial information unit holding a substantial number of reports to keep its reports in a separate collection with a separate catalogue, and not to integrate them with other library material. This is because reports are usually written about a highly specific subject, and they would tend to bulk out the library catalogue at certain points. Separate storage and cataloguing also assist in controlling access to reports and overcoming the problems of maintaining consistent treatment when cataloguing. The solution is to provide access to the reports only via the information unit which will search the catalogues and other indexes for the report. Since the unit has either done the cataloguing or indexing itself, or is familiar with the catalogues and indexes obtained from other sources, then it is in the best position effectively to find the report.

Some standard guides to report cataloguing have been produced, such as those by the US Committee on Scientific and Technical Information, the Atomic Energy Commission, and the National Technical Information Service, which should be consulted, and from these and other sources an information unit would be well advised to produce a guide for its own use. It should know the *Anglo-American cataloguing rules*, but these are for cataloguing general material.

The guides suggest that for the description and identification of technical reports the required elements of cataloguing are: (a) accession and/or report serial number; (b) corporate author; (c) title; (d) personal author(s); (e) date; (f) pagination; (g) contract or grant number; (h) availability; (i) subject index entries; (j) security classification.

It is up to the individual information unit to decide which of these are necessary as headings. The object of a catalogue is to be a useful record and there is no point in recording information which is not useful.

A report will usually require multiple entries in the catalogue under the names of the personal authors, the corporate author and under the subject, report number and contract number and a clear decision will have to be taken regarding the filing of the corporate author entry. Will the Mellon Institute be filed as such or under the University of Pittsburgh, Mellon Institute? Will the Building Research Establishment be filed as such or under Department of the Environment, Building Research Establishment? Government departments and Ministries often change their names and it is important to ensure that the catalogue contains appropriate cross reference entries.

CLASSIFICATION AND INDEXING

All collections of reports need to have subject indexes associated with them in order to be able to exploit fully the information contained in them. Any information unit should be spending a considerable portion of its time indexing reports, certainly its own company reports, so that it can provide in-depth subject access.

Methods

The method used for classification or indexing again depends on the needs of the individual information unit. In a widely based collection which does not cover the subject in great depth, there may be good reasons for employing a classification scheme such as UDC, which provides scope for searching around a subject and related subjects in other fields. There may be grounds for using a faceted classification system as was used by the English Electric Company in the United Kingdom, an alphabetical subject index, a computer-based system using computer-controlled keywords or there may be grounds for using a post-co-ordinate indexing system based on the use of keywords from a controlled vocabulary chosen by human indexers. It is now probably true that the majority of information units use the post-co-ordinate system for indexing their report collection and several descriptions of such indexes have been recorded in the literature (see Selected Bibliography).

It is not the purpose of this monograph to deal with indexing techniques and, as has been indicated, there are many publications which will provide information on which a decision can be taken as to what method to employ. However, there are several points to be borne in mind when indexing unpublished reports and these points are valid whether the indexing and retrieval methods depend on computer, optical coincidence, UDC or other techniques.

(a) Internally produced reports and other reports which carry a security grading, or have been obtained as a result of an exchange agreement between companies, should be indexed to a greater depth than published reports. Such indexing is best done by those who have to use the index to answer inquiries and who have relevant subject knowledge, though it is only fair to say that research being done on indexing procedures may disprove the need for detailed subject knowledge. There is only one point of access to this type of report and that is the internal information index. There are several access points to published reports and no information unit should waste its resources indexing material when an external service can do it speedily and effectively and at least at similar cost.

The internal report is the product of many man-hours of work and probably is the end point of a large capital outlay. All the features described in a report may well need considering for indexing. The indexer must try to anticipate any future questions which might be posed to the index. This will include considering the report from different angles: for example, the publicity manager will vaguely remember the report from one angle, the sales controller from another and the warehousing manager from yet another.

(b) Unpublished reports may include the names of companies visited, people seen, trade names, etc. These need to be brought out in the indexing process. If one is using computer methods for information retrieval, the storage facilities will be capable of absorbing these items but if an optical-coincidence method is used then it is advisable to consider the frequency with which certain names or trade marks are likely to occur. If they are not likely to occur regularly then there is no point in bulking up the system by having an optical coincidence card for them. It is just as effective

Cataloguing, Classification, Indexing, Dissemination

to use a plain card, with the relevant accession or report number written on it. This method can be criticized in that it is creating two retrieval banks where there should, at least in theory, be only one. In practice one would find little possible advantage, indeed quite the reverse, in filling the main system with infrequently used information.

(c) Contract and/or job numbers are sometimes referred to either in the title, text or reference number of the document, and questions can be posed as to what information exists regarding work on a certain contract or job. It is useful therefore as appropriate to have a contract and/or job number index of a simple type such as can be constructed on 125 × 75 mm cards. The heading will be the contract or job number and the appropriate number for the document will be written on the card.

(d) It should be an infallible rule that the various indexes produced should be compatible with each other to provide either greater depth or easier access. For example, the subject index, author index and trade names index should be of the same type to allow easy cross linkage.

Centralized versus decentralized indexing

In a large, widely-spread, national or multinational organization decisions will have to be taken whether indexing should be done centrally or whether each issuing location should do its own indexing according to a standard pattern. Theoretically, centralized indexing may be advisable, but in almost every case, practical considerations will dictate that each issuing location should index its own reports and then link into a company-wide index, either by exchange of computer tapes, index cards or printed indexes. No matter what standard procedures and checks are introduced, this decentralized procedure does lead to a lack of consistency in indexing and therefore a possible loss in recall and relevance when using the index. Information units which have adopted this decentralized approach have pointed out that this loss in efficiency is small and therefore is acceptable when the scale of other possible indexing and retrieval errors is considered.

Indexing various kinds of reports

Information units may find that indexing progress reports poses interesting problems and they may also consider that there is no necessity to index committee minutes. Both these points are worthy of consideration. Progress reports are usually resumés of research reports and it is these research reports which should be indexed in depth. The progress report need only be 'shallow-indexed' since it does not usually provide new information or new interpretation. The indexing can be done in the main information index or a 'book' index can be produced covering all the progress reports issued in a particular year. Committee minutes can and should be indexed. This can be done by producing a 'book' index to yearly issues of committee minutes, and thus a general guide to the contents, or by 'shallow indexing' the various points discussed by the committee and including these index terms in the main information index. It is also useful for an information unit to place on a report a reference to the minutes of any committee where this report was discussed. This ensures that when information is being sought and particular reports highlighted using the information index, additional, and perhaps vital, information is brought to light.

Access to reports index

Access to any reports index can be, and most usually is, via the reports centre staff, though the enquirer sometimes is given access directly to the index itself. If computer-produced or other listings are available the enquirer is usually able to consult these personally. It would be most unusual if the enquirer were given direct access to any index of the security type of report referred to later.

DISSEMINATION OF INFORMATION

Having received and indexed reports, the information unit now has to take active steps to link the reports with potential users of the information in them. The passive role would be to wait for the reports to be highlighted as a result of enquiries, but this approach is so negative that no information unit should ever adopt it. At worst it can be damaging to the organization being served because information which could be vital to the organization is not acted upon. At best it is damaging to the information unit in that it fails to bring the value of the unit to potential users and presents an image of a sleepy backroom service which is not in touch with the needs of its parent organization.

There are several methods by which information on reports received can be disseminated by the unit. These can vary according to the information-indexing and retrieval method employed and the position of the information unit in the organizational structure of the company. They fall naturally into two categories:

(a) selective dissemination, where individuals are notified of particular reports of interest to them;
(b) general dissemination, where listings are produced and the individual searches these to identify reports of value to him.

The amount of dissemination given to any document, or list of documents, will be governed by any security grading the document carries. A highly confidential document may be of interest to many people but knowledge of it can only be disseminated to a few for reasons of security.

It cannot be too strongly emphasized that even though selective dissemination is practised there should always be a reports list produced to back this up. No information unit can ever be so efficient that it will provide an individual automatically with all the information he needs.

What then are the methods of dissemination? If the information unit is linked with, or has responsibility for, the publications unit, then before a report is reproduced the distribution list can be checked and additional names added. This of course presupposes that a good knowledge of the people in the organization and their interests exists in the unit. If it does not it certainly should do and the information can be obtained by personal interview, by questionnaire and by day-to-day contact between the unit and its customers. It is worth noting that if any additional names are put into the distribution list, the author should be notified. This ensures that he knows those who are interested in his work and assists in fostering informal contacts between them. Similarly, after the report has been issued it is useful if the author is notified periodically of anyone requesting a copy of his report. This again ensures that he knows those who are interested in his work and assists in fostering informal contact between them. It is also worth telephoning the individual whose name is being added. This ensures that he needs the report, that he knows it is coming and that he appreciates that the information unit have kept his needs in mind.

Should the information unit not be in a position to see reports before they are issued, then information dissemination must wait until the reports have been reproduced and a copy is received. Checking the distribution list will again indicate anyone who should be notified about the report but who has not been sent a copy. The same steps as previously indicated should be taken to notify him of the report.

The information unit may have its indexing and retrieval system based on a computer. In this case it is possible to produce interest profiles of users of the information unit and to match these profiles in keyword terms against the terms used in the indexing of the information in the report. Many information units provide this sort of service by various means not using a computer, but the computer has the advantage of being able to handle, more easily, much more information, both from internally or externally produced services, than the individual. This method is deceptively simple for it depends very much on the accuracy of the interest profile. Before adopting this technique, it is worthwhile studying the literature and contacting an information unit which has tried the method. Questions should be asked regarding the number of interest profiles being dealt with by the system and the relevance of the information being disseminated to the potential user.

Three methods of selective dissemination have been outlined and, as has already been suggested, these should be backed up by listings of reports received. These listings of less confidential reports should be distributed widely throughout the organization and each listing should of course indicate how to obtain copies of the reports listed.

From the point of view of the information unit, it is most efficient if listings can be produced as a byproduct of indexing procedures rather than as a separate task. If indexing and retrieval are done using a computer then the computer can also produce report listings either by serial number or by general subject headings; it can also produce specialized listings by title keyword terms. These listings can be distributed to individuals or to departments and copies can be held in libraries for dissemination purposes and for retrospective searching. Several organizations, such as the Unilever Company, produce such listings. Printout can be in the form of a KWIC (Keyword-in-context) index or a KWOC (Keyword-out-of-context) index. With a KWIC index the keyword concerned is arranged to be in the centre of a title line (with keywords in one vertical row). The final product then is an index with the keywords printed down the centre of the column. With KWOC the keyword is brought out of the title of the report and highlighted separately as a heading for the entry.

It is usual for an information unit to have a card for each report held showing corporate and personal authors, serial numbers, title and date of issue. These cards can be used by a typist to produce a report list, the cards being arranged in the most suitable manner to benefit the users. Alternatively a typing operation can be saved by using the cards themselves to produce a master, by photographic or other copying techniques, and then by producing the required number of copies from this master.

It should be remembered that in creating a reports list one has created a document which should be confidential to the company and depending on its contents it may have a higher security grading than this. It is important therefore that a reports list carries some indication that it is to be treated as confidential.

Should it be decided that a listing is not required frequently then an index can be produced, perhaps every six months, utilizing title keywords. Reports are then listed against those keywords expressing the content of the report.

References

ANGLO-AMERICAN CATALOG(U)ING RULES: prepared by the American Library Association, the Library of Congress, the Library Association and the Canadian Library Association. (British text): London, Library Association, 1967. pp. 422.
(North American text): Chicago, American Library Association, 1967. pp. 422.
ATOMIC ENERGY COMMISSION (USA). Descriptive cataloging guide. Oak Ridge, 1966. pp. 78. *TID* 4577.
COMMITTEE ON SCIENTIFIC AND TECHNICAL INFORMATION (COSATI). Standard for descriptive cataloging of government scientific and technical reports. Washington, 1966. pp. 54. (Available from NTIS as AD 641 092, or PB 173 314.)
ENGLISH ELECTRIC CO. LTD. Thesaurofacet: a thesaurus and faceted

classification for engineering and related subjects, compiled by Jean Aitchison and others. Whetstone, Leics., 1969. pp. 491.

NATIONAL TECHNICAL INFORMATION SERVICE. Standard for descriptive cataloging of government scientific and technical reports. Springfield, Va., 1963. pp. 21. PB 181 605.

SELECTED BIBLIOGRAPHY

AIRCRAFT RESEARCH ASSOCIATION. Report cataloguing at the Aircraft Research Association. Bedford (England), 1971. pp. 18. *Report 27*.

ANTHONY, L. J. *and others*. Selective dissemination of information using a KDF9 computer. *Aslib Proceedings*, **20**(1). January, 1968. 40–64.

ATOMIC ENERGY COMMISSION (USA). Report number codes used by the USAEC Division of Technical Information in cataloging reports. 9th ed. Springfield, Va., Clearing House for Federal Scientific and Technical Information, 1970. pp. 182. *TID 85*.

CHRISTIANSON, E. B. Information retrieval for advertising and marketing research. *Special Libraries*, **60**(4). April, 1969. 219–222.

COMMITTEE ON SCIENTIFIC AND TECHNICAL INFORMATION (COSATI). Corporate author headings. Springfield, Va., NTIS, 1970. pp. 850. *COSATI Report 70–7*. PB 198 275.

CONFERENCE ON CO-ORDINATE INDEXING SYSTEMS. London, 1963. *Aslib Proceedings*, **15**(6). June, 1963. 160–194.

DAMMERS, H. F. SDI: some economic and organizational aspects. *Aslib Proceedings*, **23**(10). October, 1971. 517–522.

GECHMAN, M. C. *and* KIESEWETTER, G. H. Development of a corporate wide technical reports processing system. *AMERICAN SOCIETY FOR INFORMATION SCIENCE. 32nd Annual Meeting, San Francisco, 1969. Proceedings*. Vol. 6, 361–367.

GOOM, H. H. SDI systems: a United Kingdom approach. *Special Libraries*, **62**(12). December, 1971. 535–538.

GREGORY, A. SDI at Swinburne: a manual approach. *Australian Academic and Research Libraries*, **2**(3). July, 1972. 93–96.

HOGENAUER, A. V. An aviation firm catalogs its special collection. *Special Libraries*, **62**(5–6). May–June, 1971. 234–237.

HOUSMAN, E. M. *and* KASKELLA, E. D. State of the art in selective dissemination of information. *IEEE Transactions on Engineering Writing and Speech*, (EWS) **13**(2). September, 1970. 78–83.

HUTTON, G. H. Product analysis by co-ordinate index. *Aslib Proceedings*, **20**(3). March, 1968. 171–180.

JACOBS, R. M. 'Whodunnit': notes on the [cataloguing] system adopted by the DSIR, HQ Library, for the control of publications issued by corporate authors. *Journal of Documentation*, **8**(4). December, 1952. 227–231.

JOHNSON, A. Experience in the use of unit concept co-ordinate indexing applied to technical reports. *Journal of Documentation*, **15**(3). September, 1959. 145–155.

JOHNSON, A. *and* BAKER, K. J. Practical considerations in establishing and operating an optical coincidence card system. *Information Scientist*, 4(1). March, 1970. 11–25.

JOSHI, R. C. *and others*. An experiment in mechanical storage and retrieval of information in internal technical reports. *Annals of Library Science*, 16(3–4). September–December, 1970. 119–125.

KERR-WALLER, R. D. Automated Information Disseminations System (AIDS): technical evaluation. *Information Scientist*, 1(2). September, 1967. 51–71.

MEYER, R. L. *and others*. A systematic approach to current awareness and SDI. *Journal of Chemical Documentation*, 11(1). February, 1971. 19–24.

SCHLESSINGER, B. S. *and others*. A new approach to indexing technical reports in an industrial information center. *Journal of Chemical Documentation*, 9(1). February, 1969. 51–53.

SMITH, J. R. Guide to UKAEA (United Kingdom Atomic Energy Authority) documents. 5th ed. London, HMSO, 1973. pp. 48.

THOMPSON, M. S. Peek-a-boo index for a broad subject collection. *American Documentation*, 13(2). April, 1962. 187–196.

WILDHACK, W. A. *and others*. Documentation in instrumentation. *American Documentation*, 5(5). October, 1954. 223–237.

CHAPTER 4

Storage and Security Control

ARRANGEMENT

When the reports have been indexed and information about them disseminated, then of course they must be available when required. The problem therefore is how best to arrange the reports so as to provide easy access to them. The ways which suggest themselves for arranging reports in a store are by subject classification, by originating body, by report code and number, or by accession number.

Subject classification

In theory, perhaps arrangement by subject classification would seem to be the best method; in practice, certainly for large collections of reports, it is not. It would seem desirable to be able to bring all reports on a given subject together in one location. However, there are problems of classification of reports and since many reports do not deal only with a single specific topic one is faced with the problem of putting multiple copies of the report in different files, or putting signals in the various files directing the enquirers to the preferred location. The first method bulks out the collection and the second method negates the advantage of bringing like material together. This method therefore may be the correct method for small libraries with few reports but it should not be used in any other situation.

Arrangement by originating bodies

Arranging reports by the name of the originating body certainly has some advantages in that many enquirers will ask to see reports of work done at a certain named laboratory. The problem with this method is to ensure consistency in the choice of the name of

Storage and Security Control

the originating body. As was instanced in the section on cataloguing, one has to decide whether to file under Mellon Institute or University of Pittsburgh, Mellon Institute, and once decided, no deviations should be allowed. There can also be problems if an organization subcontracts some work and then issues a report under its own covers, although referring to the fact that the work was done elsewhere.

Arrangement by series codes and serial numbers

The third method is the one which the majority of report libraries use. Every report should have a unique code and number which distinguishes it from other reports. Filing by this code and number therefore gives each report one place, and only one possible place, in the file. Should an information unit receive a report which does not bear a report series code and number then one must be created for it. In practice, many series codes readily identify the originating body, and examples have been given in the section dealing with them. Thus in filing, all reports originating from one source are brought together by the series code. It can be seen that filing by series code incorporates some of the advantages of filing by the name of the originating body providing the series codes used by the various sources of interest are known.

Access to the subject matter of the reports will be either via the subject index created by the information unit or via relevant published indexes. A cross-reference index between corporate author and report-series code can be produced for those reports which do not appear in any published listing. Information units using co-ordinate (strictly, post-co-ordinate) coincidence retrieval methods will also need to be able to refer from the index number to the report code and number and will thus need to create an index to do this.

One of the drawbacks about the systems so far outlined is that room for expansion must be left at the end of each subject category or source category. This adds considerably to the total space requirements and also means that periodically, part of the report collection needs to be moved round to create more space at the end of particular sections.

Arrangement by accession numbers

One means of overcoming these difficulties is to file by accession numbers. In this method every report obtained by the information unit is given an accession number, quite simply the next number in a running sequence, and filing is done by this number.

The advantages of this method are that every report has a unique filing number which avoids any possibility of ambiguity; all additions to the collection occur at the end, thus avoiding having to leave any spaces at various parts of the collection; and the accession number can be used as the number to be marked or punched for co-ordinate optical-coincidence retrieval purposes. Weeding is facilitated since the accession number gives an indication of the date a report was received. Thus all reports received in 1972 will be adjacent to each other.

The main disadvantage of this method is that it separates reports originating from one source, and that, since this is the way in which the majority of enquirers ask for reports, the first steps in answering any such request must be to turn to an index, which the information unit must create, linking accession numbers to report series code numbers. In practice this is not a major disadvantage and is balanced by the disadvantage of the filing system based on series code numbers that one must be able to link an index number to a report number. Another possible disadvantage of using accession numbers is that they add one more number to those already on the report. However, as we have seen in the section on report series codes, if the information unit has the responsibility for allotting report-series numbers, then it can use the accession number for the serial number. This gives the advantage that indexing, filing and retrieval are all done using the same number and that anyone requesting a report does so by quoting a number which makes it easy to obtain a copy of the report from the file.

STORAGE METHODS

Reports can be in filing boxes, in filing cabinets, upright on any suitable shelving or in a lateral suspended filing system. The last system has hanging pockets which hold the reports and each pocket can have an indicator tag, to display the serial or accession numbers of the reports in the pocket. Metal shutters (with special security locks if necessary) or blinds can be used to close the filing unit. The lateral-filing system is very popular because it allows a lot of material to be filed in a fairly small space, it provides good means of access and is fairly cheap.

Separate storage for confidential reports

Open to argument is whether unpublished reports should be stored or displayed in the same way as published reports. Unpublished reports are rarely to be seen on open library shelves where published reports are likely to be displayed. They are more usually to be found in a store room set aside for the purpose, and access to the reports is via some controlling system. The point of this is that in an open library they could be examined by non-company visitors; also their whereabouts in the company could not be easily controlled, and, since many libraries now have on-site photocopying facilities freely available, copies could be made and distributed without control.

The housing of the security type of document presents its own type of problem. There must be no possibility of uncontrolled access to such reports and thus they must be kept in a store; they cannot be displayed for open access. Within the store there is the problem of whether they should be filed with the unpublished, but non-security, reports, or whether a separate store should be created for them. Each company must make its own decision although the author certainly takes the view that these reports should be stored separately because of their very special confidentiality. At all times there should be a reference copy of each unpublished report retained in the store and on this copy amendments, corrections and additions can be written and additions to the circulation list noted.

The need for duplicate sets and indexes

One of the most important things to remember about any store of unpublished reports is that somewhere there should be a duplicate set either in hard copy or microfilm. The store should be a considerable distance away, not next door, so that in case of fire or any other disaster, there is still a set of reports in existence. If this is not done then a considerable proportion of any company's 'know how' could be irretrievably destroyed. Similarly there should be a duplicate set of index cards, at a second location; or alternatively a secondary method of obtaining the information, such as copies of a six-monthly reports index, should be similarly located.

WEEDING

The useful life of an external report to a company can be limited: technical reports probably have a longer useful life, possibly up to thirty years, than commercial reports. Therefore weeding of the reports collection may be necessary to keep it within reasonable limits. Weeding can be done on a subject or time basis and also on an availability basis. One should ask: is the report stored in any national depository library where copies can be obtained on request? If so there may be no point in retaining a copy of the report after a certain period.

The first weeding method which should be tried is to microfilm old reports in the collection. This will substantially reduce storage space and allow one protection against the old adage 'any report destroyed will be wanted the day after destruction'.

In-house reports should always be kept as these cannot be replaced and while it is not necessary to keep every copy, at least one copy should always be retained. It is not, however, always necessary to keep a copy of every old report in the reports store; they can conveniently be located with the company's archives department and called upon as necessary. In this case, the information unit and the archives department should ensure that the indexes available will allow the report to be located quickly.

SECURITY GRADING

Within any one company there will be several grades of unpublished reports. The different gradings would reflect the different risks to its future viability, either commercial or technical, which the company would run if the contents of the report become known to its competitors or other unauthorized persons. Thus the five-year plan of a company would most probably have a different grading from the five-year plan of any department within the company. The different gradings can be thought in a sense to reflect the value in the market place of the report. Security reports are by definition the most important reports existing in any company and the standing of an information unit within a company can be measured by whether it is allowed to see these security reports or not.

Allotting gradings

Each report produced within a company must be considered before issue to evaluate what security grading, if any, it should carry. This evaluation can initially be done by the author in conjunction with his manager but the ultimate responsibility should be with the senior manager responsible for the work. His judgement is usually based on broad guidelines laid down by the company which may be decided by the patent situation, commercial policy, personnel policy, or by any of the other reasons for not making the report freely available. The information unit can provide advice regarding security gradings by quoting the gradings of other reports on that topic or other reports at a similar stage in another project. It is rare for an information unit alone to be responsible for allotting security gradings.

The United Kingdom Atomic Energy Authority allots security gradings to its reports by first having them scrutinized by senior technical management who give them technical approval. Then a separate section, specially appointed to do the work, scrutinizes them for their commercial value. The special staff are in close touch with patents offices and agencies dealing with commercial agreements made between British industry and overseas organizations. They are guided by a code laid down, and periodically revised, by a working party from all parts of the organization, and their task is to decide whether the material can be released to the public, or issued only on a limited basis under commercial agreements. They also decide who may see the report.

Markings

When the information in a report needs to have some restriction placed on its availability then the report must be marked in some way to indicate its availability. The markings used must convey a clear message of their meaning and of how the report should be handled and protected, and they should appear on every page of the report.

There is no universal method of designating gradings. Methods used include numerical codings, colour codings or the use of gradings such as 'Confidential', 'Secret', 'Top secret', 'Limited distribution' or 'Named distribution only'. The validity of any security-document system, however, depends on its being understood by all persons operating it, and being adhered to so that all recipients safeguard information appropriately.

A numerical grading system would operate by having different numbers to indicate different gradings and also to indicate the way that the information in the document should be controlled. Thus a document graded 1 could be available to anyone in a company but a document graded 4 could be available only to directors and would have to be kept in a security cabinet with receipts being issued when it is removed.

The cover and all pages or the margins or corners of all pages of a report could be coloured to indicate the grading. The difficulty of this system is that the colours in themselves mean nothing, and their meaning must be made clear to those operating the system and perhaps to others as well; it is also difficult to 'down-grade' reports. Colour coding can be operated in conjunction with numerical gradings, and with gradings using standard words.

Systems using standard words, such as 'Confidential' and 'Top secret', require the words to be printed boldly on the cover and each page of the report. No matter what system is used, documents can carry a note on the cover indicating the manner in which the information is to be handled.

Access

Whatever grading is chosen for a report will usually limit the initial distribution to a few specified people and it will indicate others who are allowed to ask to see a copy of the report. Thus a category 4 report may concern itself with a new warehousing and distribution system for a company and it will have been sent to certain directors. The director of research may wish to see a copy of the report, and though he was not on the original distribution list, his standing in the company would be such that he has the right to see all category 4 reports.

There will also be those who require to see a copy of a report on a 'need to know' basis. Again, people who are not on the original distribution of the report or are not sufficiently senior to be able to see the report on their own authority, may demonstrate that they need to see the report in order to do their job properly. If this need can be demonstrated then right of access can be granted. It is usual for the authority to grant right of access to be vested only in senior managers in a company; it is most unusual for an information unit to have such authority. A further method for allowing access to security documents is that each individual in a company is informed of the security gradings of documents he is allowed to see and is supplied with an appropriate order form. This, as mentioned previously, is usually on the basis of his function, e.g. a senior manager would be able to see highly rated security documents. A reports list is issued periodically and each report listed carries its security grading. This enables the individual to request a security document with the appropriate order form. If, however, he does not have an order form of sufficient security rank, then the individual has to make his request to a more senior person who, if he agrees with the request, will make out an order form carrying the necessary security rank.

RECORDS

To help control access to security documents, adequate records must be kept. The methods employed depend on several factors including a company's attitude to security, the number of documents to be controlled, the number of staff who require access to security documents, the number of staff available to keep the records, and the number and location of the various works within the company.

Typical systems

Examples of some of the methods employed by some English companies can serve as guides. They should not be copied without first evaluating their usefulness and effectiveness in the company or situation where the establishment of security document control is necessary.

Example 1. One method utilizes the following steps:

(1) An author writes a report and the contents are approved either technically or editorially, by his manager, if necessary in conjunction with others.

(2) The senior manager responsible for the project allots a security grading to the report and the security grading is written on the routing slip which is attached to the document. Against the security grading is the name of the person who has allotted that grading.

(3) The draft of the report is taken to the section responsible for security reports and they produce the appropriate number of copies. The author certifies that no other copies are in existence and that all drafts have been destroyed. Each page of the report has the security grading, report serial number and copy number stamped on it.

(4) Report record cards are produced, each card showing: (a) the report series code and number; (b) the security grading; (c) the title; (d) the author; (e) the number of pages, graphs and charts; (f) the date of issue; (g) the names of the people receiving copies.

(5) Three sets of report record cards, in different colours, are produced. One colour indicates that the card is a master record card, and is to be retained by the reports issuing section; a second indicates that the card is a record of an individual's holdings and is to be retained by the reports issuing section and a third colour designates the card which the receiver of the documents will retain. The recipient signs the master record card on receiving the report. When the cards are produced, one card is filed under the recipient's name, one card is given to the recipient as a record of his holdings, and one on which the recipient's signature is obtained as a receipt for the document, is kept as a master record. Thus there is a central record of what security reports each person holds, there is a central record of all security reports issued and each individual holding security reports has a record of those reports for which he is responsible.

(6) The unit responsible for the distribution of the report keeps a master copy. If any copies of the report are returned by holders this can be noted on the master record card and an appropriate

adjustment made to the record cards representing the holdings of an individual, and to the master record card.

Once such a system has been installed, two further matters need to be reviewed periodically. The first is that there should be regular checks made of an individual's holdings to make sure that all security documents can be accounted for. The second is that the grading of the existing documents should be reviewed at a regular period, say once a year. The level of confidentiality of the report could fall with time and then the security grading should be lowered, thus allowing the information in it to be used by a wider audience than the original one. The review of the security grading can be done by the senior manager who was responsible for allotting the original grading or by a small committee set up specially to review security report gradings.

Example 2. Another example of how security documents can be controlled utilizes steps 1 to 3 in the method outlined previously. A master copy of the report is kept in the section responsible for security control. With this copy is kept a work sheet showing: (a) recipients' names against individual copy numbers; (b) receipt number; (c) date returned; (d) copy kept on file or destroyed; (e) additional copies made after original distribution; (f) names of persons who have been allowed to read the report but who have not required a copy for retention.

When a report is issued, a receipt is obtained from the recipient and kept on file with the master copy. Later when the document is returned the original receipt is cancelled and given to the person returning the report and this acts as a receipt for the return.

Safeguards

In any system controlling security reports, no individual should be allowed to make copies of such reports. The security-reports section should be the only part of the company allowed to copy them.

Should it be necessary to refer to a security report in any other document, this should be done by quoting the series code and serial number only; no reference should be made to the title. This in itself helps to safeguard the system.

The major conflict within any security report system comes

from balancing the need to restrict the flow of certain pieces of information with the need to ensure that staff are adequately informed in areas affecting their work. To overcome this, one method would be to issue a list of recent security reports to project leaders and to senior management and to require these people to bring to the notice of their staff any security report containing information relevant to that person's work.

SELECTED BIBLIOGRAPHY

GERRARD, S. A. *and* LYLE, D. F. Handling industrial (scientific and technical) confidential report material. *Aslib Proceedings,* 18(8). August, 1966. 206–217.

JERMY, K. E. Control of commercially confidential information in reports. *Aslib Proceedings,* 18(8). August, 1966. 218–223.

TYLICKI, L. Preparation of a microfilm file of company technical reports. *Journal of Chemical Documentation,* 10(1). February, 1970. 20–22.

Other Relevant Literature

CHILLAG, J. P. Don't be afraid of reports. *BLL Review*, 1(2). October, 1973. 39–51.
GRAY, D. E. Organizing and servicing unpublished reports. *American Documentation*, 4(3). July, 1953. 103–115.
HALL, J. Technical report literature. *ASHWORTH, W., ed. Handbook of special librarianship and information work*. 3rd ed. London, Aslib, 1967. 287–308. Also in 4th ed. (ed. W. E. Batten), 1975. 102–123.
HARTIS, J. C. Technical report literature: its nature and some problems. *HOUGHTON, B., ed. Information work today*. London, Bingley, 1967. 77–87.
HOUGHTON, B. Technical information sources: a guide to patents, standards and technical report literature. 2nd ed. London, Bingley, 1972. ISBN 0 85157 126 3 pp. 119.
LEONDAR, J. C. Proceedings of the workshop on report literature and sources of information. *Special Libraries*, 59(2). February, 1968. 84–106.
WEIL, B. H. The technical report: its preparation, processing and use in industry and government. New York, Reinhold, 1954. pp. 455.
WRIGHT, J. C. Report literature. *BURKETT, J. and MORGAN, T. S., ed. Special materials in the library*. London, Library Association, 1963. 46–59.

Index to Parts I and II

Organisations, systems, methods, etc. represented by abbreviations or acronyms of four or more letters are indexed under the abbreviation or acronym which can be found in the list on pp. 225–230. Those with shorter abbreviations etc., are indexed under the full name except for a few such as SDI, UDC, widely known by initials. Joint authors' names are not indexed.

Abbot, M. T. J., 107
Aberystwyth research, 104
Abstracting, 90
    automatic, 91, 100
Abstracting periodicals, attitude to reports, 251
Abstracts, 65, 90, 251
    by author, 91
    bulletins of, 83
    content of, 90
    indicative, 90
Access
    to indexes, 270, 277
    computer, 184
    and security, 193, 282
    to reports, 193, 274, 282
Accession numbers, 85
    arranging by, 278
Acquisition of reports, 76, 243, 249, 251
Acronyms, 91
    list of, 225
Adams, H. C., 134
Adkinson, B. W., 39
Aerospace Materials Information Centre, 99
AGARD, 41, 68
    distribution centres, 68
AGARD Conference Papers, 109
AGARD Lecture Series, 53
AGARDographs, 68
Agency entries, 85
AGRINDEX, 69
AGRIS, 68, 69
AIAA, 136
AIDS, 135
Aims of the monographs, 23, 239
    of reports, 27, 237

Aircraft Research Association, 274
Aitchison, J., 98, 104
Aitchison, T. M., 101
American Doctoral Dissertations, 37
American Library Association, 60
American National Standards Institute, 41, 44
Anglo-American Catalog(u)ing Rules, 84, 266, 273
Announcement bulletins *see* Bulletins
Anthony, L. J., 135, 148, 274
Aperture cards, 157
Appendixes, 32, 49
Appropriations Committee, 76
Approval systems for reports, 256
Archives, reports as, 195, 280
Arrangement of reports in store, 195, 196, 276
Ashworth, W., 91, 223
Aslib, 18, 72, 103
    Commonwealth Index, 72
    Cranfield project, 100, 103, 104
    Information Dept., 252
ASLIB Directory, 53
ASSASSIN, 102, 106
ASTIA, 19
ATLIS, 217
Atomic Energy Commission (USA) *see* USAEC
Atomindex, 124
AUDACIOUS, 94
Auger, C. P., 223
Authors
    corporate, 85, 86, 269
    of reports, relations with, 258, 271
    personal, 40, 87

Automation, 176
Avedon, D. M., 156
Aviation Week, 76
Awareness, 117
Ayres, F. H., 187

Baffady, W., 158
Bagg, T. G., 158
Baker, G. G. & Associates, 155, 161, 187
Baker, G. G. & Associates, *Guide*, 161
Bakewell, K. B., 84
Ball, H. R., 158
Barker, R. E., 151
Barlow, D. H., 101
Batten, W. E., 223
Bauer, C. K., 174
Berlin, S., 193
Bernhardt, R., 169
Bhattacharyya, K., 101
Bibliographies, 142
  indexes to, 142
  of theses, 36
Bibliography of Medical Reviews, 64
Bierman, K. J., 187
Biological Abstracts, 66
BIOS reports, 55
BIOSIS, 66
Blagden, J. F., 97, 98
BLLD, 55, 56, 72, 121
BLLD Announcement Bulletin, 78, 125
BLLD Conference Index, 128
BLLD Current Serials, 128
BLLD Review, 128
Boolean operators, 106, 111, 133
Bourne, C. P., 93
Bousselet, P., 172
Brain, M. E., 119
British Government publications, 54
British Library, 54
British Library Lending Division *see* BLLD
British Library Research and Development Newsletter, 58

British National Bibliography, 55, 102
British Research and Development Reports, 126
British Scientific Documentation, 74
British Standards, 25, 41, 43, 51, 237, 253, 261, 265
British Theses Retrospective Index, 36
Broadhurst, R. N., 157
Brookes, B. C., 254
Brophy, P., 221
Buckley, C., 81
Bulletin Signalétique, 170
Bulletins (*see also* Lists of reports), 118, 129
  abstract, 251
  announcement, 55, 72, 118, 120
  content of, 119
  future of, 129
  news, 148
  production of, 118
Burkett, J., 54, 67, 75, 287
Burton, H. D., 134
Bush, V., 19, 20
Business Equipment Digest, 154

CADO, 19
CAIN, 64
Caless, T. W., 94
Cameras, 160, 179
  microfiche, 160
  step-and-repeat, 160
Campey, L. H., 103
CARD, 159
Cards
  aperture, 157
  catalogue, 83, 91, 118, 273
  feature, 105
  optical coincidence, 71, 105, 268
  punched, 168
  temporary, 85
Carroll, V. D., 252
Carter, C., 81
Carville, M., 108
Case Western Reserve University, 104
Cassettes, 156

Catalogues, 82, 212
  card, 83, 118
  entries for, 85
Cataloguing
  centralized *versus* decentralized, 269
  forms for, 82
  methods of, 266, 267
  systems of, 21
  rules, guides, 84, 266
Cathode-ray tubes, 151
Cavendish, J. M., 165
CCM Information Corporation, 252
Centralization, 203, 269
CFSTI, 20, 30
Channels
  open, 31
  privileged, 31
Chemical Abstracts Condensates, 107, 136
Chemical Abstracts Service, 66
Chemical and Biological Activities, 107, 136
Chemical Titles, 100, 107, 136
Chillag, J. P., 56, 287
Christianson, E. B., 274
CIOS, 55
Citation, 109
Classification, 93, 267
  arranging by, 276
Cleaning, 213
Clement, L., 67
Clerical staff, 212
  work of, 85
Cleverdon, C. W., 100, 103, 104
Clough, C. R., 106
CNRS, 170
COBLOS, 172
Coden, 136
Codes, 87
  numbering, 261
Coincidence, optical, 71, 105, 268
Collation, 88
College of Librarianship Wales, 104
Colour coding of security gradings, 282

COM, 174, 180
  applications of, 181
  costs of, 181
Commerce Business Daily, 76
Committees
  ad-hoc, 33
  minutes of, 242, 250
  reports of, 33, 242
Commonwealth Agricultural Bureaux, 70
Commonwealth Bureaux of Dairy Science & Technology, 70
Commonwealth Index of Translations, 72
Company names in indexes to reports, 268
Company reports, 241, 244
  ensuring all reach information unit, 249
  holdings of, as measure of standing of information unit, 249
  reasons for non-publication, 238
  widely available, 244
Comparison, report/article, 29
Computer Program Abstracts, 65
Computers, 61, 67, 69, 70, 71, 83, 84, 87, 88, 105, 119, 133, 272
  access to, 184
  data bases, 63, 64, 65
  indexing by, 101, 268, 272
  installation of, 175; preparation for, 174; problems of, 175
  output microform *see* COM
  programs, 106, 134
Computerization, 176
Conclusions to reports, 46
Conference on Co-ordinate Indexing Systems (1963), 274
Conferences
  international, 20
  papers of, 248
  index to, 158
  proceedings of, 85, 109
  reports of, 34
  Royal Society, 20
Confidence of managers in information units, 239, 249

Confidentiality *see* Security
Congressional Record, 61, 76
Conserve-a-trieve, 159
Consultancy reports, 245
Contacts, personal, 31
Contractors, 41
Contracts, 29
  numbers of, 88, 269
Cook J., 216
Co-operation, 145
Co-ordination, 93
  false, 95, 134
Cooper, B. M., 51
Copies *see* Photocopying
Copinger, W. A., 151
Copyright, 150
Copyright Act (UK), 151
CORE, 218
Corporate authors, 85, 86
COSATI, 41, 73, 86, 266
  cataloguing rules of, 84, 273
  fields of, 121, 171
  subject headings of, 132
COSATI Corporate Author Headings, 86, 274
COSATI Guidelines, 41
COSATI Standard for Descriptive Cataloguing, 84, 273
Cost-effectiveness, 100, 111, 218
Costing, 104, 111, 162, 184, 216
  of retrieval, 218
Costs, manual/computerized loan systems, 173
Cranfield Project, 100, 104, 109
Cremer, M., 67
Cuadra, C., 223
Current Catalog, 84
Current Papers, 87
Current research, 75
Daily List (HMSO), 54, 246
Dammers, H. F., 274
Data
  machine-readable, 183
  preparation of, 169, 183
Dates, 88
  in report numbers, 262, 264, 278
Decisions, mechanization, 185

Defense Documentation Center, 64, 101
Definitions, 17, 25, 26, 31, 73, 90, 95, 176, 237
Department of Industry (UK), 74
Depositories, 53, 66
Descriptors, 95, 133, 171
Deutsch, A., 165
Deutsche Gesellschaft für Dokumentation, 67
DEVIL, 101
Dictionary of report series codes, 87
Direct entry, 171
Directory of Federally supported information analysis centers, 74
Discussions, 34
Dissemination of information on reports, 28, 270
Dissertation Abstracts International, 36, 72
Dissertations, 36, 72
  foreign language, 38
Distribution, 27, 28, 49, 68, 271
  lists for, 271; adding to, 271
Document control sheets, 49, 80
  digests of, 174
Documents, primary, 26
  secondary, 33
d'Olier, J. M., 171
Downie, C. S., 202
DRIC, 55, 68, 110
Duchesne, R. M., 187
Dummy runs, 97
Duplicate sets
  of indexes, 279
  of reports, 279
Dutton, B. G., 221

EARS, 111
Economist Intelligence Unit, 245
Editing reports, 253, 254, 258
  relations with authors, 258
Editrec, 170
EIRMA, 246
Ejlersen, R., 67
Elton, M., 219
ENDS, 159
Engineering Index, 83

Index

Engineers' Joint Council, 95
English Electric Co. Ltd, 267, 273
ERDA, 66
ERIC, 65
ESRO, 68, 69, 136
Eunson, B. G., 172
European Association of Scientific Dissemination Centers, 120
European Economic Communities, 67
European Industrial Relations Management Association, 245
European Space Agency, 68, 69, 136
European Translations Centre, 72

FAIR, 98, 105
Fangmeyer, H., 103
Federal Supply Service, 265
Fédération Internationale de Documentation (FID), 68, 71, 93
FID News Bulletin, 71
FileSearch, 158
Filmorex, 159
Finer, R., 252
Fisher, M., 116
FLIP, 158
Flowerdew, A. D. S., 221
Food Science and Technology Abstracts, 70
Ford, G., 187
Form of reports, 38, 42
Forms, 82, 137, 145, 254
Forschungsvereinigung Verbrennungskraftmaschinen, 74
FOSDIC, 158
Freeman, R. R., 94
Friden Flexowriter, 168
Fussler, H. H., 221

GAME, 218
Gardner, K. S., 67
Garvey, W. D., 28
Geary, P. J., 143
Gechmann, M. C., 274
General Accounting Office, 60
German information centres, 67
Gerrard, S. A., 202, 286

Gilcrist, A., 98, 218
Godfrey, J. W., 52
Godfrey, L. E., 87, 263
Goom, H. H., 135, 274
Gordon, H. F., 165
Gordon, R. F., 249
Government Printing Office (US), 59, 78
Governments
 one dealing with another, 147
 reports, 54, 58, 60, 246
Government Reports Abstracts, 61, 76, 78, 96, 108, 110, 119, 263
Government Reports Index, 61, 121
Government research & development, 54
GRAI, 121
Gradings, security *see* Security gradings
Gray, D. E., 25, 287
Graziani, A., 67
Gregory, A., 274
Growes, H. F., 42
Guides
 to sources, 54
 for users, 134

Hall, A. M., 130
Hall, J., 287
Hall, J. L., 108
Hampshire, T., 154
Hanson, C. W., 222, 248
Harley, G. P., 102
Hartis, J. C., 287
Harvey, N., 81
Hastening return from loan, 139
Hayes, R. M., 187
Headings, subject, 21
Heath, T. H., 187
Heinritz, F., 83
Henderson, M. M., 97
Henry, N. I., 165
Herner, M. & S., 252
Herner, S., 223
Hersey, D. F., 101
HMSO, 54, 246
Hochschulschriften Verzeichnis, 38
Hogenauer, A. V., 274

Holdings
  BLLD, 56, 72
  DRIC, 58
  NTIS, 61
  personal, 284, 285
  SRL, 57
  TRC, 59
Holland, D., 68
Holloway, A. H., 41, 165
Holmes, P. L., 109
Honoré, S., 67
Hookway, H. T., 54
Houghton, B., 81, 287
Housekeeping, 58, 172
Houseman, E. M., 274
Hutton, G. H., 274

Identifiers, 96
Illustrations in reports, 46
Imperial Chemical Industries Ltd, 102
Index Medicus, 64, 101, 107
Index of Conference Proceedings, 128
Indexes, 121, 129, 212, 267, 275, 279
  access to, 270, 277, 279
  bibliographies of, 142
  book-form, 83
  to bulletins, 129
  computer-produced, 125
  subject (*see also* Subject), 82, 93, 267
  of theses, 36
Indexing, 93, 101, 267
  citation, 103
  comparisons of, 101
  computer, 101
  evaluation of, 103
  language, 79, 99, 103, 133
  machine-aided, 101
  subject (*see also* Subject), 93
Industrial Relations RA, 74
Industrial reports, 60
Industrial Research in Britain, 75
INFIRS, 106, 107
Information analysis centres, 73
Information centres (large), 22, 54, 59, 67, 203
  centralization of, 203
  international, 68
  specialized, 73, 97
  units and subunits of, 203, 205
Information not available, 242, 244, 249
Information retrieval *see* Retrieval
Information units (small), 238, 244, 249, 271, 278
  allotting report numbers, 264, 278
  devising coding and numbering systems, 263
  staff of, 238
  standing of, 239, 249
'In-house' *see* Reports, internal; Company reports
INIS, 68, 70
INIS Atomindex, 70
INSPEC, 76, 101, 110, 130, 135
INSPEC SDI User Manual, 136
Institut für Dokumentationswesen, 70
Institute of Food Technologists, 70
Interaction, searcher/computer, 184
Interest profiles *see* Profiles
Internal reports *see* Reports, internal
International Aerospace Abstracts, 65, 110
International Atomic Energy Agency, 71
International Conference on Scientific Information, 20
International Federation for Documentation, 68, 71, 93
International Food Information Service, 68, 70
International Information System for the Agricultural Sciences and Technology, 68, 69
International Organization for Standardization (ISO), 52, 261, 265
International Road Federation, 71
INTREX, 160

Introductions to reports, 45
IRMS, 106, 107
IRRD, 68, 70
Irvine, R., 188
ISIS, 106, 107
ISO Standards, 52, 261, 265
Isotta, N. E. C., 110

Jacobs, R. M., 274
Jermy, K. E., 202, 286
John Crerar Library, 72
Johnson, A., 105, 274
Joshi, R. C., 275
Jones, K. P., 116
JPRS, 73
JURIS, 64

Kapp, R. O., 52
Kard-veyer, 198
KARDEX, 179
Katzer, J., 111
Keen, E. M., 101, 104
Kennington, O., 221
Kent, A., 223
Kerr-Waller, R. D., 135, 275
Keywords (*see also* Terms), 100, 169
Kimber, R. T., 188
Klingbiel, P. H., 101
Klintøe, K., 216
Kruzas, A. T., 81, 223
KWAC, 100
KWIC, 100, 103, 169, 273
KWOC, 100, 169, 170, 174, 273

Laboratory notebooks, 243, 250
Lancaster, F. W., 108, 188, 218
Languages
  indexing of, 79, 99, 103, 133
  descriptor, 133
  natural, 99
Layout
  of bulletins, 120
  of request forms, 137
Leasco Systems & Research, 65
Lektriever, 159
Leondar, D. C., 287

LEX, 95
Libraries, depository, 66
Library Technology Reports, 162
Library (for particular libraries *see under* title of library)
Library of Congress, 60, 63
Library pen, 173
Licensing agreements, reports arising from, 251
Liebesny, F., 215, 248, 252
'Life' of reports, 200, 280
Limitations on distribution, 27
Lists of reports (*see also* Bulletins), 271, 272
  confidentiality of, 273
  production of, 272
Lithography, for reproduction, 43, 119, 260
Loans, 172
  hastening return from, 139
  mechanization, 173
  requests for, 137
Locating reports, 53, 249
Long Range Planning Service, 245
Loosjes, T. P., 223
Luhn, H. P., 91, 100
Luther, F., 165
Lynch, M. F., 223
Lyon, C. C., 159

McAllister, C., 172
McClelland, W. G., 221
McCracken, I. B., 107
McIvor, R. A., 173
McKenna, B., 67
Machine-readable text, 105
Mack, E., 215
Macroprofiles, 136
Magnetic tape, reports on, 249
Magson, M. S., 218
Management, 203
Management, senior, 249, 250, 281, 283
Management Services in Government, 154
Manuals, style, 42
MARC, 102, 110

Markings, security, 190, 281
Martyn, J., 219
Mason, D., 218
Masters Abstracts, 37
Mechanization, 94, 167, 173, 177
  of equipment, 178
  of indexing, 100, 102
  of loans, 173
  and microcopying, 179
  and microforms, 179
  planning of, 177
  savings in, 177
  stages of, 178
Medical and Health related sciences thesaurus, 96
Medical subject headings (MeSH), 84
MEDLARS, 63, 102, 107
MEDLINE, 63
Meetham, R., 116
Mekeirle, J. O., 81
Meltzer, M. F., 97
METADEX, 110
'Methods' sections in reports, 45
Methods assessment, 216
Methods in miniature, 162
Meyer, R. L., 275
Microcards, 157
Microcopying, 195, 201
Microfiches, 57, 69, 139, 150, 156, 161, 169, 179, 249
  acceptance of, 197
  as safeguard against loss, 279
  cameras for, 160
  copying of, 161
  economics of, 162
  handling of, 180
  production of, 160
  SDIM service, 61
  and space saving, 195, 280
  storage of, 197
Microfilm, 155, 179
Microforms, 155
  retrieval systems, 157
Micro-opaques, 157
MIL specifications, 58
Minicard, 159
Minicomputers, 173

Ministry of Defence (UK), 81
Minutes, committee, 242
MIRACODE, 158
Mongar, P. E., 71
Monthly Catalog, 56, 59, 246
Murdock, J. W., 74
Murphy, J., 188

NACA *see* NASA
NASA, 18, 64, 69
  indexes, 123
  RECON, 65, 69, 109
  subject categories, 123
National Agricultural Library, 64
National Bureau of Standards, 97
National Institutes of Health, 30, 76, 96
National Library of Medicine, 63, 101, 203
National Microfilm Association, 165
National Referral Center, 20, 60, 61
National Reprographic Centre for documentation, 162, 165, 249
National Science Foundation, 27, 76, 223
National Technical Information Service *see* NTIS
National Translations Center, 72
NATO, 68
'Need to know' (*see also* Security), 137, 193, 263
Negus, A. E., 108
Nekon, J., 42
Nelson, C. E., 186
Neville, H. H., 116
Newcastle file handling system, 170
Newton, J., 70
NLM Current Catalog, 64
Non-publication, reasons for, 15
Notebooks, laboratory, 243, 250
Notice of Research Projects, 63
NRCd, 162, 165, 249
NRLSI, 57
NTIS, 20, 28, 60, 61, 65, 78, 120, 266, 274
Nuclear Safety, 66
Nuclear Science Abstracts, 23, 78, 110, 124

Index

Numbers
  accession, 85
  in codes, 263
  contract, 88, 269
  project, 88

Oak Ridge National Laboratory, 27
Objects of the Monographs, 23, 239
  of reports, 27, 237
OECD, 56, 72
Office of Technical Services, 20
Offset lithography for reproduction, 43, 119, 260
Olive, G., 101
Oltheten, T. H., 68
ONERA, 75
On-line systems, 162
  searching, 108, 111; economics of, 111
Operators, Boolean, 106, 111, 133
Optical character recognition, 169, 171
Optical coincidence, 71, 105, 268
Origin of reports, 53, 241
Originating bodies, 53
  arrangement by, 277
Orr, R. H., 30
OSRD, 20
OSTI, 55, 74, 103
Overhage, C. F. J., 160
Overton, C. D., 216
OVID, 108

Packages, computer program, 106
Pandex (tape service), 252
Paper quality and sizes, 261
PASCAL, 170
Passman, S., 27
Patent Office Library, 57
Patten, M. N., 172
PCMI, 157
  ultrafiche, 160
Pelzer, C. W., 70
Pemberton, J. E., 54
Periodical Publications in the NRLSI, 57
Personal authors, 87
Personal contacts, 31

Personal holdings of reports, 284, 285
Pfoutz, D. R., 223
Photocopying, 126, 150
  economics of, 155
  equipment for, 154
  permanence of, 154
  processes of, 153
  'second generation', 154
  services of, 126
Photolithography, 119, 260
Pickford, A. G. A., 98, 105
Plumb, P. W., 166
Power Reactor Docket Information, 66
PRECIS, 102
Precision in information retrieval, 99
Predicasts, 245
Price, D. S., 216
Primary publication, 26
Process sheets, 84
Production
  of announcement bulletins, 118
  of microfiches, 160
Profiles, 132, 272
  compilation of, 134
  review, 134
  search, 133
  subject interest, 132
Program packages, computer, 106
Progress forms, 254
Progress sheets, 85
Projects
  numbers for, 88
  officers for, 32
  planning system for, 250
Prosser, C., 221
Public Information Act (US), 76
Publication (for publications of particular organizations *see under* the organizations), 26, 59
  primary, 26
Publication Board (US), 19, 55
Purpose of reports, 27, 237

Qualified Products List, 58

Quality control, 169
QUOBIRD, 108
QUODAMP, 108

R & D Abstracts, 59, 78, 125, 177, 263
R & D organizations, 74
Rand Corporation, 55
Rank-Xerox Corporation, 154
Ratio, recall/precision, 99
Reader-printers, 156
Recall in information retrieval, 99
Recent Advances, 35
'Recommendations' sections in reports, 46
RECON, 65, 69, 109
Records of reports, 283
Reference copies of internal reports, 279
References
  agency, 88
  checking, 49
Regulatory Adjudicatory Issuances, 66
Reintjes, J. F., 160
Release conditions, 78
Repertoire des thèses, 38
Reports (for reports issued by particular organizations, see under the organizations)
  AD, 55
  article comparison, 59
  annual, 33
  BIOS, 55
  cataloguing see Catalogues, Cataloguing
  centres see Information centres
  CIOS, 55
  committee, 33, 242, 250
  company see Company reports
  conference, 34
  consultancy, 245
  content of, 31
  contract, 31
  contractors of, 41
  definitions of, 17, 237
  documentation pages of, 88
  editing of, 253, 254, 258
  external, 244, 251
  final, 33
  foreign language, 79
  form of, 38, 42, 248
  Germany, 19
  government, 246
  indexes to, indexing of see Indexes, Indexing
  industrial, 60
  interim, 29
  internal (see also Company reports), 27, 241, 243, 249; approval systems for, 256; distribution lists for, 249; need for detailed indexing, 268; reference copies of, 279; types of, 253; value to a company of, 242, 268
  introductions to, 45
  Japan, 19
  and joint projects, 251
  licencing agreements for, 251
  lists, confidentiality of, 271, 272, 273; production of, 272
  location of, 249
  microfilming of; as a safeguard, 279; for spacesaving, 280
  multiple copies of, 150
  nature of, 25
  numbering of, 261
  objects of, 27, 237
  of other companies, 244
  origins of, 241
  parts of, 38
  processing of, 84
  production of, 40
  progress, 28, 29, 31, 32
  purpose of, 27, 237
  R & D, 237
  records of, 283
  reference numbers of, 86
  release of, 30, 31
  reproduction of, 259
  series, 55, 86; arrangement by, 277; codes for, 87, 261, 263; numbering within, 261, 263; searching by, 263; new titles of, 38

sizes of, 43
sponsored, 257
state-of-the-art, 34, 141; compilation of, 142
text of, 44
title pages of, 44
types of, 22, 27, 29, 238, 253
unique copies of, 147
units, confidence of managers in, 239; staffing, 238;
university, 247
value of, 17, 237, 268
visit, 35, 268
wartime, 18
weeding of, 199, 280
writing, 40; guidelines, 42
Requests, 82, 137, 146
assessment of, 141
forms, 137, 145; layout, 137
handling, 138
information, 138, 141
management of, 137, 141
passing on, 140
special, 78
subject, 138, 140
urgency of, 139
Research Association reports, 247
Research Grants Index, 76
Research in Education, 65
Research
contract, 31
current, 75
operational, 219
organizations for, 74
Restrictions, 26, 119
'Results' sections in reports, 45
Retrieval, 104, 268, 272
on-line, 184
optical coincidence, 71, 105, 268
Retrieval networks, 107
Retrieval systems, 157, 268
Rigby, M., 94
RIOT, 108
Robertson, S. E., 111
Robinson, F., 188, 221
Ronco, P. G., 25
Rosenblum, M., 140
Rosenborg, S., 26

Ross, J., 173
Royal Aircraft Establishment, 132
Royal Society Scientific Information Conference, 20
Research and Technology Operating Plans (RTOP), 124

Safeguards, security, 189, 285
Safety, nuclear, 66
Salton, G., 101
Sargent, C. W., 83
Sauter, H. E., 162
Schieber, W. D., 107
Scheffler, F. L., 99, 104
Schlessinger, B. S., 275
Schmeckebier, L. F., 59
Schuler, S. C., 119, 171
Schultz, C. K., 104
Science Abstracts, 130, 135
Science Citation Index, 103, 109
Science Reference Library, 57
Scientific research in British universities and colleges, 75
SCISEARCH, 99, 111
SCORE, 218
SCOUT, 218
SDI, 63, 69, 118, 130, 131, 135, 136, 169, 171, 173, 271, 273
commercial, 135
computerized, 132
manual systems in, 131
methods of, 271
SDIM, 61, 78
Sealy, T., 156
Searching
economics of, 111
on-line, 108, 111, 185
Searle, R. H., 173
Security, 189
access, 193, 282
'classification', 150
'declassification', 192
downgrading, 192
handling, 150, 190
indexing, 268
marking, 190, 281
of material, 189
protection, 190

Security—*continued*
  records, 283
  safeguards, 285
  of secondary documents, 192
  in storage, 190, 194, 198, 279
  transmission, 194
Security gradings, 191, 280
  allocation, 281
  and distribution, 271
  colour coding, 282
  of internal reports, 281
  marking, 191, 281
Selected Reports Announcements, 126
Selective dissemination of information *see* SDI
Self-help by users, 146
Senate Report, 101
Senior management, 240, 250, 281, 283
Series, report *see* Report series
SHARP, 171
Sharp, J. R., 102
Shaw, R. R., 19, 157
Sheppard, M. O., 163
Simons, E. W., 52
Simpson, D. J., 174
SLIC, 102
Smith, J. R., 54, 275
Smith, R. C., 54, 171
Software, 184
Sources, 53, 243
  Government, 54
  guides, 54
Space in report stores, 194, 277
Spacemiser, 198
Sparck Jones, K., 103
Special Libraries Association, 66
Special requests, 78
Specialized information centres, 73, 97
Specifications, 58
Spencer, S. R., 188
SSIE, 61, 62, 75, 124
SSIE Science Newsletter, 63
Staff, 208, 238
  ancillary, 213
  assessment of, 215
  classes, 208
  clerical, 212
  for company information units, 238
  organizing, 209
  supervisory, 211
  technical, 209; committees, 211; exchanges, 210; qualifications, 210; specialization, 210
  training of, 214
  translating, 166, 210
Stahl, N., 166
Standard Title Service (ESA), 69, 136
Stanford Research Institute, 245
STAR, 65, 75, 78, 87, 110, 123, 136
  content of, 123
  indexes, 123
State-of-the-art reports, 34, 141, 142
Stationery, multiple, 139
Statutory organizations, 74
Stencil reproduction, 259
Step-and-repeat camera, 160
Stevens, M. E., 158
Storage arrangements, 157, 194, 198, 276–8
  by accession numbers, 278; originators, 276; series, 277
  for classified documents, 279
  costs of, 196
  equipment for, 196, 197
  for indexes, 198
  methods of, 278
  separate, for confidential reports, 279
Style manuals, 42
Subject
  analysis, 93, 98
  categories, 96, 124
  classification, 93, 267; arranging reports by, 276
  headings, 21, 132; medical, 84, 108
  indexes, 82, 93
  interests (*see also* Profiles), 132
  searching, 105
Sub-units, 205
  autonomy of, 208

functions of, 206
in research establishments, 207
SUPARS, 111
Swihart, S. J., 188
Syntactic analysis, 101
System 4000, 160
Systems
  batch retrieval, 107
  cataloguing, 21, 64
  computer programming, 106
  indexing, 64, 93; evaluation of, 103; intellectual systems, 104; machine, 105
  numbering, 261
  on-line, 162
  paper tape, 170
  post-coordinate, 94; advantages/disadvantages, 94
  pre-coordinate, 93
  project-planning, 250
  SDI, manual, 131

Tables in reports, 46
Tallman, J. E., 18
Tape typewriters, 119, 167
Taube, M., 21, 94
Taylor, L., 216
Techlink, 59
Technical Abstract Bulletin, 64
Technical editors, editing, 253
  progress systems, 254, 256
  relations with authors, 258
Technical memoranda, 65
Technical notes, 65
Technical reports, 65
Technical Reports Centre, 58, 59, 110
  holdings of, 58
  publications of, 59
  services of, 59
Technical Services for Industry, 74
Technical translations, 65
Teletypewriters, 172
Terminals, 183
Terms
  bound, 94, 97
  broader, 96
  narrower, 96

number, 97
related, 96
subject, 193
'use for', 96
TEST, 95, 96
Text, machine-readable, 105
Thesauri (*see also* Terms), 21, 95, 97, 171
  amendment to, 98
  construction, 97
  faults of, 97
  terms, number, 97
Thesaurofacet, 91, 267, 273,
Theses, 35, 72, 247
  bibliography of, 36
  index of, 36; retrospective, 36
Thomas, P. A., 116
Thompson, M. S., 275
Tinker, L., 188
Titles, 69, 87
TITUS, 172
Torkington, R. B., 188
Townley, H. M., 103
Trade association reports, 247
Trade names in indexes, 268
Translation
  management of, 144
  panels for, 143
  staff, 210
Translations, 72, 143
Transliteration, 87
Tyler, A. W., 159
Tylicki, L., 286
Types of reports, 22, 27, 29, 235, 253
Typewriters, tape, 119, 167

UDC, 71, 93, 267
UKAEA, 54, 281
UKCIS, 107, 136
Ultrafiches, 157, 160
Uniterms, 94, 105
Universal Copyright Convention, 166
Universal Decimal Classification, 79, 93, 267
Universities, colleges, 75
  reports by, 247

'Unpublished', definition of, 17, 238
UPDATE, 172
US Government publications, 59, 172
US Highways Research Information Service, 71
USAEC, 55, 66, 266, 274
  depository libraries, 66
Users, 136, 144
  channels for, 145
  foreign, 147
  guides for, 134
  needs of, 148

Value of reports, 17, 237, 268
Van Velze, P. L., 109
Vanwijngaerden, F., 67
Varian 620, 174
Veit, F., 166
Vernimb, C. O., 159
Vernon, K. D. C., 97
Vessey, H. F., 119, 166, 171
Vetting reports, 254, 256
Vickers, P. H., 168, 217
Vickery, B. C., 98, 216, 223
Visual display units, 109

Walkins, P. S., 202
Walkley, J., 116
Warheit, I. A., 188

Wars, influence of, 18
Weeding, 195, 198, 280
  at intake, 199
  policy of, 200
  of unique copies, 201
Weinberg, A., 20, 66, 73
Weil, B. H., 42, 223, 287
Weissman, H. M., 25, 42
Wessel, C. J., 217
Western Reserve University, 104
What's available in the atomic energy literature, 66
White, C. M., 81
Whittemore, B. J., 26
Wildhack, W. A., 275
Wilkin, A. P., 217
Williams, B. J. S., 157, 158
Wilson, B. J., 53
Wilson, C. W. J., 168, 172, 188
Wood, D. N., 148
Word ranking, 91
World Index of Scientific Translations, 72
Wright, J. C., 287
Wright, R. C., 132

Xerox, 154

Zentralstelle für maschinelle Dokumentation, 70
Zoller-Phillips, G., 67

166598

DATE DUE